Flossmoor Public Library
1000 Sterling Avenue
Flossmoor, IL 60422-1295
Phone: (708)798-4006

INVENTING MADE EASY

INVENTING MADE EASY

The Entrepreneur's Indispensable Guide to Creating, Patenting and Profiting From Inventions

Tom and Roger Bellavance

Quiet Corner Press, L.L.C.
Moosup, Connecticut 06354

Although the author and publisher have made every effort to ensure the accuracy and completeness of information contained in this book, we assume no responsibility for errors, inaccuracies, omissions, or any inconsistency herein. Any slights of people, places, or organizations are unintentional.

First printing 1999

———————————————

ISBN 0-9665069-7-9

LCCN 98-67181

———————————————

ATTENTION CORPORATIONS, UNIVERSITIES, COLLEGES, AND PROFESSIONAL ORGANIZATIONS: Quantity discounts are available on bulk purchases of this book for educational purposes. Special books or book excerpts can also be created to fit specific needs. For information, please contact Quiet Corner Press, L.L.C., 318 Sterling Hill Road, Moosup, CT 06354-2034, (800) 917-6689.

Product manufacturers and sellers often utilize trademark protection to signal the proprietary nature of their products' designation. We have sought to identify all trademarked designations in this book with capital letters (i.e., Kleenex).

This publication is designed to provide accurate and authoritative information in regard to the subject matter covered. It is sold with the understanding that the publisher is not engaged in rendering legal, accounting or other professional service. If legal advice or other expert assistance is required, the services of a competent professional person should be sought. (Source: From a Declaration of Principles jointly adopted by a Committee of the American Bar Association and a Committee of Publishers.)

ACKNOWLEDGMENTS

The authors wish to give heartfelt thanks to all those individuals and organizations whose contributions helped to make this book all that it is. Your knowledge and patience is greatly appreciated. To our family, we extend our gratitude for their encouragement and support during the many months of researching and writing *Inventing Made Easy*.

Our deepest gratitude goes to those creative talents who provided artwork for the book and promotional campaign; Roger LaRocque, illustrator par excellence, as well as photographers Guy Grube and Charleen Herrick. A special thanks goes to Audrey Cross for her lightning fast and accurate manuscript typing. We would be remiss if we did not offer our thanks to Michael A. Cantor, Kathryn Guinan, Donald L. Gammon and Jason Bitgood for their expert advice.

Lastly, we both extend our appreciation to our many friends and colleagues who believe in us and bless us with unflagging support and encouragement.

* * * * *

To our anonymous "angel" in Irving.
You've been so helpful
from the very start.
Thanks
for the proof.
Such shocking secrets!
We're dying to read your tell-all book.

HOW TO CONTACT
THE AUTHORS

We encourage our readers to contact us with comments and constructive criticism. The authors look forward to hearing from you with ideas on how to improve future editions. Let us know what new topics you want covered in the next edition. We value your feedback. Our goal is to make the next edition even better than the first. Inquiries regarding the subject matter and inventions detailed in this book may be directed to the address below:

Tom and Roger Bellavance
Quiet Corner Press, L.L.C.
318 Sterling Hill Road
Moosup, CT 06354-2034

CONTENTS

SECTION II

SECTION III

*"A man of genius makes no mistakes. His errors
are the portals of discovery."*

—James Joyce

PREFACE

Throughout history, inventors have made their mark upon human development. One of the first inventors was most likely some protohuman who picked up a stick or stone and used it as a tool. From this simple beginning, an inevitable cascade of inventions came to be. Survival of the fittest has ensured that the act of inventing defines our humanity.

Some say that everything worthwhile has already been invented. Yet, the creative drive will not be denied. We are all hard-wired for creativity and invention. Humanity will continue to succumb to the inexorable urge to create something new or innovative.

The authors must confess, we're a couple of Connecticut Yankees. We seem destined to persevere in keeping the tradition of "Yankee Ingenuity" alive. If there is a better way to do something, we try to find it. Sometimes we wonder if this drive is a blessing or a curse. A curse . . . a curse . . . a curse . . . would that more had such a blessing!

Anyone who has ever had an idea has probably fantasized about getting a patent and making millions of dollars off it. We are sorry to say, it's not that easy. Taking your idea and transforming it into reality is one of the hardest things you could ever try to do. Starting your own business to sell your invention makes the whole process doubly difficult. Failure is all too easy unless you have a guide to show you how.

Inventing Made Easy: The Entrepreneur's Indispensable Guide to Creating, Patenting and Profiting From Inventions is your personal guide to creativity, driving an inspiration from concept to reality, inventing, prototyping and market testing leading to validation and finally business start-up and marketing for sales and success.

Consider us your mentors. Let us show you the ropes. This book teaches how to harness your creativity to dream up winning ideas. We take you step-by-step through the maze known as the patent process. You can explore your options as you read about the many ways to make money with your inventions. Our savvy marketing tips will teach you how to successfully promote and sell your products. We intend to save you a tremendous amount of time, money and heartache. Our book exposes many of the secrets in this mysterious field of endeavor.

Much of the information in this book was acquired through the school of hard knocks. Mistakes were made . . . but we learned from them. So can you. We only wish a book like this existed when we were novice inventors. We gladly would have paid thousands of dollars for the invaluable information you'll find between these covers.

SECTION I

*"The man with a new idea is a crank
—until the idea succeeds."*
—Mark Twain

CHAPTER 1
Protecting Your Idea

The Burst of Inspiration

Where do ideas come from? The germ of an idea percolates in your creative subconscious. Your mind blends an amalgam of concepts, ideas and experiences, continually forming new and novel associations until that fortuitous moment: Inspiration strikes. A great idea bursts from your subconscious. A truly great idea shatters the bounds of conventional thinking, revealing possibilities never before considered.

The adrenaline rushes as the idea overwhelms you with its elegance. Your mind seems to operate at warp speed as the images flood your consciousness. You revel in the moment as you emotionally experience your insight.

You scramble to write it all down. Your frantic search may lead you to use a piece of scrap paper, a napkin or the back of an envelope. As you jot down every detail you bask in the deliciously warm afterglow of creative genius. Wonderfully focused, you are oblivious to all else.

Creative entrepreneurial inventors routinely experience this profound moment. Chances are, you've experienced moments like this yourself. When you get those great ideas, what do you do with them? Will this idea become the basis for a new product or invention leading to a new business opportunity? Quite possibly it may. If so, what do you do next? Instinct tells you to protect your idea. Your precious brainchild may become a target. Rest assured, if it is truly a great idea, there will be legions of people out there who live for the opportunity to steal it. Many savor the challenge. As a general rule, the more valuable your idea is, the more likely it will be at risk for being stolen.

If you consult with an attorney, he or she will advise you to seek proprietary protection for your idea. You may use either a patent, copyright or trademark to protect the idea. The right one to choose depends upon the nature of the idea.

A copyright will protect the writings of an author against copying. What is protected is the form of expression rather than the subject matter. If you copyright the description of your invention, others may manufacture or use the invention or even write a description of your invention in their own words. Copyrights are of little use for protecting a patentable invention.

According to the Department of Commerce's pamphlet, *General Information Concerning Patents,*

> a trademark relates to any word, name, symbol or device which is used in trade with goods to indicate the source or origin of the goods and to distinguish them from the goods of others. Trademark rights may be used to prevent others from using a confusingly similar mark but not to prevent others from making the same goods or from selling them under a non-confusing mark.

For example, if you ask someone for a Kleenex™, what you are technically saying is you want a Kleenex brand facial tissue and not some other brand of facial tissue. Many companies can manufacture and sell facial tissue, but only the Kimberly-Clark Corporation, owner of the registered trademark Kleenex, may manufacture and sell Kleenex brand products.

If your great idea is for a new or novel product, then you should seek to patent your invention to protect it. If you have never patented an invention, a multitude of questions should flood your mind. What is a patent? What will a patent do for me? What steps do I take to get my idea patented? How long will it take? How much will it cost? How effective are patents in protecting my invention? Can I make money on my invention? The whole process can seem rather complex and daunting. We have the answers to your questions and a rich well of experience to tap. Let us be your guide as we explore some of our painfully acquired wisdom. The patent system can be treacherous, but with our help, it *can* be easier, less time-consuming and less expensive. Take our word for it, from two guys who have been there . . . done that.

What Is a Patent?

According to *General Information Concerning Patents*, "A patent for an invention is a grant of a property right by the Government to the inventor acting through the Patent and Trademark Office." As one of the 14 bureaus in the Department of Commerce, the U.S. Patent and Trademark Office examines and issues patents, disseminates patent information and promotes an understanding of intellectual property protection. What is granted is "the right to exclude others from making, using or selling the invention." The right conferred by the patent for a term of 20 years from the date of application extends throughout the United States and its territories and possessions.

By statute, anyone who "invents or discovers any new and useful process, machine, manufacture, or composition of matter, or any new and useful improvements thereof, may obtain a patent."

Because a patent is a form of personal property, it may be given away, sold, mortgaged or bequeathed in a will. Permission may be granted to others for the use of a patented invention (licensing) in exchange for royalty payments. Three types of patents exist: utility, design and plant.

Utility Patent: This class of patent is the most important, most common and most useful to inventors. It covers the functional aspect of an idea, clearly describing its useful nature. For illustrative purposes, consider a computer. The hard drive, circuit boards and modem or component parts thereof are protected by utility patents.

Design Patent: This class of patent covers an invention's unique design or appearance. If the appearance is functional, then a utility patent should be chosen instead of a design patent for protection of the idea or concept. Ask yourself if your invention's novel feature serves a functional purpose or an ornamental purpose? If changing the novel feature results in a change in the operation of the invention, then you need a utility patent. Again, using the example of a computer, the computer case may possess unique and ornamental features. A design patent would be appropriate to provide protection for this design.

Many experienced inventors feel, for the most part, design patents are a waste of time and money unless the design is incredibly distinctive. Circumvention of the design patent is often easily accomplished. All too many inventors are persuaded by their patent attorney or agent to get a design patent. Sure, it satisfies your ego, but it also empties your wallet. If it does not provide you with protection, you are wasting your time.

Plant Patent: This class of patent protects both sexually and asexually reproducible plants. The Plant Variety Protection Act provides monopoly protection for sexually reproducible plants that utilize pollination and seeds for propagation. Plant patent protection can also be obtained for asexually reproducible plants that are propagated by the use of grafts and cuttings. Examples of plant patents include flowers with improved disease resistance and sweet corn with increased levels of complex sugars to enhance flavor and increase shelf life. Changes in patent law now allow both sexually and asexually reproducible plants to be granted monopoly protection by utility patents as well. Science and technology in engineering plant life forms are advancing faster than the law can keep up with. For the absolute latest on plant patent law, contact the Patent Office or consult with a patent attorney who specializes in this rapidly changing field.

The recent GATT (General Agreements on Tariffs and Trade) Treaty signed December 8, 1994, resulted in new legislation affecting the term of patents. Previously, utility patents enjoyed a 17-year grant of protection from the date of issue. Now, all utility and plant patents filed with the Patent and Trademark Office after June 7, 1995, remain in force for a period of 20 years from the filing date. The design patents' terms remain the same, expiring 14 years from the date of issue.

Utility Patents

When most people speak of patents they are generally referring to utility patents. This most common type of patent relies upon its claims to describe a device's function and interrelation of its parts. For illustrative purposes, we have included the author's Hook Pen patent. Refer to it as we discuss the parts of a patent.

Upon examination of a utility patent you will notice it has five main sections: frontmatter, abstract, specification, drawings and claims.

The *frontmatter* of the patent begins with the title of the invention. It continues with the name and address of the inventor(s), patent application number and date filed in the patent office. Patent search information including field of search is listed next. References are cited for both U.S. and foreign patent documents that closely relate to the patented invention. The frontmatter concludes with the patent office's primary examiner and the inventor's patent attorney, agent or law firm.

The *abstract* is a brief explanation of the nature of the invention. This section is concisely worded to explain how the invention works. The abstract provides an overview that is expanded upon in the next section.

The *specification* goes into great detail to describe the physical and/or chemical composition of the invention. The parts of the device and their interrelation are explained by the text and reference to the patent drawings. This section begins with the listing of the formal name of the invention then launches into the background of the invention. The summary of the invention is presented along with a brief description of the drawings. Next, a full description of the invention provides the reader with a clear understanding of the embodiment of the invention.

The *drawings* are technical blueprints that visually display the technology. Traditionally, cutaway views of the object are used to fully illustrate the external as well as internal structure. Parts of the patented invention are numbered and referenced in the specification and claims for clarity of explanation.

The *claims* are specifically worded to give the owner of the patent the legal protection of monopoly rights for the invention. They describe in exact and minute detail the precise nature of the invention. Your patent attorney or agent will utilize exquisite care to give your invention as many claims as possible with the appropriate language to maximize your patent protection. The more claims the better to ensure your legal rights. Your patent's claims count more than any other section of the patent when it comes to legal protection.

United States Patent [19]

Bellavance

[11] E   Patent Number: Re. 32,656

[45] Reissued   Date of Patent: Apr. 26, 1988

[54] **WRITING INSTRUMENT WITH FASTENING MEANS**

[76] Inventor: Roger T. Bellavance, P.O. Box 866, Moosup, Conn.

[21] Appl. No.: 84,554

[22] Filed: Aug. 12, 1987

[51] Int. Cl.⁴ B43K 24/00; B43K 7/12; B43K 29/00; B43K 25/00

[52] U.S. Cl. .... **401/104**; 24/11 R; 24/11 M; 70/459; 401/99; 401/109; 401/195; 401/52

[58] Field of Search .... 401/99, 195, 104, 105, 401/106, 52, 109; 70/456 R, 459; 24/3 K, 10 R, 11 R, 11 M

[56] **References Cited**

U.S. PATENT DOCUMENTS

387,042	7/1888	Bohren	401/110 X
803,839	11/1905	Merrill	70/459
1,795,555	3/1931	Greenwood	70/459
2,400,679	5/1946	Biro	401/106
2,715,888	8/1955	Liguori	401/105
2,928,373	3/1960	Esterow	401/105
3,120,837	2/1964	Johnson	401/111
3,288,115	11/1966	Hechtle	401/110
3,344,484	10/1967	Zepell et al.	24/11 P

FOREIGN PATENT DOCUMENTS

1007666	5/1957	Fed. Rep. of Germany	401/105
3300038	7/1984	Fed. Rep. of Germany	401/195
72880	4/1960	France	401/104
245096	6/1947	Switzerland	24/11 M
273976	3/1951	Switzerland	401/105

Primary Examiner—Steven A. Bratlie
Attorney, Agent, or Firm—Fishman & Dionne

[57]   **ABSTRACT**

A writing instrument, having a mechanism for alternately retracting and protracting its writing point, comprises a shackle alternately closed and opened by that mechanism, for releasably fastening to an associated object.

26 Claims, 1 Drawing Sheet

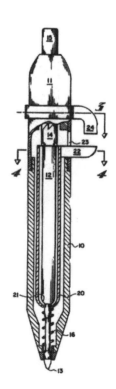

Hook Pen Patent, page 1.

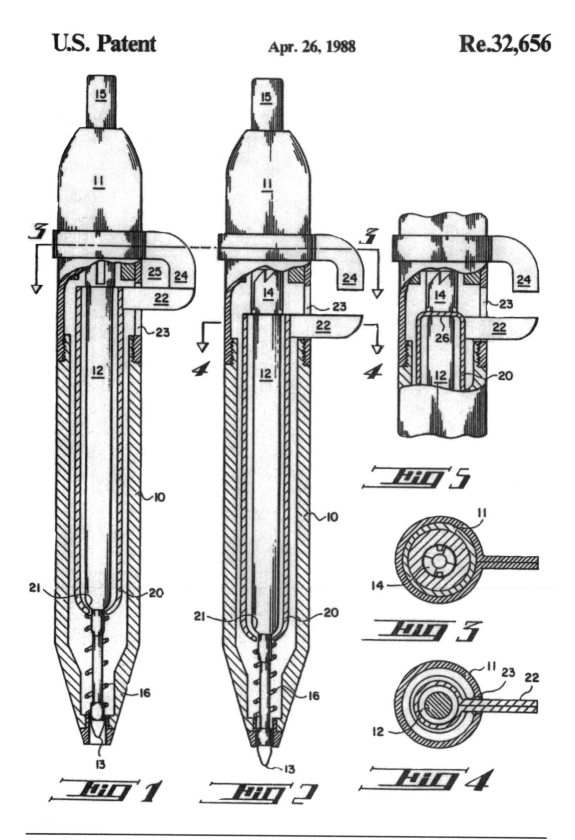

WRITING INSTRUMENT WITH FASTENING MEANS

Matter enclosed in heavy brackets [ ] appears in the original patent but forms no part of this reissue specification; matter printed in italics indicates the additions made by reissue.

BACKGROUND OF THE INVENTION

1. Field of the Invention

This invention relates generally to writing instruments, and more particularly to writing instruments in which the writing point may be axially displaced to alternately protracted and retracted positions by successive axially inward displacements of the end, of the writing instrument, remote from the writing point.

Such writing instruments have been highly developed over a considerable period: an early example is disclosed in U.S. Pat. No. 387,042, July 31, 1888, to Ulrich Bohren; more recent improvements are disclosed in U.S. Pat. No. 3,120,837, Feb. 11, 1964, to William F. Johnson and in U.S. Pat. No. 3,288,115, Nov. 29, 1966, to Emil Hechtle. These instruments, particularly those utilizing a ball-type writing point, are extensively preferred. One reason for this preference is that they do not require a separate point cover or cap which can be mislaid or lost.

2. Prior Art Problem

However, the entire instrument may inadvertently be separated from a desk, clipboard or notebook with which it is intended to be used. To obviate this difficulty, such writing instruments are frequently provided with some sort of leash, frequently of light chain, by which they can be tied to associated objects with which they are to be used. Such leashes, unfortunately, tend to impede the task of writing.

It would therefore be useful to devise a writing instrument which fastens reliably to an associated object when it is not being employed for writing, and which is not encumbered when it is so employed. It is the principal object of this invention to provide such an instrument. It is a further object of this invention to provide an instrument of the simplest character.

SUMMARY OF THE INVENTION

According to this invention, the stated objects are achieved by utilizing the axial displacements of the writing point, to alternately protracted and retracted positions, to produce corresponding displacements of a pawl to alternately open and close a side of a shackle which can receive a fastening member, such as a ring, which is borne by an associated object. Thereby, pressing the end of the instrument to protract its writing point to the exposed position automatically displaces the pawl to open the side of the shackle, freeing the instrument from the associated object. Also, pressing the end of the instrument again to retract the writing point to the covered position automatically displaces the pawl to close the side of the shackle, thereby allowing the shackle to engage a received fastening member to fasten the instrument to an associated object.

These and further objects of this invention, as well as the means for attaining them, are set forth in the following Specification and Drawings, wherein:

BRIEF DESCRIPTION OF THE DRAWINGS

FIG. 1 is a schematic view, mostly in lengthwise cross-section, of a writing instrument according to this invention, with the writing point in the retracted position;

FIG. 2 is a similar view of the same instrument, with the writing point in the protracted position.

FIG. 3 is a cross-section of the instrument through the fixed part of the shackle;

FIG. 4 is a cross-section of the instrument through the pawl of the shackle; and

FIG. 5 is a fragmentary schematic view, mostly in lengthwise cross-section, of an alternative embodiment of this invention.

DESCRIPTION OF THE INVENTION

Reference is made to FIGS. 1 and 2, which illustrate a preferred embodiment of this invention. The writing instrument has a conventional outer case comprising a barrel 10 and a cap 11 fastened thereto by a threaded joint. It also has a conventional cartridge 12 of the so-called "Parker" type provided at one end with a ball-point writing element 13 and at the other end with a rotary ratchet cam 14. That cam is engaged and operated by the usual mechanism (not shown) so that as pushbutton 15 is repetitively pressed, cartridge 12 and its writing element or point 13 are successively retracted and protracted as illustrated in, respectively, FIG. 1 and FIG. 2, with retraction force being provided by compression spring 16.

The preferred embodiment further comprises a bushing 20 which surrounds and rotates easily upon cartridge 12. Bushing 20 is reduced in diameter at one end to engage diameter step 21 of cartridge 12, against which step it is urged by compression spring 16. The other end of bushing 20 is provided with a pawl 22 which passes out through a slot 23 in cap 11. As shown in FIG. 4, bushing 20 may be constructed as a butted tube integrally connected to two tabs bent outwardly to form pawl 22; these tabs may be joined by adhesive bonding or electric spot welding. It should be clear that the thickness of bushing 20 and the magnitude of its clearance have been exaggerated in the Figures in the interest of clarity.

The preferred embodiment also comprises a shackle arm 24 which, together with pawl 22, defines a shackle having an opening 25; this shackle is shown closed in FIG. 1, in which writing point 13 is shown retracted, and is shown open in FIG. 2, in which the point is shown protracted. As shown in FIG. 3, shackle arm 24 may also be configured as a butted tube integrally connected to two outwardly-bent tabs, and may be joined to itself and to cap 11 by adhesive bonding or electric spot welding.

Opening 25 may receive a fastening member, such as a ring, which is borne by an associated object with which it is desired to employ the writing instrument. For example, it can readily fasten to a ring of a looseleaf ring binder, and thus be less likely to be mislaid, since a single motion retracts the writing point and also fastens the writing instrument to the ring.

The illustrated preferred embodiment utilizes a cartridge of the so-called "Parker" type, which has rotary ratchet cam 14 mounted directly on the upper end. In another common form of mechanism, illustrated in FIG. 5, cam 14 is mounted together with the rest of the mechanism within cap 11; the cartridge, comprising just

3

the ink chamber and the writing point, is positioned axially by abutment of chamber end 26 with rotary ratchet cam 14. In this embodiment, bushing 20 does not need to engage a diameter step 21 as shown in FIGS. 1 and 2, but may merely engage chamber end 26. Indeed, since it is then unnecessary that cartridge 12 be able to rotate, bushing 20 could then simply be fixed to cartridge 12 as by adhesive bonding; in such an example, bushing 20 and pawl 22 become part of the disposable cartridge.

Given the foregoing teaching, those skilled in the art to which this invention pertains may readily devise further embodiments. For one example, the illustrated form employing pushbutton 15 may be replaced by a form using an enveloping outer cap; also, one may use other well-known mechanisms for protracting and retracting the writing point. Moreover, the shape of shackle arm 24 and pawl 22 may be changed without loss of function; for example, pawl 22 could have an L-shaped external portion, and the mating portion of shackle arm 24 could be straight. Further, the shackle arm may be fixed to the outer case by being integral therewith, as by being a notch in the outer case or a protuberance molded thereon.

Yet other variations and modifications of the illustrated embodiments may be achieved without departing from the spirit and scope of the invention as defined by the following claims:

I claim:

1. A writing instrument having an outer case which contains an elongated cartridge having an axis, said cartridge bearing a writing point at one end and engaging, at the other end, a mechanism for alternately moving said cartridge axially to position said writing point to alternately a retracted position within said outer case and a protracted position protruding outside said outer case, said writing instrument further comprising:
a rigid shackle arm, fixed to said outer case;
a bushing, enveloping said cartridge within said outer case and adapted to be moved axially by said cartridge; and
a pawl, borne by said bushing and movable substantially solely axially thereby, said pawl protruding through a slot in said outer case to define, with said shackle arm, a shackle which is open when said writing point is in a protracted position and which is closed when said writing point is in a retracted position.

2. A writing instrument according to claim 1 in which said bushing is easily rotatable upon said cartridge.

3. A writing instrument according to claim 1 in which said bushing is fixed to said cartridge.

4. A writing instrument according to claim 1 in which said bushing has a section of reduced diameter which engages a section of changing diameter of said cartridge.

5. A writing instrument according to claim 4 in which said section of reduced diameter is urged, to engage said section of changing diameter, by one end of a spring, the other end of which bears upon the inside of said outer case.

6. A writing instrument according to claim 1 in which said cartridge comprises a chamber end opposite said writing point, and said bushing engages said chamber end.

7. A writing instrument according to claim 6 in which said bushing is urged, to engage said chamber end, by one end of a spring, the other end of which bears upon the inside of said outer case.

4

8. A writing instrument according to claim 1 in which said shackle, when closed, defines an opening sufficiently large to engage a fastening member affixed to an associated object.

9. A writing instrument having an outer case which contains an elongated cartridge having an axis, said cartridge bearing a writing point at one end and engaging, at the other end, a mechanism for alternately moving said cartridge axially to position said writing point to alternately a retracted position within said outer case and a protracted position protruding outside said outer case, said writing instrument further comprising:
a rigid shackle arm, fixed to said outer case;
a bushing, enveloping at least a portion of said cartridge within said outer case and adapted to be moved axially with said cartridge; and
a pawl, borne by said bushing and movable substantially solely axially thereby, said pawl protruding through an opening in said outer case to define, with said shackle arm, a shackle which is open when said writing point is in a protracted position and which is closed when said writing point is in a retracted position.

10. A writing instrument according to claim 9 in which said bushing is easily rotatable upon said cartridge.

11. A writing instrument according to claim 9 in which said bushing is fixed to said cartridge.

12. A writing instrument according to claim 9 in which said bushing has a section of reduced diameter which engages a section of changing diameter of said cartridge.

13. A writing instrument according to claim 12 in which said section of reduced diameter is urged, to engage said section of changing diameter, by one end of a spring, the other end of which bears upon the inside of said outer case.

14. A writing instrument according to claim 9 in which said cartridge comprises a chamber end opposite said writing point, and said bushing engages said chamber end.

15. A writing instrument according to claim 14 in which said bushing is urged, to engage said chamber end, by one end of a spring, the other end of which bears upon the inside of said outer case.

16. A writing instrument according to claim 9 in which said shackle, when closed, defines an opening sufficiently large to engage a fastening member affixed to an associated object.

17. A writing instrument having an outer case which contains an elongated cartridge having an axis, said cartridge bearing a writing point at one end and engaging, at the other end, a mechanism for alternately moving said cartridge axially to position said writing point to alternately a retracted position within said outer case and a protracted position protruding outside said outer case, said writing instrument further comprising:
a rigid shackle arm fixed to said case;
a pawl operatively connected to said cartridge and movable substantially solely axially with said cartridge, said pawl protruding through an opening in said outer case to define, with said shackle arm, a shackle which is open when said writing point is in a protracted position and which is closed when said writing point is in a retracted position.

18. A writing instrument according to claim 17 wherein: said pawl is operatively connected to said cartridge via bushing means.

19. A writing instrument according to claim 18 wherein: said bushing means is supported by said cartridge within said outer case and is adapted to be moved axially with said cartridge.

Hook Pen Patent, page 4.

5

20. A writing instrument according to claim 18 in which said bushing means is easily rotatable upon said cartridge.

21. A writing instrument according to claim 18 in which said bushing means is fixed to said cartridge.

22. A writing instrument according to claim 18 in which said bushing means has a section of reduced diameter which engages a section of changing diameter of said cartridge.

23. A writing instrument according to claim 22 in which said section of reduced diameter is urged, to engage said section of changing diameter, by one end of a spring, the other end of which bears upon the inside of said outer case.

6

24. A writing instrument according to claim 18 in which said cartridge comprises a chamber end opposite said writing point, and said bushing means engages said chamber end.

25. A writing instrument according to claim 24 in which said bushing means is urged, to engage said chamber end, by one end of a spring, the other end of which bears upon the inside of said outer case.

26. A writing instrument according to claim 17 in which said shackle, when closed, defines an opening sufficiently large to engage a fastening member affixed to an associated object.

* * * * *

Documenting Your Ideas

One of the essential first steps in the invention process is proper documentation of your idea or invention. Many good reasons exist for retaining comprehensive documentation.

1. If you don't write your idea down, you are bound to forget it, or at the very least, forget important details. Perfect recall is a rare talent. Get in the habit of keeping a pen and notepad with you at all times for when inspiration strikes. Keep them in your car, in your bathroom and by your bedside. You won't forgive yourself if you forget a brilliant idea. These brainchildren are all too often ephemeral, easily lost amidst the distractions of a busy life.

2. Remember to log your idea in your Invention Notebook. Using ink, describe your idea or invention in as clear and detailed a manner as you can. Make sketches of your ideas. You must sign and date your entry.

   Additionally, you want two independent and *completely trusted* individuals to sign and date each page to verify they have "witnessed and understood" your concept. An alternative to having two trusted individuals sign off in your Invention Notebook is to use the Patent and Trademark Office's Disclosure Document Program, which will be discussed shortly.

3. By writing your idea down, you force yourself to think your idea through. Before you can communicate your idea to others, you must first be able to describe it to yourself with the details crystal clear in your own mind.

4. A technical log of your ideas, research and experiments is essential to record the development of your invention. This documentation may be needed to help prove you invented something should your patent be challenged, for tax purposes or for licensing negotiations.

Some inventors believe "post office documentation" will adequately meet their legal documentation needs. They are wrong. It is never an option. Post office documentation involves making a copy of your idea, properly dated, then sealing it inside an envelope. You send this envelope back to yourself via registered mail. You do not open it but store it in a safe place. This method to establish you owned the idea at the postmarked date is a poor method of documentation—it is so easy to cheat. Simply send the envelope back to yourself *unsealed*. At some later date put your invention papers in the envelope and seal it. Presto! You have backdated invention records. Patent law regards this sealed envelope method of documentation to be essentially *useless* as evidence of your date of conception.

Another documentation method, also not recommended, is the use of a notary public. Some inventors routinely have their invention notes stamped by a notary, but the downside to this option is the potential lack of confidentiality. You have no assurance the notary public will keep your material confidential. Additionally, the notary cannot testify as a witness to your invention's date of conception or progress of work should you go to court in a patent matter. The material has to be read and understood and the notary public doesn't do this.

It is natural to have serious concerns about having two independent witnesses sign and date your Invention Notebook. Obviously, you must select these two individuals with great care. Trusting them implicitly is a given. They must keep your ideas completely confidential.

Will they "permanently borrow" your idea? Sure, it can happen (very rarely). If you choose your friends well, you should have no worries. The truth is most ideas at the conceptual stage possess little value. It is only after a monumental amount of time and effort your idea grows in value to become worth something. The work required to transform this idea into reality is more than most people are willing to invest their time in. It is tremendously difficult. If someone takes your idea, they may find the development of that idea more of a curse than a blessing. There are easier ways to get money.

As an alternative to having two trusted individuals document they witnessed and understood your idea for an invention, you may wish to utilize the Patent and Trademark Office's Disclosure Document Program. For a $10 filing fee, the Patent and Trademark Office (PTO) will accept and preserve your papers disclosing your invention for a period of two years. This disclosure is accepted as evidence of the date of conception of your invention. At the end of the two-year period the PTO destroys your Disclosure Document unless a patent application has been received.

The Disclosure Document only establishes evidence of the date of conception of your invention. It does not confer upon you any patent rights. You must still file a patent application if you wish to obtain patent protection. The papers will be stamped with an identifying number and returned with the reminder the Disclosure Document may be relied upon only as evidence of the date of conception and that an application must be filed in order to provide patent protection. Many people feel the Disclosure Document Program to be unnecessary. We agree. Having two independent witnesses sign off in your Invention Notebook costs you nothing, unlike the PTO's Disclosure Document Program. Additionally, live witnesses are better able to testify as to the facts surrounding your invention's conception and better establish evidence of conception should you have to go to court.

In addition to keeping records in your Invention Notebook, you may be in the habit of doing so on your computer. This is fine. However, bear in mind that computer entries can be altered at any time. You can add to, delete or insert information at a later time. This subverts the purpose of an invention record. Obviously, information can be falsified, including the all-important date of conception of the invention. For this reason you should use a paper record such as an Invention Notebook. An unalterable and verifiable paper trail can prove its value sometime down the road if you need to prove date of conception. If you need to go to court you will be glad you have your proof on paper.

Since the use of personal computers has grown so prevalent, however, we should spend a moment discussing information management. As a computer user you are given the responsibility of ensuring efficient and secure methods of information storage. Surely you have heard the familiar admonition to always backup your work on a disk. Do it often—several times a day. A hard disk crash will break your heart! We all get a little lazy sometimes but let's be honest—we can do better, can't we? So let's all remember to back up our work.

Those of us with more substantial information storage needs can rely upon disk backups only so much. Computer users seeking to conserve memory turn to tape backups and zip drives. These storage mediums hold vastly more information than any disk.

Date of Conception

When considering documentation we must stress the importance of documenting certain important dates. These dates may have legal ramifications upon your claim to patent rights. Proving the date of conception for your invention may very well be crucial to receiving patent protection. Creation of this paper trail is absolutely essential. The date you conceive of the idea for your invention must be recorded along with the description of it. This will be the earliest date in your paper trail.

Disclosure Documents

When you file your related patent application within the two-year period, you must include a separate letter referring to the existence of your Disclosure Document. The separate letter must specify the patent application, title of your Disclosure Document, its number and date of receipt by the PTO.

Your Disclosure Document must give a highly detailed description of your invention's concept and operation. This 5- to 25-page document you prepare will be the basis of setting limits on your patent protection as described in the patent application's claims. Much of the information in the Disclosure Document comes straight out of your Invention Notebook. Be certain your disclosure's description is complete enough to cover every conceivable application for your invention.

If you cannot or are unwilling to have two independent witnesses sign and date your Invention Notebook, then the Disclosure Document Program is your best alternative. As the requirements for this document are rather specific and exacting, you should inquire with your patent attorney or agent or with the PTO for information on how to complete this document.

Invention Notebooks

Always properly document your inventions as you think of them. An Invention Notebook should be used to record your ideas as well as document all subsequent work you do on the project. Document your efforts to build, test and market your inventions here. Use a separate notebook for each invention to keep each project isolated from each other. Section III of this book contains a ready-to-use Invention Notebook for your next project.

Your notebook must contain permanently bound pages that are consecutively numbered in an unalterable sequence. Removing or adding pages must not be possible. Perfect-bound or smythe-sewn notebooks are acceptable but loose-leaf binders are definitely not. Engineering notebooks are available with cross-hatched pages, ideal for sketching your engineered drawings of your invention. Many have preprinted lines at the bottom of the pages for inventor's and witnesses' printed names, signatures and dates. If you choose, you can have an ink stamp made up that reads, "Witnessed and Understood by Me" followed by a space for the witness' printed name, signature and date. Use the stamp for each witness who signs off in your notebook.

You should sign and date all entries the same day you make them. If you neglect to, insert a brief note indicating when you made the entry and explain that you signed at a later time. Witnesses should likewise sign and date on the same day you made the entry in the notebook. Make sure they read and understand the entries. Obviously, trust is a major concern. *You must trust them completely.* It is best that relatives and close friends who might be mistaken for co-inventors *not* sign your notebook.

What information should you enter into your Invention Notebook? Enter the same information as you would expect to find on a U.S. patent, for starters.

1. Who it belongs to. Print your name and address. Always use ink to register entries.

2. Name(s) of your invention. Include ideas for trademarks.

3. Abstract or primary function of your invention.

4. A complete, detailed physical description of your invention. The description should include functional, mechanical, structural, chemical and compositional elements.

5. Artwork. Start with sketching to illustrate important points about the invention's design and function. Include photographs of mock-ups and models. Paste these photographs in the notebook using permanent adhesive and draw a lead line from the paper onto the picture to help establish that the photos were not exchanged or tampered with at a later time. Include a written reference to the picture in the notebook.

6. Describe how this invention is new or novel and therefore deserving to be patented.

7. Describe all possible construction or manufacturing possibilities. How can it be made? Try to think what your competition might do to make it cheaper or better. How would they get around the patent?

8. List every benefit this invention offers. What advantages does it offer over previous developments?

9. Record all information on your marketing efforts. Details of discussions or negotiations for assignments and/or licenses should be entered.

10. Make a reference to all research, meetings and correspondence conducted regarding your invention. Include your patent attorney's, manufacturers' and potential licensees' interactions.

The Invention Notebook is an indispensable tool used to collect every scrap of information related to your idea that you plan to patent. Log any brainstorms or notions on your idea. Log all activity and interactions related to the development of the invention. If you research companies in the field of the invention, do a preliminary patent search at the library, consult with a patent attorney, engage the services of a consultant, get advice from your accountant, line up a manufacturer for production and so forth, all these activities should be logged. The paper trail may help you later on.

A vital part of the patent process includes "due diligence," or the continued and persistent march toward market versus conceptualizing an idea, sitting on it and doing nothing with it. It is imperative you continue with progress on your idea, prove it actually works (known as "reduction to practice") and finally filing a patent application. In certain legal situations your patent rights may be jeopardized if you fail to show due diligence.

Document your invention by writing down a clear and complete description of your idea. Explain how it works. Sketch your concepts on paper. Don't worry if it is not professional quality. The idea is to record a visual representation to the best of your ability. A professional draftsperson will clean it up later.

Always use nonerasable ink—never pencil—to make entries in your notebook. These handwritten entries must be permanent and nonalterable. If you make a pencil sketch outside of the notebook, make a photocopy of it then paste it into the notebook. This makes it permanent and unalterable. Also remember not to leave spaces in your notebook. All entries should be in sequential order. Do not make notes on separate sheets of paper to be entered into the notebook later. Always make your entries directly into the notebook at the time they occur to you.

Keep your entries in chronological order. Enter all thoughts, data, results and so forth with plentiful descriptions and elaborate detail. Incorrect entries should be crossed out. Corrections should immediately follow.

If at any future time your patent is challenged, your Invention Notebook will prove to be a crucial piece of evidence on your behalf. Your goal must be to create a secure piece of evidence. You accomplish this by making it impossible to modify your invention record after the original entries have been made. A proper record of documentation can spell the difference between keeping or losing your patent rights.

Date of Reduction to Practice

As soon as you conceive of your invention you should strive to design, build and test it as soon as possible. This is known as an Actual Reduction to Practice. Proving only on paper that the invention works or filing a complete patent application qualifies as a Constructive Reduction to Practice. Both are important in patent law and either one is adequate to satisfy the PTO's requirement for a timely reduction to practice for an invention.

The legal benefit of an early date of reduction to practice may become evident if your patent is contested by an "interference" or if "prior art" shows up from before the date of filing of your patent application. In either situation you may lose your patent rights or win them depending upon how early you can prove your date of reduction to practice. In an interference, the PTO receives two patent applications for essentially the same invention from two different inventors. This is not an uncommon experience. About 1 percent of all patent applications face an interference. Since only one patent can be granted, the PTO must determine in an "interference proceeding" who invented the concept first. The concerned parties must submit evidence showing when the invention was made. Whoever has first reduced the invention to practice wins the patent rights. If prior art (the invention is already patented or published) shows up in a publication from before your filing date, all may not be lost. If you are able to prove you built and tested your invention before the publication date, thus satisfying the requirement to reduce your invention to practice, you preserve your patent rights.

The One-Year Rule

If you decide to offer for sale, complete a sale, commercially use or publicly disclose by exhibition or in print or electronic media your invention, then you must file a patent application within one year. Should you neglect to file within this one-year period, the PTO will not allow you nor anyone else to file a patent on your invention. The public disclosure of the idea violates the PTO's requirement your invention be considered "novel." Additionally, if you wish to obtain foreign patents for your invention, you should file in the United States before you sell, offer for sale, commercially use or exhibit, publish or publicly disclose your invention. You may then freely disclose the invention in the aforementioned ways as long as you file for your foreign patents within one year of your U.S. patent filing date.

"For an idea that does not at first seem insane, there is no hope."

—Albert Einstein

CHAPTER 2
Patenting Your Idea

Patent Searches

The next big step in protecting an idea for an invention is to determine if the idea is potentially patentable. A patent search must be performed to determine if any prior art exists. *Black's Law Dictionary* defines prior art as "any relevant knowledge, acts, descriptions and patents which pertain to, but predate invention in question."

You may wish to perform the patent search yourself. Some inventors tend to be a bit paranoid, reluctant to disclose their ideas to anyone. If you decide to go this route, expect to spend a good week performing the search. You may do this at the Patent Public Search Room at the Scientific and Technical Information Center of the Patent and Trademark Office at Crystal Plaza 3, 2021 Jefferson Davis Highway, Arlington, Virginia. If this location is not convenient, you can conduct searches at one of many Patent and Trademark Depository Libraries (PTDLs) scattered across the country. This book's Appendix contains the full list of PTDLs and their addresses and phone numbers. The wisdom of conducting your own patent search is highly questionable, however, if you have never done so before. In this case, it is better to engage the services of a professional.

A professional patent searcher or patent search organization may be located through your local inventors group or by their listing in the *Yellow Pages*. A comprehensive search may take seven to ten hours. Patent searchers charge hourly rates of $30 to more than $60 per hour in the Washington,

DC area. You can expect to pay anywhere from $175 to $500 for a quality search. A quality search is a comprehensive one. If your patent search is not comprehensive, it is next to worthless.

Should you decide to contract directly with a professional patent searcher, you may well save a significant amount of money. When you hire a local patent attorney or agent he or she must either travel to Arlington, Virginia, or hire an associate in the DC area to perform the patent search. The end result is you pay for two patent professionals to do the work or pay travel expenses for your local patent professional. Know your options and don't throw your money away.

You have a choice. You may hire a lay patent searcher or a patent attorney or agent in the DC area. Lay patent searchers may be found in the *Yellow Pages* of the Washington and Virginia telephone service areas under the heading of "Patent Searchers." If you are looking for a patent agent or attorney to conduct your patent search, you may find one by checking the listings in the PTO's publication *Attorneys and Agents Registered to Practice Before the U.S. Patent and Trademark Office*. This publication can be purchased from the U.S. Government Bookstore, or can be found at all the Patent and Trademark Depository Libraries or can be accessed on the PTO's electronic Bulletin Board System.

Whomever you consider to perform your patent search, interview him or her by telephone first. A brief conversation will give you a sense of whether or not you can work with this person. As with choosing any professional, try to get a personal referral from someone you know and trust. It could be a colleague, an inventor or a friend who can suggest a particular patent professional with whom they have had good experience.

Your professional patent searcher will need specific information from you to conduct a comprehensive, accurate search. To do this, your chosen searcher needs a complete and clear description of your invention. Include your drawings as well. Some people choose to send copies of their Invention Notebook entries. Others make up a disclosure document. Either way, do *not* include any dates on these papers. If someone spots your invention notes and wants to steal your idea (a very rare occurrence) it becomes much more difficult for them to antedate your patent.

Some inventors insist upon the use of confidentiality or nondisclosure agreements. If you are dealing with patent attorneys, be aware they are bound by the attorney-client relationship to confidentiality in all patent and invention matters. However, don't feel shy about insisting that patent agents and lay patent searchers sign and honor your confidentiality agreement. You are poised to invest a significant amount of time and money in your brainchild. At this point it has zero protection other than secrecy. You deserve the peace of mind that comes from having a signed confidentiality agreement. Keep one thing in mind: A signed agreement is only as good as the signatory's word. Choose wisely to whom you show your inventions.

We recommend you draw up an invention disclosure document when you intend to submit an idea for a patent search. See our invention disclosure document for the H_2O Anchor Mulch concept we proposed for a patent search. *(Pages 22, 23, 24)* Study this document as an example of how you should draw up your own invention disclosure document. The document should include the title of invention, purpose, description, novel features, ramifications, documentation of building and testing, advantages of the invention and artwork such as sketches and pictures.

As is often the case in patent searches, a number of prior art patents were found in the search for our H_2O Anchor Mulch concept. Significant prior art exists resulting in limited patentable novelty in the invention concept described in our disclosure. U.S. Patent No. 4,833,822, which belongs to P. DiGrassi, prevents us from obtaining broad patent protection. For illustrative purposes, we have included the DiGrassi patent. Examination of it will reveal that it is nearly identical to our H_2O Anchor Mulch concept.

However, all is not lost. By designing and applying for patent protection for a filler adapter device with snap fittings that can engage the tubular segments of the mulch pad in series, and specifying the diameters and material composition of the tubular segments, narrow protection could probably be secured. Whether or not this narrow patent protection would be economically practical or commercially viable is open to debate.

This example goes to show how it may be possible to design around someone else's patent and obtain a new patent. Many people come up with ideas that are, unfortunately, already patented. Don't be too discouraged if this happens to you. It is quite common. In our case, life handed us a lemon, so we made lemonade. Instead of patenting and marketing the H_2O Anchor Mulch, we used the materials developed to illustrate a point for this book. It was not a complete waste of time after all. *(See DiGrassi's Mulch Patent, page 25.)*

INVENTION DISCLOSURE FOR PATENTABILITY SEARCH

TITLE:
H$_2$O ANCHOR MULCH

PURPOSE:
To provide a plastic garden mulch that is self-weighted with water.

DESCRIPTION:
A landscape fabric similar to the WEED-X brand product is used. Plastic bladders which hold water weight the fabric edges down. Twist-off caps at both ends of the mulch allow you to fill the bladder with water and drain it for storage. The plastic garden mulch is fiber reinforced and permeable to water and air but impermeable to light. The edges of the fabric are folded over to wrap around the plastic water bladder. The fabric is overlapped with itself and the two layers are fused to each other to contain the bladder. Holes for the end caps are made in the fabric. The fabric near the hole is bonded to the cap and bladder for a tight seal. The mulch ends are sealed to secure the plastic bladder. See sketch 1.

SKETCH 1:

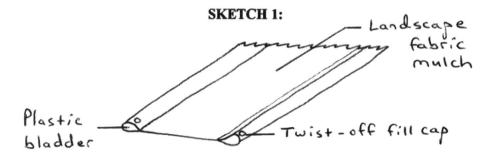

POSSIBLE NOVEL FEATURES:
It is believed that the use of a water weighted bladder to secure landscape mulch to the ground is an entirely novel feature.

RAMIFICATIONS:
A possible alternative design involves the use of heavy gauge plastic mulch. This mulch is impermeable to water, light and air. The plastic is folded over completely upon itself to create a double layer. The mulch's top layer is bonded to the bottom layer at three points. These points extend the length of the mulch:
{a} Six inches more or less in from one edge.
{b} Six inches more or less in from the other edge.
{c} Bond the free outer edge.

An optional construction technique would bond all the plastic together between points {a} &{b}. Holes are made at the end of each strip of mulch for the twist-off cap. Heat seal or bond in some other fashion the cap to the mulch. Bond the ends of the strip of mulch to

---

create an airtight and water-tight bladder for filling with water. Perforate the walking path in the center of the mulch to allow drainage of pooled water from rainfall or irrigation. See sketch 2.

SKETCH 2:

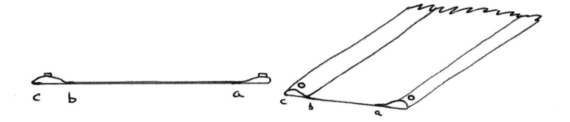

RAMIFICATIONS (continued):

A second alternative construction technique involves one strip of mulch overlaid by another strip of mulch. the plastic sheets are bonded to each other at four points along the length of the strip of mulch. The rest of the construction technique is identical to the previous example. At point {d} the free edge of the plastic is bonded in an identical manner as point {c}. Refer to sketch 3.

SKETCH 3:

RAMIFICATIONS (continued):

A third alternative construction technique involves only one plastic sheet of mulch. Both edges are folded in to create pockets. These edges are bonded. Caps are added at both ends and the ends sealed. The walking path is perforated to allow water drainage. See sketch 4.

SKETCH 4:

BUILDING AND TESTING:

Picture of working model taken in September of 1996 by Tom Bellavance. Photo accompanies this disclosure.

ADVANTAGES:

Holds down plastic mulch in your garden between rows of plants. Simply filling the bladder with water weights the mulch down. Can be secured quickly and with great ease even by people with physical infirmity or the elderly. This method is superior to other methods of anchoring such as burying the edges in dirt, using metal staples to pin the mulch to the ground or using heavy rocks or lumber to anchor the edges of the mulch. Easier to pick up than any other mulch method: just open caps, drain water, replace caps, roll up the mulch and store it. Other benefits include superior tear resistance and thicker, more durable material than others, allowing multi-year use.

OTHER BENEFITS OF H$_2$O ANCHOR MULCH:

Controls weeds.

Boosts soil temperatures.

Conserves soil moisture. Less watering required.

Eliminates the majority of hoeing and cultivating.

Improves yields.

Earlier harvests.

Deters soil insects.

Reduces problems with soil-borne diseases.

Plants grow faster, more lush, and healthier.

Doesn't kill beneficial earthworms like tillers and cultivators do.

Gives plants improved drought resistance.

Conserves soil. Reduces wind and water erosion.

Keeps gardeners' feet clean of mud and dirt.

Allows 100% of fertilizer, organic matter and nutrients to go into your garden crops.

Less time and attention needed to garden.

Eliminates the need for pre-emergent chemicals for weed control.

Prevents root damage from tillers and cultivators.

Eliminates messy and unsightly weed debris.

No pollution of your land by plowing plastic mulch into the soil.

Mulch doesn't whip in the wind damaging tender young plants.

Can easily flop the mulch away from plants to weed then flop the mulch back up against the weeded row.

United States Patent [19]

DiGrassi

[11] Patent Number: 4,833,822

[45] Date of Patent: May 30, 1989

[54] **MULCH STRIP**

[76] Inventor: Paul DiGrassi, 70 Bull Hill La., West Haven, Conn. 06516

[21] Appl. No.: 140,727

[22] Filed: Jan. 4, 1988

[51] Int. Cl.⁴ A01G 13/06
[52] U.S. Cl. 47/9; 47/2
[58] Field of Search 47/56, 9, 14, 15, 16, 47/2, 25

[56] **References Cited**

U.S. PATENT DOCUMENTS

1,372,996	3/1921	Eckart	47/9
2,015,471	9/1935	Genuit	47/9
2,030,267	2/1936	Pratt	47/9
2,058,934	10/1936	Yohe	47/26
2,909,328	10/1959	Babyak	47/25 X
2,974,442	3/1961	Womelsdorf	47/26
3,154,885	11/1964	Waterman et al.	47/26
3,205,619	9/1965	Henry	47/9
3,206,892	9/1965	Telkes et al.	47/9 X
3,727,345	4/1973	Smith	47/2
3,857,195	12/1974	Johnson	47/25 X
4,023,506	5/1977	Robey	47/26
4,044,501	8/1977	Frydryk	47/26
4,071,974	2/1978	Tripp, Jr.	47/9 X
4,120,797	10/1978	Huebner	210/522
4,241,671	12/1980	Joyner et al.	110/188

FOREIGN PATENT DOCUMENTS

2504352	10/1982	France	47/28 R
2544960	11/1984	France	47/9
611117	5/1979	Switzerland	47/9
487619	1/1976	U.S.S.R.	47/9

Primary Examiner—Robert A. Hafer
Assistant Examiner—Kevin G. Rooney
Attorney, Agent, or Firm—Jerry T. Kearns

[57] **ABSTRACT**

A mulch strip consists of an elongated base sheet formed from a flexible plastic material having a pair of parallel fluid reservoir tubes extending along the length of the base strip, down opposite side edges of the strip. Each of the fluid reservoir tubes is provided with a hose fitting for connection with a conventional garden hose for filling the reservoir tubes with water. In use, the water filled tubes serve to hold the mulch strip in place, and form a channel for retaining rain water on the surface of the strip. The fluid reservoir tubes also collect heat and serve to keep the ground beneath the strip warm after sunset. A plurality of concentric perforations are spaced along the length of the base sheet for the insertion of plants into the ground through the base sheet. Spaced peg holes are provided around the periphery of the base sheet which allow pegs to be inserted through the holes to retain the mulch strip in place. The fluid reservoir tubes may be provided with a male hose connection at one end and a female hose connection at an opposite end so that a series of mulch strips may be connected together in end to end relation. In this fashion, a plurality of connected mulch strips may be filled without repeated reconnection of the garden hose.

1 Claim, 3 Drawing Sheets

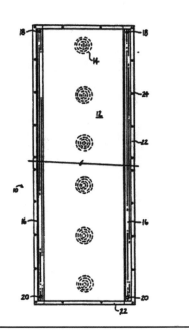

DiGrassi's Mulch Patent, page 1.

Performing Your Own Search in a Patent and Trademark Depository Library

Many inventors choose to perform their own search at one of the Patent and Trademark Depository Libraries scattered across 49 states, The District of Columbia and Puerto Rico. Wise inventors know one of the first steps after conceiving of an idea for an invention is to perform a patent search. If prior art exists, you need to know this to avoid wasting any more time on that idea. You need to kill these ideas before they assume a life of their own and steal all your time and money.

However, you should be forewarned that a patent search conducted at a PTDL may not be as complete as can be performed at the PTO in Arlington, Virginia. Despite some shortcomings though, this is a great place to start, but be aware of the following PTDL deficiencies:

1. PTDLs may not have all patents issued from the genesis of the PTO.

2. No PTDLs have physical separation of patents by subject matter into searchable classifications.

3. No PTDLs have foreign patents.

4. No PTDLs have literature other than patents from which to search.

These deficiencies are bound to affect the thoroughness of your search. For this reason it is wise to use PTDLs only as a starting point in your search.

PTDLs boast one major strength: Their staff is highly trained and trustworthy. You can (and must) totally entrust and divulge your concept to them. They will not violate that trust. You do not need to have them sign a nondisclosure or confidentiality agreement. Don't be paranoid and think they may steal your idea. They, more than most, are well aware of what it takes to successfully bring a new concept to market. It takes time, money, contacts, experience, skill, talent, inspiration and luck. It doesn't hurt to have plenty of chutzpah and panache as well.

Learn how to conduct a patent search from the helpful staff and see if your invention is already patented by someone else. If you are lucky, you won't see it in the records and you can take your next step—hiring a professional to conduct an intensive search at the PTO. The modest fee is certainly worth it for the peace of mind you get knowing a comprehensive search was performed by an experienced professional.

Another option is to go to your patent attorney or agent, who can arrange a search for you by a professional patent searcher. Expect your attorney or agent to add a premium to the fee charged to him or her by the patent searcher. Don't throw away good money needlessly—you will need it later. Better to contract the services of an independent patent searcher yourself and turn the results over to your patent attorney or agent for an opinion.

If your patent search turns up no prior art or competing inventions, then it is time to file for a patent. A word of caution: Don't procrastinate. All too often an invention is thought up at the same time by numerous people. Call it coincidence or whatever. Odds are, someone is thinking along the same line as you are about a particular idea. If you dither, they may be first to file. This has happened many times.

Case in point: An obscure and struggling inventor, plagued by financial woes, worked in feverish secrecy on an idea for an improvement in telegraphy. Alexander Graham Bell didn't have much faith in the future of harmonic telegraphy but fervently believed in his concept of telephony. His father-in-law, a shrewd lawyer and financial backer, insisted a copy of Bell's telephony specifications be placed with a Washington attorney. Fearing treachery from abroad and following his instincts, Bell's father-in-law instructed the Washington attorney to file a patent application in Bell's name on the morning of February 14, 1876. This was done without Bell's knowledge.

Only a few *hours* after Alexander Graham Bell's patent application for the telephone was registered, another inventor, Elisha Gray, who was known as the foremost "electrician" in the United States, submitted a caveat for the invention of his telephonic device. The subsequent development of phone systems would have been profoundly different. Instead of telephone service by Ma Bell, we might have had a Ma Gray in our cultural lexicon. Alexander Graham Bell came that close to slipping into historical obscurity.

Patent Attorneys and Agents

You may wish to prepare and file your patent application with the Patent and Trademark office yourself. It's perfectly legal to do so. You can obtain the required forms right off the Internet. Visit the Patent and Trademark Office's Web site at http://www.uspto.gov. According to the PTO, all forms are available in Adobe PDF format for viewing and printing. You will need Adobe's Acrobat reader installed on your computer; it is available for free.

Unless you are well versed in patent law, Patent and Trademark Office practices and have substantial knowledge in the scientific or technical areas involved in your particular invention, have a patent attorney or agent do it. The do-it-yourself route may very well result in a patent grant but may not adequately protect the particular invention. If your patent is not adequately protected, then you've wasted your time and money. Look for an experienced professional. Take the same care in making this decision that you would when screening a medical professional or accountant.

The PTO publishes a comprehensive directory of registered patent attorneys and agents. You may purchase the directory *Attorneys and Agents Registered to Practice Before the U.S. Patent and Trademark Office* from the U.S. Government Printing Office for a modest fee. You can place credit card orders by calling (202) 512-1800.

The National Council of Patent Law Associations (NCPLA) consists of 40 local and regional patent law associations. For a list of active patent attorneys, contact them at NCPLA, Crystal Plaza 3, Room 1D01, 2021 Jefferson Davis Highway, Arlington, VA 22202.

Contact your local, county or state bar association's lawyer referral service. Check the *Yellow Pages* for their listings. When you call them, tell them the nature of the legal services you need performed. They will refer you to an appropriate legal professional in your area.

Additionally, you may wish to get referrals from other inventors. Contact your local inventors association. Many excellent patent attorneys and agents are affiliated with inventors associations or the members can refer you to a good patent professional they have used.

Check the *Yellow Pages* for associations of patent attorneys and agents as well as individual listings of patent attorneys and agents. One of the best ways to screen attorneys is to go to your local library and consult the *Martindale-Hubbell Directory of Lawyers and Law Firms*. This publication rates attorneys by peer review. Their peers evaluate them based upon legal ability, experience, ethics, reliability and other qualifications important to consumers. Be certain to ascertain that the attorney or agent is a registered patent professional. Those attorneys or agents not recognized by the PTO to conduct this practice cannot represent inventors before the Patent and Trademark Office.

How do you go about choosing an honest lawyer? In a speech before the American Bar Association, Chief Justice Warren Burger once stated that in his opinion 95 percent of all lawyers should be disbarred. Some people say it's not hard to find a good lawyer, but it's hard to find an honest one. Sadly, the legal profession does suffer from a serious image problem. Personally, we've been blessed with several excellent attorneys to represent us, but they were not easy to find. We wish you good luck in your search for representation and present the following guidelines.

Interview several prospective patent attorneys in the customary free or low cost initial consultation. You need someone with the requisite professional expertise in your field of invention as well as an ability to communicate with ease and understanding. Ask these questions as you interview the attorney:

1. How many years have you performed patent law? Summarize experience.
2. Do you have a specialization in a certain field? State qualifications.
3. How many other clients do you represent?
4. What course of action do you suggest?
5. What is the step-by-step process?
6. Do you anticipate any difficulties?
7. How long does the patent process take?

8. What will it cost me? What is your hourly fee? What are my payment options?

9. Who is your search firm and what do they charge? How quickly can they do an accurate search?

10. Can you give me several inventor and business references?

11. Exactly what services will I receive?

Check the attorney's background by making an inquiry with the state and local Chambers of Commerce. Has the attorney ever been accused of professional misconduct or unethical business practices? Make a similar inquiry with the Better Business Bureau. Make certain there are no complaints about the patent attorney's business practices. For a comprehensive list of Better Business Bureaus in the United States, refer to the Appendix. It's always a good idea to interview several of the attorney's clients. Find out how effective the attorney was for them. Are they pleased with their representation? Find out if the attorney lectures or performs teaching duties at a college or university. These professionals are often a notch above the rest.

Always insist on an agreement of representation in writing. The written contract will spell out your lawyer's duties to you, the nature of the work to be performed and the way you are to be billed. This retainer agreement should be understood completely before signing. It should not be written in an excruciating form of legalese that a reasonable person cannot understand. Some states have Rules of Professional Conduct that require an attorney who has been retained by a new client to provide to that client a written agreement of the services to be provided and the fees to be charged.

Pay special attention to how and for what you will be billed. Make sure the specifics are on paper. Expected activities you will be billed for are phone calls, legal research and preparing letters, among many others. Ask if you are responsible for the lawyer's business expenses such as photocopying, postage, parking fees, mileage and so forth. Be sure to determine who pays for travel time.

If a retainer fee is charged it should be applied against work performed on your patent case. Retainer fees are often negotiable whereas the hourly fees most lawyers charge are often not. Insist upon seeing a sample bill and make sure you fully understand all the charges. Request a fully itemized monthly billing statement you can review for accuracy.

You must take responsibility for keeping on top of the lawyer's work. As a client you have a responsibility to follow certain guidelines to promote a good working relationship with your patent attorney. Ask your patent attorney to send you copies of all documents and correspondence. Set up a working file for your patent and keep copies of important legal paperwork in this file. Always read and understand any legal document before you approve or sign it. Keep informed and ask questions of your attorney if you don't understand something. Always evaluate the quality of your attorney's work.

Learn to communicate with your attorney. When he or she talks, listen and take notes. Better yet, ask if you can record your conversations so you have completely accurate recall. Speak up if anything is bothering you about the patent process. Always be honest and disclose information the attorney needs to know.

While on the subject of audio recordings, you may wish to use a tape recorder for logging ideas as well as interviews and telephone calls. You won't miss a word with this handy piece of technology. We advise you to record everything you possibly can. The benefits will become obvious as time passes and memories dim.

A word of caution: The law, which varies from state to state, may require you to obtain permission from the other party on the phone to record your conversation. Some states allow you to record a phone conversation if you are one of the participating parties in that conversation. Other states are not so lenient and prohibit such activities. Permission may be in writing or may be given at the start of, and part of the recorded conversation. Some but not all telephone recording systems emit an audible beep tone every 15 seconds. Your state's Office of the Attorney General can provide information on the legality of recording telephone conversations. Refer to the Appendix for state-by-state listings of Attorneys General.

Even if it is not illegal, it is considered good manners to ask permission to tape record. Most people have no problem with having their interview or business meeting taped as long as you are up front with them.

The cheapest telephone recording system, and a handy one at that, consists of a tape recorder connected to your telephone by a telephone pickup device. This device attaches to the receiver by a suction cup and plugs into your tape recorder. Radio Shack telephone pickup model #44-533 is simple and effective and costs about $4.

Your patent attorney has certain responsibilities to you. These responsibilities relate to professional ethics and facilitation of a smooth working relationship. A good patent attorney will always:

- Keep clients fully informed on the progress of patent matters.
- Return telephone calls, faxes, letters and email in a timely fashion.
- Listen to clients and address their concerns.
- Draw up and file patent applications without delay.
- Provide accurate, detailed and timely billing for legal services rendered in accordance with a written fee agreement.

One caveat: If your attorney has your papers for a month or two and has done nothing on your patent application—take your papers and run! Either the attorney is too busy to do a quality job on your patent or just doesn't care about you. You may be considered small potatoes and your patent application will linger at the bottom of the pile. Some large patent law firms will not give the independent inventor much respect. They make their money off large corporations in defending their intellectual property rights in court. The bottom line is that corporate clients make these law firms rich; independent inventors don't. Whose patent work do you think gets priority?

Refusing to allow your patent application to linger on a patent attorney's desk also endorses due diligence. You should make a determination up front whether the first choice for your patent attorney will serve you as you expect. If you have doubts, move on. Time's a-wasting! You are by no means desperate. You're not asking for a handout. Yes, you may be a novice inventor, but all pros start out that way. Insist upon professionalism. No, demand it!

When you go to the attorney's office, go organized. Preparation is the key. Plan an agenda for your meeting. Organize your documents and have your questions written down. Obtain necessary photocopies ahead of time. This can save you money. Remember, time is money for your attorney.

What should you bring when you go to hire a patent attorney? Bring copies of the record of invention from your Invention Notebook. These papers must describe your invention in explicit detail. You should define your idea broadly enough to prevent others from making a minor substitution of one or several elements. This allows them to take advantage of your idea and call it their own.

Your claims must be complete, clear and specific but also broad enough (but not too broad) to prevent them from finding a way around your patent and busting your monopoly. According to *General Information Concerning Patents*, "claims are brief descriptions of the subject matter of the invention, eliminating unnecessary details and reciting all essential features necessary to distinguish the invention from what is old. The claims are the operative part of the patent. Novelty and patentability are judged by the claims."

Also bring detailed drawings of your invention to your attorney. Working prototypes are not required although they certainly are useful for visualization purposes for your attorney's benefit.

The patent drawings for the application will be performed by an in-house or freelance skilled draftsman. Patents may require numerous sheets of drawings. Expect to pay around $100 per sheet for the services of a bonded draftsman.

Patent attorneys charge around $2,500 to $15,000 to prepare a patent application. More complex inventions require more work so naturally you must expect to pay more. You should consult with several attorneys and get estimates of expected charges. Get it in writing! You don't want to experience fee creep where the attorney squeezes you for more money with excuses you don't want to hear. Agree upon and establish a cap on prices. A price cap keeps the attorney wonderfully focused. If the attorney balks, move on. Don't be afraid to shop around for the best price. Always remember, it's a buyer's market!

If the inventor is what the PTO terms a "small entity," that is, if you are an independent inventor or affiliated with a small business concern or a non-profit organization, the PTO *reduces its fees by half.* You simply file a small entity declaration to qualify for this status. There is a specific small entity declaration form for each of the three groups. Independent inventors are those who are unaffiliated with large companies. Small business concerns are those with fewer than 500 employees. Nonprofit organizations include colleges and universities, nonprofit scientific or educational groups and other groups that qualify as tax exempt. Your patent attorney can provide you with the appropriate form.

After your attorney sends your patent application to the PTO, you begin the waiting game. After a few weeks, the PTO sends your file number to you. You refer to this file number in any future correspondence with the PTO. As the wheels of government turn slowly, expect the application process (known as the patent pendency time) to last about 20 months.

Always insist your attorney send you copies of all documents and correspondence prepared on your behalf. Remember to safeguard all of your patent documents. Keep copies of all your and your attorney's papers in a fire-proof safe. The Sentry Fire-Safe security storage file is a first-rate product designed specifically for this purpose. We use it and heartily recommend it. It gives us piece of mind. Were a fire ever to break out, years of work would be safeguarded. Your most important and sensitive documents should, of course, be kept in a bank safe deposit box.

"Our doubts are traitors and make us lose the good we oft might win by fearing to attempt."
—William Shakespeare

CHAPTER 3
The Patent Process— After Filing

After the Patent Is Awarded

Aren't you the lucky one! You've beaten the odds. Out of all the people out there with a hot idea for an invention, you are one of the very few who have acted and been granted a U.S. patent. During any point in the long and arduous process, your invention might have been tripped up. Any one of many calamities might have occurred. The patent search might have turned up prior art. Someone else might have beaten you to patenting the idea. Your patent attorney or agent might have made critical errors in the patent application process. The PTO's examination process might have determined the invention to be unpatentable subject matter or that the invention is not novel. You survived this minefield. Congratulations!

Upon allowance and issue of the patent you have three months to make payment of the issue fee. You've kept the most intimate details of your invention completely secret for all these months. On the day your patent is granted, your patent file becomes available to public inspection. *The Official Gazette* of the Patent and Trademark Office publishes your invention including the invention's main drawing and first claim. Your secret is secret no more. Your technology is out there where those companies who seek eco-

33

nomic advantage can attempt to design around your patent. If they can come up with a single additional claim, they will be able to get their own patent and bust yours in the process. Due to the inherent weaknesses in the design of the patent system, you run the risk of losing your rights of monopoly for your invention.

Not surprisingly, some people elect not to patent their technology but to keep it a trade secret. By keeping proprietary information secret, your business can maintain a competitive advantage over others. With a trade secret, you avoid the full disclosure of your invention's innermost workings, which can rob you of protection for your technology. Treating this information as a trade secret instead of patenting it prevents the release of this sensitive information to the public.

Trade secrets can remain secret in perpetuity rather than only a 20-year patent-in-force term. Manufacturing processes, chemical formulas and recipes are typically the sort of intellectual property that can be protected by the trade secret route. Because of their value, businesses will go to great lengths to protect and preserve their trade secrets.

Employing trade secrecy to protect intellectual property affords you several advantages. There is no disclosure of the details of your invention to the public. You can protect the trade secret forever versus being limited to a 20-year term with a patent. The trade secret route is fast, easy and inexpensive as opposed to patenting, which can take months or years, is difficult in process with uncertain results and costs significant money.

There are disadvantages to trade secrecy that you must recognize. Chief among them is the possibility that someone else can independently invent the same concept and patent it as their own. You have no legal rights to the invention if this occurs. In fact, they can sue you for patent infringement! Trade secrets must be constantly and scrupulously protected. This often can be quite a challenge, particularly if you have disclosed your trade secret to employees. The temptation to share this secret information for a price can be too great to resist. There is legal recourse if someone acquires your trade secret by illegal means. However, if someone discovers your trade secret honestly and ethically, such as by independent discovery, you no longer can protect the proprietary information.

The ability to discover your trade secret by reverse engineering of your invention should prevent you from considering utilizing the trade secret route. If thorough examination by technical means allows your secrets to be divined, your secrets are not safe. Sophisticated analytical tools now in use make reverse engineering easy.

Whether the trade secret route is right for you or not depends upon the nature of your invention, your company and your market. Consider carefully before deciding to patent and therefore advertise to the world your most sensitive trade secrets.

Patent Rights—What Rights?

What right does the U.S. government grant to the patent holder? The patent grant confers "the right to exclude others from making, using or selling the invention throughout the United States." The U.S. government grants a monopoly. It doesn't grant a right to make, use or sell the invention. We are free to do that dependent upon the rights of others and our conformance to whatever general laws of commerce and society that exist. The right of exclusive commercial exploitation allows the patentee the options of manufacture, marketing and sale of the invention or licensing others to do so.

Maintenance Fees

A fairly recent invention by the Patent and Trademark Office are the Maintenance Fees, which are required to maintain the patent in force during its 20-year life. For patents awarded to applications received after December 12, 1980, a fee is due at 3.5, 7.5 and 11.5 years from the date the patent was granted. Due at 3.5 years is $1,050. Due at 7.5 years is $2,100. Due at 11.5 years is $3,160. These figures are from the PTO fee schedule as of October 1, 1997. No notice is mailed to the patent owner that payment is due. It is up to the patent owner to make payment on time or within a six-month grace period immediately following the due date or your *patent will expire*. Maintenance fees will be covered in depth in Chapter 7.

Self-Promotion

Promoting yourself and your accomplishments should become second nature to you. You must spread the word about your newly patented invention as part of your marketing efforts. Don't be shy. Become a braggart. You've accomplished something unique and rare. You have successfully conceived of and developed a brand new invention. This is truly a rare achievement and you should be proud of yourself. So promote . . . and prosper.

After the PTO issues the date and number of your patent, it is time for you to begin promoting. Start with a press release, which is more correctly referred to as a news release or media release. Remember, you'll be sending the release to the electronic media as well as the print media. Be certain to concentrate upon your local media as well as trade magazines. Providing wholesalers and distributors with your news release can also be productive. Send them the news release and a copy of your patent. Including camera-ready artwork of your product is a clever idea.

You should target your prime prospects with a press kit. A glossy press kit filled with your news release and other promotional material gets attention. By making this additional information available you increase the odds of getting your story published. Although most editors enjoy receiving a well-produced press kit, a minority actually despise them. They toss these kits into the circular file. These editors are no-nonsense news gatherers who have no inclination to wade through what they consider to be a pile of fluff. Do not be discouraged. Most editors enjoy receiving these packets of information. These extra details only serve to make a better story. Consider including the following material in your press kit:

- News release.
- Publicity photo of the inventor and personal biography.
- Camera-ready artwork of inventions, products or company logos.
- Cover letter or personalized note to pitch your story idea.
- Copy of patent.
- Product samples.
- Fact sheets to provide technical background information.
- Promotional information such as brochures and audio and video tapes.
- Prepaid return postcard to request further information or an interview.
- Copies of previous news articles (blurbs, product reviews, feature stories).
- Creative packaging.

Premium or gift items have been known to be included in press kits. Premiums may include imprinted pens, pencils, notepads and so forth. It is not unheard of for editors to be offered something more substantial in an attempt to draw attention to the press kit—a basket of fresh-baked muffins? A bottle of scotch?

Issuing a news release allows you to garner publicity and promote your invention. This is essential as you commence marketing the invention. You will learn it is prudent to issue a news release any time a newsworthy event happens to you, your invention or your company. For illustrative purposes, we have included a sample news release used to publicize the author's Hook Pen. When the PTO awards you a patent on your invention, let the world know! News releases are so valuable in promoting your invention and yourself. The best part is—they cost so little. They are unbelievably productive for something that is almost free. You get enormous bang for the buck!

Do you want to know a secret about the news articles you read in newspapers? It is estimated 75 percent of the stories come from news releases. Companies and organizations provide the majority of the news you read in their effort to publicize and promote themselves and their products and services. The media need these news stories just as much as you need the publicity. Without the contribution news releases provide, there would not be much to report.

An entrepreneurial inventor who blindly sends out massive numbers of news releases at one time is bound to face disappointment. The scattershot approach is usually destined for failure. Always target your media selection.

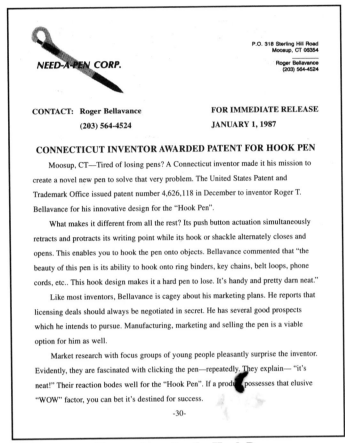

News release for the Hook Pen.

Look for publications and media outlets compatible with the subject matter in the release. Address your release to the appropriate editor. Look for editors who cover topics related to yours.

Select a dozen media outlets and concentrate your efforts on them. Make most of them local ones. When given a choice, an editor is more likely to run an article on a local business rather than one that is not. Readers want local news. You would be wise to call the media outlet's editorial offices and verify the name of the appropriate editor to receive the release. Get their address so you can properly direct your news release to this person. It is a great idea to personalize a cover letter or enclose a handwritten note to this editor.

Consult a good book on advertising to learn how to write an effective news release. Check the Bibliography/Recommended Reading section in the back of this book for several advertising titles we recommend. Keep in mind the following information when writing your news release:

- Open with a provocative headline to immediately grab attention. Capitalize and center the headline below the dateline.

- Keep it short—one page only. Use double- or one-and-one-half-spaced type.

37

- Present the most important information in the first few paragraphs. Editors usually cut material from the back end of a story first.
- Always cover the journalist's who, what, when, where, why, how and how much as soon as possible in the release. Write with the journalistic style of news stories.
- Be to the point and conversational. Don't get overly technical.
- Highlight the invention's major benefit.
- Type "For Immediate Release" at the top.
- Always include ordering information if your product is ready for or on the market. Make sure it is a quality product and ready for the market. Although many editors will not include ordering information in the article, some will allow its inclusion. (It's fantastic when they do!) Remember to code this information so you can track responses.
- Include artwork such as a sketch or picture of your invention. Don't forget to send along a professionally taken, well-composed photo of you, the inventor.
- Make it easy for people to reach you. Include your name, address, phone number, fax number and email address if you have it. This information plus the date goes at the top.
- Saturation coverage works. Don't forget your local media—hit 'em hard.
- Target your releases toward media outlets your research has indicated would be interested in your product.
- Make your release newsworthy—entertain and use drama. It should not read like an advertisement.
- Quote yourself in the release.
- Follow up your news release mailing with a call to the editor asking if he or she needs more information to publish the release.
- Laser print the news release on high quality company letterhead.
- It is customary to type "30" or "###" or "END" at the end of the release.
- Allow adequate lead time to coordinate publication of the story with any time-sensitive event you are planning. Contact the editor's office for lead-time estimates.
- Use the correct format.

Always follow up with a telephone call to the editor. Confirm receipt of the news release and offer to provide more information if the editor needs it to run the story. Make the editor's job as easy as possible by sending a newsworthy story that includes all the facts a journalist would have included. Sometimes it is all too easy for the writer of the release to forget to include essential facts. We've all done it. Sometimes we just can't see the forest for the trees.

Persistence pays off. If your first news release doesn't get picked up and run, issue another. Keep issuing them on a routine basis whenever you have a newsworthy event to publicize. With persistence, you will eventually see it in print.

Send your news release to the following media outlets to have a shot at getting your invention mentioned in their columns:

- New York Times Patent Columnist
  229 West 43rd Street
  New York, NY 10036

- Julia Angwin
  States News Service
  Fax (202) 737-1851

Instead of a news release, you can write your own news or feature story to be picked up by newspapers. Do it by first writing your own news story about your invention or business. Remember to follow standard journalistic style and conventions. It should read like any other news or feature story you spot in any newspaper.

Your next step is to contact one of several agencies that distribute camera-ready news or feature stories. They will format and distribute your story for a small fee. Expect to pay a little over $1,000. These stories can be distributed to well over 10,000 U.S. newspapers. Typically, several hundred newspapers will pick up the story. Consider the power of this promotional strategy. What would it cost you to run paid advertisements in several hundred newspapers? The answer is—too much! Many people do not read advertisements but they do read news articles. By utilizing a different format you can get your message noticed.

If your invention is ready for or already on the market, this promotional outlet will give you awesome exposure. If your marketing strategy includes direct marketing to consumers, placing ordering information in the story can result in significant sales.

Besides camera-ready news and feature stories, publicity services also distribute multi-media releases and news releases. Some distribute news releases electronically to newsrooms all across America (print and broadcast). Many provide usage reports and clipping services as well. Clipping services are valuable. Anytime an article is printed about your subject (invention or company), this service provides you with a copy. Copies of these articles are perfect for your further promotional activities. Include them in press kits and sales materials such as direct marketing letters. Check with these publicity services to see what they can offer you:

- Metro Creative Graphics
  31 West 34th Street
  New York, NY 10001-3099
  (212) 947-5100; Fax (212) 714-9139

- North American Precis Syndicate
  405 Lexington Avenue, 59th Floor
  New York, NY 10174
  (212) 867-9000
  Fax (212) 867-9010

- PR Newswire
  810 Seventh Avenue
  New York, NY 10019
  (800) 832-5522

Product Marking

If you have a product already on the market based on an invention that is filed for but not yet patented, it is customary to mark it with the legend "Patent Pending." This serves as a warning to others that it is about to become a patent-protected product and thus off limits to them should they desire to manufacture, sell or use that or a similar product. You are telling them don't bother to tool up for production or purchase some knockoff and import it because their investment may suddenly go bad when patent protection kicks in.

A note of caution: Do not be tempted to mark your product Patent Pending or refer to it as such in any of your literature if you have not filed a patent application. You will be breaking the law and the U.S. government will nail you. Lawbreakers can expect a $500 fine and possible prison time.

When your patent is granted, you need to change the markings on your product as well as your marketing and sales literature. Patent law offers patent holders a choice. According to federal statute 35 USC 278, you can choose to mark the legend "Pat." or "Patent" with the patent number immediately following on your product. Your other choice is to make no mark at all on your product or simply mark it "Patented" without referring to your patent number. Your choice in this matter will have serious repercussions should you face the evil specter of infringement.

If your product is properly marked with your patent number and infringement occurs, you can sue the infringer for damages from the date you first marked your product. The infringer doesn't even have to see your notice. You can potentially recover from day one of your patent term. Should you decide not to mark your product or only mark "Patented," you must first notify the infringer that infringement is occurring. If you sue for damages, you cannot recover from the beginning of your patent protection but only for the period after you notified them of the infringement or after the date you filed suit against them, whichever is earlier. In many cases, you will not be aware of infringement activity until some time has passed. Even though you have a patent, the infringers can get away with using your intellectual property rights during this prenotification period.

Many inventors debate the pros and cons of whether or not to mark their products with their patent number. One school of thought is that if the number is marked, a potential infringer can easily order your patent from the PTO and design a new product and patent it, thus superseding yours. Some inventors and the companies they work for believe they are protecting their products and markets by not making it easy for competitors to gain access to proprietary information. Another school of thought says you might as well mark the product with the patent number. You get the benefit of being able to recover damages from infringers all the way back to day one of the patent. The infringer doesn't have to be notified of their illegal activity. The patent holder doesn't have to worry about noticing the infringement immediately to get the opportunity to recover damages fully. The fact is, if an infringer is interested in a patented but unmarked product, it is a simple process to get the patent. A simple patent search will turn up all prior art, including your patent. They can examine your claims and attempt to design around them to get their own patent.

We believe proper marking of your product with your patent number is really in your best interest. It gives you a stronger position from which to fight infringement.

Seeking a Licensing Deal

Immediately after filing your patent application is the time to seek a licensing deal with a manufacturer. You neither need nor want to wait a year or two until the PTO issues your patent. The manufacturer that licenses your invention will want the advantage of as long a patent-in-force term as possible to protect their market. This also allows them the option of obtaining foreign patent rights before time runs out to do so. Foreign patents cannot be obtained after your invention is awarded a U.S. patent. Only during the U.S. patent application time or patent pendency time can you obtain a foreign patent.

You may decide a licensing deal is the best way for you to profit from your invention. Let's explore this option. A license confers upon a licensee the right to use a patented invention for a negotiated period of time. The ownership of the patent still remains in the inventor's name. The licensee renders compensation to the inventor in the form of a royalty payment and up-front money to cover costs. You should insist on a minimum guaranteed royalty or lump sum payment to prevent your licensed manufacturer from shelving your invention. This is especially important if you are granting an exclusive license. You get paid even if the company doesn't manufacture or sell the invention. Additionally, you should insist upon a clause in the license agreement stipulating that if nothing is done with the invention for a set period of time (two years is reasonable), the license expires and the invention rights revert back to you.

It is shocking how many patents are killed by unethical companies who lock them up in a licensing deal and then shelve them. This is one strategy some companies use to stifle emerging competition. By taking the patent out of circulation, their product line and bottom line are not threatened. If they do not actively market and sell your invention, your royalty payments will be reduced or even nonexistent. Make certain any agreement you sign includes a no-shelving clause for your protection.

Royalty arrangements vary greatly depending upon how well you negotiate (actually your attorney should negotiate for you) and how much you are willing to give away to secure other important concessions in the license agreement. One strategy is to start out asking for 10 percent. Negotiate downwards. If you end up with 1 to 3 percent you've done okay. This is by and large the average range.

Of vital concern to you is of what figure you are getting a percentage. Are we talking about a percentage of the gross revenues? Net revenues? Net income? Income before extraordinary items? Many options exist. You must be cautious when negotiating the agreement. Some companies can get very creative with their accounting. If you settle for a percentage of the net, you may end up with little or nothing.

The Hollywood movie business is a wonderful example. Some movie studio accountants manipulate the books to show a zero net or even a loss for a particular movie project. Anyone expecting a percentage is out of luck. In the movie industry, if you agree to a percentage of the net, you are a fool.

Selecting the appropriate category upon which your percentage is based will determine the financial success or failure of your licensing program. Choose well, for it can mean the difference between life in mediocrity or life in Maui.

Another strategy is to spread out the royalty payments over a number of years. The initial payment might start at 5 percent for the first year. Subsequent payments decrease by a half percent per year for several years until you reach 1 or 2 percent, then continues at that rate for the rest of the term of your agreement.

The initial year or two for sales of the invention will be small, but hopefully growing. Even at a higher royalty percentage, the payment to you will be modest. By the time the product is really getting established in the marketplace, the royalty percentage will have come down. This is a decent arrangement for both you and the manufacturer.

A more advantageous royalty agreement would be to have the royalty payments, in percentage terms, match the product's lifecycle. A typical product lifecycle starts slowly, builds over time to a peak and then declines to a steady or slightly declining mature level. In this scenario, your percentage starts low, rises as sales increase, peaks and then declines to a steady rate. Using this royalty payment structure, you realize a net gain over the previous scenario. By taking a lower percentage the first year but a higher percentage as sales peak, you will not be leaving money on the table. Instead, it goes in your pocket.

Finding Prospects

It's time to do your homework. You need to find prospective manufacturers who will be good prospects for licensing your invention. Look for manufacturers who deal with products similar to your invention. The same resources we are about to mention can be used to research and locate manufacturers if you want them to manufacture your invention for you to distribute and sell. These manufacturers should possess certain characteristics:

- The company should have a history of honest and ethical business practices.

- The company should be financially sound.

- The company should have strong marketing and sales expertise.

- The company should be local so you can keep in close touch with them and offer your services as a consultant if needed. This is not a hard and fast rule. Often, it is unrealistic to expect to find a qualified manufacturer in your local area who is willing to license your patent.

- The company should be small or mid-sized. Huge companies generally suffer from NIH (Not Invented Here) syndrome. Their research and development department will be heavily biased against you.

- The company should already manufacture and market a related product line.

To find these types of companies you need to go only so far as your local library. Numerous directories exist in which you can find listings of companies, their profile including product lines, sales history, contacts, corporate officers and other valuable company information. Resources you need to check are the following:

Dun & Bradstreet Million Dollar Directory
Moody's Manuals
Standard & Poor's
Value Line Investment Survey
Business Periodical Index
Directory of Corporate Affiliations
Dun & Bradstreet Business Information Reports
Encyclopedia of Business Information Sources

In addition, the *Thomas Register of Manufacturers* cannot be beat for company research. This vast compendium of corporate listings is available in nearly every public library. The *Thomas Register of Manufacturers* lists the industrial goods and services of U.S. companies. There are three sections:

- The main *Thomas Register*: This collection of volumes contains company listings by type of product they manufacture. The company name, address, phone numbers, company profile and information on their product line are listed here.

- *Company Profiles*: Companies in this register are listed by name rather than organized in a listing by their products.

- *TOMCAT Guide*: Many companies listed in the register have their product catalogs in this valuable section.

Publications exist in which you can gain exposure for your invention if you are seeking a licensing deal or sale of patent. Independent inventors, corporations and university research and development centers advertise their ideas here attempting to interest companies and investors (such as venture capitalists) in their invention. Refer to the following information services:

American Bulletin of International Technology
Patent Licensing Gazette
Selected Business Ventures (published by General Electric Company)
Technology Mart
National Technical Information Service

Approaching a Manufacturer

When you have selected one or several prospective manufacturers it is time to prepare your presentation for them. Remember, contact a manufacturer to seek a licensing deal *after* your patent application has been filed in the PTO. Never send an unprotected idea. Be forewarned, however, the PTO must have received your patent application and initiated the examination process before you contact any manufacturer with a licensing offer. Make certain your patent application file number is in your possession.

According to the U.S. Department of Commerce, "If the inventor describes the invention in a printed publication or uses the invention publicly, or places it on sale, he must apply for a patent before one year has gone by, otherwise any right to a patent will be lost." You must heed the one-year rule. Always make sure your invention is patent pending or patented to protect your rights to it.

You should prepare a compelling and highly descriptive presentation package showcasing your invention, emphasizing what it does and its benefits to the company and/or the consumer. Be certain to indicate "Patent Pending" on your literature.

Don't think you can try to bluff a manufacturer by marking "Patent Pending" on your invention brochure when you haven't yet filed. You may be tempted to try to get a licensing deal set up before spending money on a patent. You may think, if I can't make the deal, I won't bother to file and instead, promote another invention. Big mistake. Marking "Patent Pending" on an invention or even referring to the invention as "Patent Pending" is a crime punishable by a $500 fine if you have not filed a patent application with the PTO.

By this time, you should have an actual working model of your invention. Have a professional photographer who specializes in commercial work photograph the model. Pictures are worth a thousand words so take advantage of this medium to show your invention and what it does. Have several dozen 5-by-7 or 8-by-10 inch glossy prints made for submissions.

Your presentation package will include a letter of introduction, brochure, product outline, patent drawings, laser copies of the picture of your prototype if you have one and SASE (self-addressed stamped envelope) for a reply if you do not make the presentation in person.

Your best strategy is to make a live presentation. In this case, go with a working model. Your brochure will accompany your working model and photographs. The brochure will include your contact information such as name, title, address, telephone and fax numbers, email address and a brief professional history. The most vital information is the invention's description. What is its function? *Do not reveal how it works at this point in the negotiations.* Why is it superior to other products on the market? List the benefits of the invention to both the manufacturer and consumer.

Every invention has its pros and cons. Highlight the positive features. Be ready to explain how to mitigate the negative factors. Anticipate the questions the manufacturer will ask. Provide the answers. Be able to discuss the invention's selling points. Demonstrate why it will have consumer demand.

Since you have filed the patent application for the invention, indicate it is "Patent Pending." Cite any other proprietary rights such as trademarks that have been applied for or already granted.

Three choices exist for method of presentation. First, you can mail or messenger your invention's brochure, pictures, patent without claims and signed waiver to the company president or other individual who will evaluate the invention. This is a poor sales technique if you are trying to license or sell the invention. The second choice is to rely on an invention marketing company to present your invention to industry. This is generally a bad idea. No one can make a presentation as well as you can. You, the inventor, have the knowledge, passion and will to succeed. The third and best choice is to make a live presentation of your invention to the company representative who is the decision-maker. A face-to-face presentation is more powerful and compelling. Your effectiveness is enhanced and success is much more likely.

Your first step is to write a brief letter to the company president in which you offer to demonstrate your invention to them. Your letter should be succinct, explaining who you are, what you have done and how the invention can benefit their company. Indicate you will call in a few days to request an appointment for a live demonstration of the invention to the president.

Preparation is the key for an effective and compelling live demonstration. Practice beforehand. Make certain you have polished your public speaking skills in order to present a more effective demonstration.

Assemble all your materials. In addition to all the others mentioned previously, inclusion of a working model or prototype is advisable in certain circumstances. Most often, bringing out the working model or prototype is done only after several meetings and negotiations have begun. You do not want to reveal too much too soon. An element of a trusting business relationship has to have been begun to reveal the working model. Consider the model or prototype a trade secret at this stage of the negotiations.

Never reveal the invention's claims until after signing the licensing deal or sale of the patent. If you reveal the claims prematurely, the company may be able to design around your patented invention. By adding just one additional claim of their own they can obtain a new patent that supersedes yours. Don't make this terrible mistake. You can easily lose your hard-won patent.

Use plenty of visual aids during your presentation. Schematics, charts, diagrams, photographs and printed materials all help to persuade the company decision makers. Do not include a model or prototype at this stage if how it works can be deduced from examination of it.

The heart of your presentation must explain several key points about your invention. This information is absolutely necessary to the success of your presentation. As you convey this information to your audience, you offer them convincing reasons to buy your pitch. This is what they need to hear:

- Function. What your invention does.
- Advantage. Why it does it better than anything else on the market.
- Form. What this invention will look like as a marketable product.
- Appeal. Why the product will appeal to the consumer.
- Profit. How the company can profit from the sale or use of the invention.
- Compatibility. How the invention fits in with the company's product line.
- Emotional involvement. This is vital! The excitement must be infectious. You must appeal to their thirst for prestige and desire to be an industry leader.

For the first meeting, it is usually not necessary to be accompanied by your patent attorney. However, if the company invites you back and they make you an offer, you have entered the negotiation stage. At this point, you definitely need your patent attorney by your side to offer advice and guide you through sensitive, often time-consuming and always complex negotiations.

The Deadly Waiver

When you submit your idea or invention to a corporation, their legal department will usually insist you sign a "waiver." Many inventors consider them nothing more than an opportunity for you to relinquish your rights to your invention. Many of these legally binding documents essentially strip you of all of your rights except for those patent law confers upon you. The waiver makes it possible and indeed, easy, for a company to steal your idea. These infamous agreements are toxic to inventors. If you decide to submit your idea or invention to a company and you decide to sign one of these agreements, see a patent attorney before you take any action.

To be fair, there are some companies whose waivers are fair and reasonable. After all, they need to protect themselves from lawsuits too. Their concern is an inventor may sue if the company's research and development team independently invents a similar invention.

Many of the clauses in the waiver cede the company every advantage and leave you with nothing. Worse, some waivers are worded in such a way that anything you invent in the future will be subject to this agreement. Always make sure the name of your invention is listed on the waiver and the agreement is binding only with this one invention. Additionally, some waivers neglect to mention a time frame for which the waiver will be valid. Limit the period for which the agreement is binding. If you don't, well . . . forever is a long time.

You should never send a company full specifications to your invention or the claims listed on your patent application. They get this only after signing the licensing agreement. If they get it before, it may be relatively easy to do you one better. They need only one additional claim to get a new patent of their own. With this new patent they will own the monopoly rights to the invention. You are out of the loop. And you just gave away your invention.

Insist the company send back to you all the documents you sent them. You want a paper trail connecting you, the inventor, with the company. A signed waiver is not enough of a paper trail to prove you have revealed your invention to them.

Obviously, any sane inventor should not hold waivers in high regard. If possible, avoid signing them. Smaller-sized companies are less likely to require you to sign a waiver. You may want to target your efforts toward them and avoid the giants who are likely to treat you shabbily. Some companies may consent to signing a waiver which you have drafted. It should be very simple and very fair for both parties. Your patent attorney can advise you should you go this route.

Seeking Licensing Through Invention Brokers

Independent inventors can contact patent brokers who market patents and negotiate licensing deals or sales to those seeking new commercial products. Warning! These are shark infested waters. There are many, many, *many* disreputable invention submission companies out there. Remember, if they make their money by charging inventors fees, you don't want to do business with them. Be wary of those who advertise on radio or television.

Some invention brokers and developers work on a contingent-fee basis. These are generally considered to be reputable. These firms represent you as they search for a manufacturer or distributor for your invention and the eventual sale or license thereof. Unless the invention broker is successful in selling or licensing your invention for a percentage of your rights, you will not incur any cost. The following is a list of invention brokers and promoters who operate on a contingent-fee basis:

- Arthur D. Little, Inc., Invention Management Group
  Acorn Park
  Cambridge, MA 02140
  (617) 864-5770

- Battelle Development Corporation
  505 King Avenue
  Columbus, OH 43201
  (614) 424-6424

- Product Resources International
  1414 Avenue of the Americas
  New York, NY 10168
  (212) 687-4741

- REFAC Technology Development Corporation
  122 East 42nd Street
  New York, NY 10017
  (212) 687-4741

Be sure to seek out only reputable brokers. Unscrupulous brokers have caused untold havoc and heartache to inventors. Always check with the appropriate consumer protection agencies when considering doing business with any broker.

It is critical you obtain several references and interview them. Questionable companies often have a slick response to this important "reference" question. Con artist alert! Don't let their representative slough it off. Don't let them intimidate you. If you don't feel comfortable and they cannot satisfy this point, drop them like a hot potato. Move on to another who hopefully is an honest one.

Have your patent attorney review and approve any legally binding agreement with these organizations in order to protect your rights. To learn more about invention promotion firms, refer to Chapter 6 where we delve more deeply into this controversial topic.

"Iron rusts from disuse; water loses its purity from stagnation and in cold weather becomes frozen; even so does inaction sap the vigors of the mind."

—Leonardo da Vinci

CHAPTER 4
How to Make Your Creativity Flow

Basic Rules

The conception of many inventions lies in the recognition of a problem needing a solution. Recognizing a problem is often the first and biggest step in solving it. Identifying the problem is often more of an effort than devising a solution. Creative inventors become adept at scrutinizing their lives, examining every task as an opportunity to identify a need for a creative solution.

Stimulate your *right brain* faculties. There is a time to abandon your linear thinking, which is centered in the left side of your brain. Should you encounter a road block in the solution of a problem, you need to open yourself up to nonlinear thinking and expression. After immersing yourself in the problem, take a break and allow your subconscious to work on the problem. Very often, the solution appears in a flash of insight.

Meditation and relaxation techniques often set the stage for creative events. Biofeedback, yoga or transcendental meditation can help you unlock creativity. A sauna, hot shower or bath will allow your body to relax. Some claim the soothing heat dilates the blood vessels in your body, causing blood to be drawn away from your analytical brain to permit your creative subconscious to take over. Additionally, the sense of general well-being is more conducive to unlocking your creative potential.

You can use powerful techniques to enhance the creative process. Don't let your ideas come to you in a haphazard manner. Cultivate them. A trickle of ideas will soon become a flood. Remember these important rules for effective generation of ideas:

1. State the problem. By defining the problem and writing it down, you've gone a long way to solving it.

2. Never compartmentalize. Form connections between your knowledge and experiences. Abandon your preconceived notions.

3. Never jump to conclusions or prejudge an idea.

4. Learn everything you can about your problem.

5. Choose an effective mental technique to tap into your reservoir of creative ideas.

How to Look at a Problem

When studying a problem the first step is to define it clearly. However, many of us make certain assumptions about the problem that lock us into noninnovative solutions. You must learn to examine some of the "facts" or "truths" about your problem. See through them to the true heart of the matter. How can you solve a problem if you don't know its true nature? Take your superficial assumptions and ignore them. Often, when you strip problems down to their true essence, they are in fact quite different than they appear on the surface. The lesson is to learn to look at the situation from a different point of view. More often than not, when framing a problem, the constraints you use are faulty. Conventional thinking will never result in a paradigm shift leading to new solutions.

A paradigm can be defined as a system model or pattern of thought. A paradigm shift is a revolutionary change in conventional thinking resulting in a new model.

Consider this example. Years ago, before bottle bill laws were enacted, many communities suffered from serious roadside litter problems. Bottles and cans were tossed out of vehicles creating an eyesore and litter problem. Outraged communities enacted severe fines for litterbugs. Few were caught. Very few fines were paid. The litterbugs were not deterred. The litter problem continued because most lawbreakers were cautious not to be witnessed breaking the law. They did not expect to be caught.

The legislators incorrectly assumed the threat of a fine would keep criminals in line. The real problem was in changing peoples' behavior. Lawmakers didn't fully grasp the effect human nature has on regulating behavior. The true problem stripped down to its barest essence was simple. How to make potential litterbugs want to keep their cans and bottles in their vehicles and not improperly dispose of them? By making cans and bottles worth a nickel with the bottle bill, potential litterbugs had a potent reason not to litter. Immediate and absolute economic self-interest prevented most from discarding the cans and bottles. At five cents apiece, many were unwilling to throw away the cash in hand. Better yet, if they were thrown away on the roadside by someone who didn't care about the nickel, others would have an economic interest to pick them up to redeem them. As a result, roadside litter from cans and bottles became almost nonexistent.

Dreams

You can utilize your dreams to develop ideas and solve problems. Information tends to percolate in your subconscious mind and solutions often pop out in your dreams.

Research indicates human brain chemistry differs markedly between the wakeful and sleep states. Ordered, rational thought simply doesn't take place during sleep. Conscious inhibitions disappear. A bonafide altered state of consciousness exists. The brain fuses information from the day's activities with stored knowledge and experiences. Dreams contain symbols and metaphors directly related to your life experiences. The following six steps guide you in mining ideas from your dreams:

1. Keep a writing pad and pen— a tape recorder is even better—near your bed. At bedtime, review your problem. Tell yourself you will wake up at the end of your dream. Sometimes good ideas will come to you when you are in that magical half-awake, half-asleep state.

2. Think of sleep as a luxury you deserve. Allow yourself a good night's sleep. A well-rested mind is twice as creative as an exhausted one.

3. Wake up after your dream ends. Keep your eyes closed because visual input pollutes your dream, causing it to fade. Rerun the dream through in your mind.

4. Write down or tape record your dream. Don't wait until morning because most of the details will have evaporated by then.

5. Get the rest of a good night's sleep.

6. When you awaken in the morning, review your notes. Add anything you forgot or dreamed after your note taking. The next evening, review your dream again in your mind as you lie in that half-asleep state. You may be able to resume your dream, elaborating on the previous night's dream. With practice, you may be able to learn lucid dreaming where you control your dream just as a director controls a film. You direct the action and plot. Even if no ideas sprout from your dream, it can be tremendous fun.

51

The semi-wakeful state you experience just before falling asleep and upon waking is referred to by psychologists as "twilight time." The human mind perceives and processes information differently from the way it does in the fully wakeful state. Many people achieve brilliant insights during this period.

Brainstorming

Dreams work well as a source of ideas for an individual. What tool is available to a group of people searching for a creative problem-solving idea?

Brainstorming is a well known and highly effective mental tool in which a group of people offer and exchange ideas to stimulate new concepts. This creativity is infectious, causing a cascade of new ideas, paradigm shifts and innovative solutions. The rules for brainstorming are simple:

1. Present a problem to the group.

2. Keep it visual. Write the group's objectives on a bulletin board or chalkboard. Ask for solutions. As ideas are offered, write them down for all to see. Ignore convention.

3. Never judge your own nor anyone else's idea. Sometimes it is the silliest utterance which can lead to a gem of an idea. Don't allow anyone to feel foolish. You need everyone's input.

4. Look for relationships between ideas—synergy. Making connections between previously unrelated ideas defines the creative act.

5. Seek as many ideas as you possibly can. More is always better.

6. Never force it. A leader who pressures the group to perform merely poisons creativity.

7. The latter part of the brainstorming session usually produces the best and most creative solutions.

Observe Nature

A seemingly infinite diversity exists in nature. From this wealth of creation have come a bounty of ideas as long as humankind has possessed the curiosity to observe. Leonardo da Vinci was a keen observer of nature. He understood nature brims with gifts for the inquisitive and observant. He closely scrutinized the world around him. Making careful records of his observations, he imitated nature in his inventions. Much of da Vinci's success was due to his rare ability to divine the hidden structures in nature.

Often, what we believe to be a unique discovery has already been utilized in nature. Humans discovered the usefulness of sonar just before World War II but bats and dolphins have exploited this innate ability since their species' origin. Nature possesses such beauty and wisdom that it's a shame to pass it up. A complex program of research and development has already been undertaken in nature's research lab. We merely have to identify those elements which can be useful to us and exploit them for our benefit. Through careful scrutiny we can identify these opportunities.

Biomimetics is an emerging field of scientific study in which efforts are made to emulate nature's successes to provide us with useful new materials. Millions of years of evolution and natural selection have produced materials in nature that await our discovery and exploitation.

You never know what you'll find in a tar pit. For eons, unfortunate creatures venturing too close have gotten stuck and met their doom. Petroleum flies seem to be an exception. They land on the tar with impunity and do not stick like everything else does. Something protects the flies from sticking. The reason may be biomechanical. The structure of the fly's legs may be a design that allows them this capability. Alternatively, a biochemical mechanism may be responsible. The flies may produce and exude some material from their bodies that gives them a nonstick coating. Here we see another example of nature's Teflon.

Deriving the invention of Velcro from the structure of the cocklebur seems easy in hindsight. The cocklebur's diminutive hook structure allows it to attach itself to objects for transport away from the mother plant. This unique structure of the seed pod was well recognized by scientists in the 1800s. Yet decades passed before Swiss engineer and inventor Georges de Mestral noticed the cocklebur's structure, linked it to a need for a solution to a problem, then made history with his invention of Velcro in 1948. Derived from the French words *velours* and *crochet*, this unique fastening system known as Velcro brand hook-and-loop fasteners makes our lives easier.

Isolating a cure for cancer from some obscure rain forest plant can present more of a challenge, particularly as ignorant humans persist in decimating this planet's valuable biodiversity. Nature possesses elegant solutions to our problems if only we care to look.

The Burst of Inspiration

Inspiration can be a funny thing. Sometimes it's just a hunch you get. Other times, it bursts forth into your consciousness and you know with absolute certainty it's right. The adrenaline rushes at the thrill of discovery. How do you get results like this? Allow the conscious manipulation of your problem to be taken over by your subconscious.

How to attain that "eureka" moment in creative thinking? Follow these guidelines:

1. Immerse yourself in the problem. Research it. Look at all the angles and consider every possible solution.

2. Forget the problem. Engage yourself in another activity. Do not allow your conscious mind to be concerned with this problem. Let it rest. This is known as the incubation phase.

3. When your subconscious mind has processed the problem, the answer will burst forth. This is your eureka moment.

4. Write your ideas down and savor the good feeling of your creative moment.

Question Everything

To young children, everything is brand new, seen through unjaded and inexperienced eyes. They possess a child's wonder and sense of puzzlement. Any parent can tell you about that certain age where every word out of their child's mouth is "why?" Children luxuriate in creativity because of the richness of their experiences as they undergo their steep learning curve.

As an adult, this childlike wonder has long been stamped out in most, courtesy of our educational system. Children, who are born with an innate sense of creativity, seem to begin to lose it at the time they start first grade. Studies indicate an increasingly structured life coupled with the development of intellectual discipline and social pressures stifle creativity.

Traditional educational systems emphasize an orderly, logical mode of reasoning. Fear of failure or making mistakes inhibits most people from attempting creative acts. This is bound to have a profound effect on creative thinking and ability. It's sad one of the most valuable and desirable human traits—creativity—ends up being discouraged or eradicated with such brutal efficiency. Do we value it so little? Flexibility and curiosity coupled with the wisdom we acquire with age and experience are the mark of great creative thinkers.

Creative thinking requires the ability to ask questions. You must allow yourself the freedom to ask "what if?" Make this your favorite term. Don't feel foolish about utilizing this critical problem solving skill. You are foolish only if you stop asking questions. Who, what, when, where, why and how are the magic words leading to enlightenment.

Self-Motivation

A key skill an inventor or entrepreneur must master is self-motivation. There will be times when your energy or inspiration for a project runs out of steam. Don't wallow in this time-wasting quagmire. There are ways you can get back on track.

Perhaps a book on a great inventor such as Thomas Edison fills you with inspiration. R. W. Clark's book, *Edison, The Man Who Made the Future* never fails to fire us up. Reading about the other entrepreneurs' successes may inspire as well as give you information to better achieve your goals.

Check out one of the several television programs showcasing inventions. The Discovery Channel's *Beyond 2000* and *Invention* as well as many of The Learning Channel's shows feature the latest inventions and innovations born of fertile minds. These shows entertain and inform you. They showcase cutting-edge technology that often astounds. It's a great idea for any inventor to watch to keep up-to-date with inventive developments. It is not uncommon to generate innovative ideas based on the technology featured in the shows.

Pick up the latest copy of *Popular Science* magazine or *Popular Mechanics* magazine. These two periodicals are must reading if you invent for hobby or business. They are chock full of fascinating articles and the latest techno-gadgets.

Inventor's Digest is a national magazine devoted to the art and business of invention. Join 10,000 other inventors who read this magazine and appreciate the information and immense benefits it offers. Sign up for a subscription by writing to *Inventor's Digest*, c/o JMH Publishing Company, 310 Franklin Street, Suite 24, Boston, MA 02110, or call (617) 367-4540.

Dream Merchant magazine offers crucial small business marketing and sales information for new ideas, products and services. This publication deals with the business of inventing. Profiting from your ideas is this periodical's emphasis. They do it well. For subscriptions, write to *Dream Merchant*, 2309 Torrance Boulevard #201, Torrance, CA 90501, or call (310) 328-1925.

The *American Heritage of Invention* magazine celebrates America's astounding history of innovation and invention. For subscriptions, write to *American Heritage of Invention*, 60 Fifth Avenue, New York, NY 10011, or call (212) 206-5588.

Income Opportunities magazine bills itself as "the original small business / home office magazine." This magazine is all that and more as it provides a wealth of information perfectly tailored for inventors who run a small business. For subscription orders and inquiries, write to *Income Opportunities*, P.O. Box 55206, Boulder, CO 80328-5206. Be certain to bookmark their terrific Web site at http://www.incomeops.com.

Visit America's preeminent museum of invention at the Patent and Trademark Museum located at 2121 Crystal Drive, Arlington, VA 22202. Hours are from 8:30 A.M. to 4:30 P.M., Monday through Friday or by appointment. For more information or to arrange a tour of the PTO, call the Office of Public Affairs at (703) 305-8341.

Visit the Inventure Place: National Inventors Hall of Fame, another museum of invention, located at 221 South Broadway, Akron, OH 44308. You can call them at (800) 968-IDEA. Visit their Web site at http://www.invent.org.

Join an Inventors Association. Networking with other inventors affords you numerous benefits. Mutual support, sharing of information, generating a large circle of contacts and tapping a deep well of expertise are the most important of these benefits. Not to be overlooked is the tendency for your involvement with the group to fire you up, to fill you with enthusiasm, to motivate you in your quest for your goal. Refer to this book's Appendix for the most extensive listing in existence of Inventor's Associations and related organizations.

Maybe you've set your sights on some sort of material reward for yourself if you attain success. Good for you. You deserve a reward for your hard work and courage in taking a risk. It might be a sports car, a pool or an exotic vacation. Think about that reward. Savor it. Imagine the reality of having it. Realization comes very quickly that if you don't get off your butt and just do it, you will never attain your goal. You must make it happen!

Most people can learn to manage their time better. Never before have people complained so bitterly about having too much to do and too little time. A close examination of your life will probably reveal a surprising amount of wasted time. Learn to identify this waste and cut it from your life. Be ruthless.

Do you read newspapers and magazines from cover to cover? Adopt the attitude if you can't remember what you read, then you wasted your time reading it. Quickly scan the headline and first paragraph of the articles. If it is of no interest, skip it. Become a discriminating reader. It wouldn't hurt to take a speed reading course, either. The Evelyn Woods Reading Dynamics course is a one-day seminar that does wonders for reading speed and comprehension.

Dynamic reading is a smooth, efficient, effective and rapid reading technique superior to the linear sub-vocal reading method we have all been taught. Reading dynamics is a vertical-visual reading method. Our eyes move across and down a page while reading, with words read triggering thoughts, thus bypassing a great deal of sub-vocalization. A multiple reading process is utilized to provide greater comprehension, retention, speed and flexibility. Pre-reading allows you to note the material's structural features and gain a brief appraisal of the content. The main reading is performed at a rate and level of comprehension which satisfies your purpose, followed by creating a recall pattern (hierarchical visual outline). Post-reading is an optional step for in-depth or study reading.

The hand is taught to be used as a pacer to curb regressions, enhance perceptual ability, direct concentration and control reading rates. It is important to allow your rate to be flexible to suit your material and purpose for reading it. It is important to absorb patterns of words, rather than reading and sub-vocalizing each word individually.

With practice, this becomes an effective technique that improves reading ability, rates and comprehension. Memory, retention and recall are also improved with the help of an effective method of taking notes. This is a powerful method for improving learning and study skills which we highly recommend.

Addicted to television? Can you honestly say the shows you view are so extraordinarily good you must see them? Let's be honest. Most television programming is just candy that rots your brain. TV mesmerizes. TV doesn't require you to think. It's habit forming. Admit it, you spend too many wasted hours each day glued to the idiot box. Free yourself from its numbing influence. Cut just one hour of viewing per evening. Go to bed early. Get up one hour early. You now find you have one extra hour to work on your idea, invention or whatever project you choose. An hour a day adds up quickly. In one year, this extra time amounts to nine, 40-hour work weeks. Imagine what you can accomplish with this time!

Make checklists. Separate the things to do into two categories. The first category is made up of all those things that are absolutely necessary for you to do. The second category is made up of all the other tasks you only think you need to do or simply would like to do. Too often, the tasks in the latter category are diversions you invent to avoid working on your project. Don't trick yourself into subverting your own efforts. Learn to prioritize these tasks properly. These things usually belong at the very bottom of your list of priorities. Never pass up the opportunity to delegate these chores to someone else. It is probably better to pay some kid a few bucks to mow your lawn or wash your car than for you to do it yourself. These kinds of tasks sap a tremendous amount of time out of our all-too-brief lives. Do you really think Edison or Einstein obsessed over mowing a lawn or washing a car? Not likely. Their work consumed them. They didn't allow unimportant tasks to interfere with their life's work, their passion.

Procrastination cripples. Understand that you suffer from procrastination because the thing you avoid doing is emotionally unpleasant. Self-help books addressing the problem of procrastination abound in the marketplace. Look in the self-help section of your local bookstore. If you have problems with this, take out your priority checklist and mark down: Buy a self-help book on procrastination. Do it now. Yes, you heard us right. Put this book down and do it now! Just don't put off going out and buying one!

Overcoming the Fear of Success

As a reader of this book, you are clearly interested in becoming successful. As an inventor, innovator or entrepreneur, you consciously work toward attaining worthwhile goals. But do you unconsciously sabotage your chances for success? Does success terrify you on an unconscious level?

Early childhood experiences reinforced by cultural and family double messages often result in self-sabotaging behavior that bedevils your quest for success. By success, we mean doing what you really want to do in your personal and professional life, excelling at it and feeling good about it. Material trappings of success may or may not accompany this idea. You may fear success because your unconscious mind feels you don't deserve it. Perhaps, when you were young, someone important in your life told you that you would never amount to anything or never showed much faith in you and your abilities. You believed them because it is always easy to believe the bad stuff, isn't it? A lifetime of programming is difficult to conquer. Overcoming the fear of success cannot be accomplished by following any set formula due to the complexity and differences in each person's underlying psychology. Identifying the problem is the first and biggest step. With luck and plenty of self-analysis you will be able to recognize and overcome your hidden fears.

Organization and Research

Organization is a skill that greases your skids on the rough path to success. Chaos is an enemy which subverts your efforts. If you don't already have it, set up a home office for your work. It doesn't need to be fancy with the latest technology featuring every bell and whistle. It can be as simple as a desk in a quiet place where you can tap into your creativity.

Pay attention to good lighting and good ergonomics for your comfort and good health. Eye strain, headaches, backaches and carpal tunnel syndrome need not be your reward for putting in long hours working on your project. If your project requires long hours of computer work, eye strain may be a possible result. Computer eye strain or "computer vision syndrome" is a consequence of glare off the screen. Your eyes work harder as a result. Symptoms include headaches; neck, shoulder and back aches; and dry or irritated eyes. More serious vision difficulties may be experienced such as blurred vision, double vision and light sensitivity.

Steps may be taken to mitigate these unpleasant effects. Taking frequent breaks to rest your eyes is the best idea. Learn to get in the habit of looking up from your work often to focus your eyes on a distant object for ten seconds. When concentrating, it is common for us to stare so intently that we forget to blink our eyes. Blinking is essential for moistening and lubricating the eyes. Lubricating eye drops can help if this is your problem. Remembering to blink more often is easy advice to give but harder to remember to do.

For those of us who spend lots of time on a computer, keeping our eyes healthy is a prime concern and constant challenge. It is possible to maintain healthy vision and even improve it. Marilyn Roy's book, *EyeRobics: How to Improve Your Vision*, explains vision, defects such as nearsightedness and farsightedness and techniques you can use to improve your vision without contact lenses or glasses. Published by Peanut Butter Publishing of Seattle, the paperback edition is available for $14.95 by calling (206) 281-5965, or it may be found at major chain bookstores such as Barnes and Noble, Borders and Waldenbooks.

Good lighting is essential. Ambient lighting should be equalized to reduce glare. High contrasts of light should be avoided. Computer screen covers that reduce screen glare are commercially available. Another bit of good advice is really very simple. Move your body. Seated stone-like at a desk, staring into the computer screen while pounding the keyboard is tough on your muscles. Taking frequent breaks (one every 15 minutes) to move, stretch and massage your muscles is highly advisable. Don't neglect your forehead, temples, scalp, neck, shoulders, forearms and hands. Always remember these are your problem sites. Neglecting them will not pay in the long run.

Check out the Occupational Safety and Health Administration's (OSHA) Internet Web site on ergonomics and prevention of repetitive stress injuries for workers. Employers and employees alike should look for their Web site at http://www.osha.gov/ergo.

A good filing system will prove essential. You need to organize all those great ideas you will dream up. Additionally, you must organize all the material you come across in your research. Don't be surprised if you find you require a whole bank of filing cabinets.

In our experience, everything we see, hear and experience is ongoing research. When reading a newspaper or magazine, cast your idea net out. When an article catches your eye, scan it. If it is of interest to you, read it, clip it, date it and save it. Into its appropriate file it goes. Many writers and entrepreneurs utilize this research-gathering technique to good advantage. These files become invaluable sources of information.

It goes without saying your local library contains a wellspring of information. Get to know your librarians. Their job is to serve the public so don't be shy in asking for their assistance. They are a most valuable resource and their knowledge can save you precious time.

You may be contemplating patenting an idea for a product and starting up a business. Our advice is, if at all possible, get work experience in the field in which you plan to patent. You can be guaranteed, in the course of this work, you will discover crucial information that never would have occurred to you. Whether or not you possess this information may just make or break you. You put yourself at a severe disadvantage if you fail to avail yourself of this easily attainable knowledge. Furthermore, the contacts you make in the industry will serve you well. An integral factor in business success has long been and still remains word of mouth and who knows who. This is how the game is played. You place yourself at a monumental disadvantage by not networking with industry movers and shakers.

If you work for a company, you must be very cautious you don't sign away your rights to inventions developed on your own time during the term of your employment. Many companies require employees to sign an agreement that assigns all of your inventions to the employer (excluding all your inventions developed prior to your employment). Typical employment agreements require an employee to legally transfer all inventions to the employer under specific conditions. The invention must be conceived of and developed on company time, utilizing company resources. The invention must have been developed in the normal course of your employment duties. The invention must relate to the nature of the company's business. Finally, the invention must be conceived of and developed during the period you are employed by the company. Agreements normally specify you promise to hold the employer's trade secrets and customer and supplier information in confidentiality.

Sometimes employees are not required to sign one of these agreements. The employee retains ownership of all their inventions but is not compensated for them except by their normal salary. This is commonly referred to as "shop rights." The invention can be used only by the company because it was developed on company time with company resources. Whether or not you sign an employment agreement, it is vitally important that you understand the rules. Knowing your rights under the law will keep you out of trouble should you patent an invention during or after employment for a company.

"If you are not a millionaire or bankrupt by the time you are thirty, you are not really trying."

—Nolan Bushnell

CHAPTER 5

How to Profit from your Invention

This chapter discusses five separate strategies for profiting from your inventions. The first strategy, licensing your patent, was discussed in Chapter 3. We now introduce four more options. Outright sale of the rights to a patent is not very common. Many inventors love this option, however, because they are 100 percent finished with the product and can start a completely new project. Test marketing, starting small for proof of concept and the full-scale business start-up involve the tremendous challenges of manufacturing and distributing your own products.

Licensing

This is the inventor's dream. License your invention to a company with deep pockets and sit back and collect your fat royalty checks. Licensing grants them the right to use your patented process and/or manufacture and/or distribute the invention. The license is for a set period of time. At the expiration of this licensing period the contract may be renewed if both parties desire. Contract provisions usually allow the license to be revoked under certain conditions stipulated in the agreement. The inventor retains ownership of the patent at all times.

Sounds great but it's not quite that easy. You've got to have a great idea and match it with a company with a need for that idea. Doubly difficult is the task of convincing them that your invention is indispensable to them. As we all know, the devil is in the details. You, partnered with your attorney, must successfully negotiate terms that provide you the maximum benefit.

Trying to interest a company in licensing your invention to manufacture, market and sell the product is not easy. If you are fortunate enough to do so you may receive a cash advance up front for expenses, minimum guaranteed royalties for a specific number of years and then regular royalties paid periodically on every product sold for the duration of the patent. The nice thing about a license is, if sales skyrocket, your royalties will as well.

We believe guaranteed royalties must be part of the deal. With guaranteed royalties, you are assured a minimum payment whether or not the company makes any sales. This provision prevents them from shelving the invention. Some companies like to license an invention then shelve it to eliminate competition in the marketplace. They do not want you selling this product if it competes with their product line.

Another way to profit from your invention is to provide a consulting service to the company licensing your invention. Who better than you to be a consultant on this project? No one knows the ins and outs of the invention's technology better than you. Providing a consulting role can prove quite lucrative and lead to unique and stimulating challenges in your career.

Outright Sale

Another option after receiving your patent is to dump it. Sell the product and all patent rights to one company. From that time forward, you have nothing more to do with the invention. The company has total control of the invention. They can sell it or they can shelve it. You research, locate, contact and negotiate with companies using the same tools and techniques as you use for licensing your invention rights.

Your patent is your personal property. You may elect to sell it, mortgage it, bequeath it in a will or donate it. The transfer or sale of a patent is referred to as an assignment. All or a part interest of a patent may be transferred. The ownership of the patent as well as the basic rights that go along with it become the property of the assignee. The assignee, when becoming the part owner of a patent, shares the same rights regarding the patent as the original patent owner. They too have the same right to sell, mortgage, bequeath or donate it or their part interest just the same as the original patent owner. When 100 percent of the interest is sold, the assignee owns 100 percent of the rights.

Many inventors find the prospect of an outright sale of their own invention unthinkable. They want to retain some control over their "baby"—their million-dollar idea. They feel the need to nurture it to its full potential. Other inventors are so prolific that outright sales of the invention and patent rights are the optimum way to go. Their fertile minds are brimming over with new ideas. They can't wait to get on to the next hot new project. Becoming bogged down with concerns about manufacturing, marketing and sales is a plague to be avoided. To be honest, most inventors are not adept at business and are lousy salespeople. All too often they seem to possess a kind of tunnel vision that gets in the way of other endeavors. It is a rare individual who can take an idea from prototype to production while setting up a company and successfully marketing and selling the product.

Test Marketing

Some entrepreneurs don't bother to get a patent right away. It is normal to have doubts about your invention concept or product as you develop it. Many people want to get an idea of how well it will do in the marketplace before investing their valuable assets of time and money. Often, you can manufacture a small quantity of your invention at a very modest cost. Test market it to see if there is a demand for your product and if you can sell it. If there is strong demand for the product, you proceed with the patent application. If the product fizzles in the marketplace, you drop it. Move on to something new.

Bear in mind that if you follow this course of action and decide to patent the invention if sales do well, you have only one year from the date you first sold the invention to patent it. Patent law requires you to file a patent application within one year after you make your invention available for sale or publish the details of the invention. You cannot obtain patent protection after this time. You will also lose the opportunity to file for all foreign patent rights due to their absolute novelty requirement. Any public exposure of your idea will prevent you from obtaining a valid foreign patent.

The possibility exists that someone will see your product, realize its value, discover it has no patent protection and proceed to file a fraudulent patent application. You will probably have to seek legal recourse to prove you own the proprietary rights to the idea. To prove the existence of prior art you will need extensive and accurate documentation of your invention's conception and development.

Despite these disadvantages, test marketing can work for some products. If competitors cannot discover the nature of your invention by examining your product, you have a trade secret. As long as you withhold this trade secret information, you will have a monopoly. You can test market, manufacture and distribute your product.

Start Small for Proof of Concept

Instead of licensing or selling the rights to the invention, you can start up a small business to manufacture, market and sell your product. Don't think big. Think small. Make a working prototype then go into production on a limited scale. Keep it lean. Spend very little money. Produce a small amount of product to keep your inventory down. Be your own salesperson. Your goal is to create a small yet strong market for your product. You are proving your product sells and reorders are coming in.

When your business reaches this point, then you are ready to approach other companies with an offer to license or sell your product or even your entire company. With a limited investment, you've proved a market exists for your product and its value can be calculated. You've proven the worth of your invention. A proven invention is worth significantly more than an unproven one.

The Business Start-up

If you are ready to escape the "Dilbert zone" and seize your dream, this is the chapter for you to read. You do not have to be an inventor to benefit from the valuable information this section offers. More and more people realize the advantages of starting their own businesses and being their own boss. No more going to work in a twilight zone atmosphere. No more slaving long hours to enrich someone else. Be advised, however, this option is the hard way. If you are a glutton for punishment, then this is the way to go. Some do it and succeed. The majority try and fail.

By starting your own company you are embarking on an adventure. This bold spirit of entrepreneurship has helped make America the miracle it is. By starting your own company you are helping to propagate the miracle.

New and small entrepreneurial firms now generate 95 percent of radical innovations. These "gazelles," responsible for 50 percent of all innovations since World War II, manage to outperform America's giant corporations that lumber along complacently. The U.S. Commerce Department reports these new and expanding firms now generate the lion's share of all new jobs in the United States.

To succeed in business you need the requisite skills. In addition to the inventing skills and creativity, you need to be capable of setting up and operating a business. Financing is one of the first and biggest considerations. Do you have access to the resources? Most new businesses fail because of inadequate start-up capital. You must hire and manage employees. You must comply with business taxes and regulations. You need to know how to effectively market your invention and be adept at sales as well. Commercial space must be obtained. Do you buy, lease or build? Production equipment must be procured. You have to deal with suppliers, inventories and shipping. Your business insurance needs must be carefully considered to protect your investment and yourself. A myriad of other concerns have to be dealt with. If you are fortunate enough to know business, you are way ahead of the pack.

A variation of the business start-up is to invent a product but have it made by outside vendors. The product should fit into another company's product line. When you approach them, you promote the product as being compatible and complementary to their existing product line. The goal is for both of you to profit as it increases sales of their existing product line.

Starting Your Business

Do you have what it takes to be successful in starting your own small business? The successful entrepreneur should possess certain qualities. Ask yourself the following questions. Be brutally honest as you evaluate yourself.

1. Do you possess a competitive spirit?
2. Do you enjoy interacting with people?
3. Do you enjoy leading others and decision making?
4. Do you possess determination, stamina, self-discipline and will power?
5. Are you highly organized, capable of careful planning to meet your goals?

If you can answer positively to these questions, you have a pretty good shot at business success. Your personality may fit the classic entrepreneur profile.

Entrepreneurship is best defined as taking an idea then creating and building something of long-term value from it. The idea itself is worth next to nothing. Only by building an enterprise and tapping your personal energy, creativity and skills can your idea evolve into something of value.

If you are the sort who marches to the beat of a different drummer, then the dream of owning your own business may be within your grasp. However, personality is not enough. To convert your dream into reality requires certain skills and experience. When starting a business, you have to follow a carefully constructed plan. This is critical to attaining success. Your business plan will be your blueprint to starting, building and managing your venture. Without it, failure is almost preordained. You must possess the basic business knowledge to run your company. You must know how to manage, finance, keep records, analyze your markets, make sales and pay your taxes. You must possess a grit and determination to meet the challenge you've imposed upon yourself. You must be wholly dedicated to your venture and capable both physically and emotionally of getting the job done right, no matter how many hours it takes.

Inventors earn high marks for possessing the precious attributes of creativity and innovative skill. Regrettably, most lack general management skills, business know-how and industry networks. Managers typically possess general management skills, business know-how and industry contacts but are often deficient in creativity and innovative skills.

The successful entrepreneur enjoys all of these personality traits, skills and assets.

You have to ask yourself; where will I obtain the capital to finance the start-up of my business? First, you should look to yourself as a source of start-up capital. You should be willing to tap your personal assets if you truly believe in your inventions. Some people are quick to suggest approaching family and friends for loans or investments of capital in exchange for partial ownership. Involving your family or friends in your business is too often a recipe for disaster whether you are successful or your business fails. If your business fails, you may face their recriminations. If you are successful, you may face their surprising jealousy. These investors often feel that you are not working hard enough or should not be taking a vacation when there is work to be done. Many cannot resist meddling in your business affairs.

The Small Business Administration offers numerous loan programs and services to meet entrepreneurs' business needs. Call (800) 8-ASK-SBA to request information on their financial assistance programs. Most people turn to banks when they need capital. Loans are also available from credit unions, loan and finance companies and life insurance companies (borrow against the cash value of your policy). Look for additional help from Community Development Organizations.

Venture capitalists offer a significant source of funding in exchange for partial ownership in your business venture. Venture capitalists are professional investors. Obtaining financing through these institutional sources is difficult for small start-up companies. Competition for their money is ferocious. Between 1992 and 1996, 275,000 fast growing companies competed for less than 4,000 venture capital awards.

Lastly, look for financing from some non-traditional sources. Seek out an "angel." These informal investors provide $5 billion to $10 billion annually to U.S. start-ups and emerging businesses. Typical investments range from $20,000 to $50,000, which is significantly less than professional venture capitalists are interested in providing.

Financial angels can be advisory entities who possess not just money but expertise in the industry in which you are building your business. The know-how these angels can provide is often significantly more valuable than the capital they invest. They can be professionals with significant assets (doctors, lawyers and other professionals) and are often self-made millionaires who seek investment opportunities. They may be someone you know. It could be a family member or acquaintance who believes in you and your prospects.

Finding your angel is the trick. Informal investors do not hang out a sign advertising their presence. They tend to be an anonymous and diverse group. Look to your business associates such as accountants, bankers, attorneys and other entrepreneurs for referrals. The key is networking. Put the word out to everyone you know. Let word of mouth bring you your financial angel.

The Angel Capital Electronic Network or ACE-Net allows both angel investors and companies to register with the hope they can find a match that fills their needs. More information about ACE-Net can be obtained from the Small Business Administration. Information is also available on the Internet. Explore the SBA Web site at http://www.sba.gov.

If you obtain a referral, your next step is to meet with the potential investor. Your goal is to dazzle the person with a winning presentation. For the potential investor to properly evaluate your proposal, you must provide a comprehensive business plan, product designs and prototypes (with an outline of steps taken to provide proprietary protection) and present your management team. If you get the green light the angel's attorney will draft an investment agreement. Have your attorney review the contract. Read and understand it. Be certain you can live with the terms.

Selecting a Business Entity

After you have thoughtfully considered the feasibility as well as the pros and cons of owning and operating your own business, you make your decision. If you are ready to dive head first into forming your own business, get ready to face one of the most important decisions. Choosing the legal structure for your business must be done carefully. You must consider a number of factors when deciding upon a business entity:

- Cost and complexity of business formation.
- Difficulty of tax preparation and record keeping.
- Business liability concerns for the owner.
- Who controls the business entity.
- Expected life of the business.
- Flexibility of ownership.
- Ease of attracting financing.

Small business entities in the United States fall into one of these broad categories: sole proprietorship, partnership, corporation, S corporation and limited liability corporation (LLC). Be certain you consult with an attorney and accountant when making this vital decision. Their advice can save you tremendous amounts of time and money. They can point out tax advantages, liability protection and other benefits certain to affect all aspects of your business.

A sole proprietorship is the most common business entity as well as the easiest and least costly to set up. Only one individual may own and operate this unincorporated business. The owner has total control over the business. Tax preparation is uncomplicated with the business income and expenses included in the owner's individual tax return. There is no double taxation on business profits as with corporations. A sole proprietor is exposed to unlimited personal liability for the business' liabilities. This means your personal assets are put at risk should you incur business debts. Legally, there is no separate business entity; the owner and the business are one and the same.

To start a sole proprietorship, choose a business name, register it with a dba (doing business as), also known as filing a fictitious name certificate, have your attorney draw up a few simple forms, check local zoning regulations, obtain the required permits, licenses and tax registrations, open a business checking account and open your door for business.

A partnership is an agreement between two or more individuals working together as co-owners of a business, jointly owning the assets, liabilities, profits and losses. Though it can be formed with an oral agreement, your attorney will recommend written articles of partnership to specify each owner's contributions. The agreement will state each partner's roles, explain provisions for continuity, who makes the day-to-day business decisions and how profits and losses will be distributed.

A partnership enjoys the benefits of ease of formation and low cost to maintain the organization. Attracting capital is easier than a sole proprietorship. The partnership enjoys pass through taxation. Each partner's share of profits or losses flows down from the partnership to the individuals. There is no double taxation as with corporations. The Internal Revenue Service requires a partnership tax return to be filed, but no taxes are paid as this is for informational purposes only. As with sole proprietorships, partnerships also subject you to unlimited personal liability for business debts. A new twist is added here, because each partner is legally responsible for the acts of the other partners. The joint partners are "jointly and severally liable." This means if your partner incurs debts and cannot pay and you have assets, those assets may be seized by your partner's creditors.

A corporation is a separate legal entity distinct from the owner(s) for tax and legal purposes. The complicated legal formalities and tax treatment make the corporate entity the most complex business entity. Because the corporation is a separate legal entity, the owners (shareholders or stockholders) enjoy limited liability. In most cases, the corporation's debts are not transferable to the owners unless the owners "guarantee" certain corporate obligations, intermingle personal and corporate funds or fail to follow statutory requirements for running a corporation. Generally, shareholders are insulated from business losses if the business is operated properly. Other benefits include the ease of raising capital, stability in case of the death of a shareholder and ease of transfer of ownership by sale of stock.

A big downside to the corporate entity is the high cost and high level of complexity to set up and run it. The biggest downside is the double taxation stockholders must endure. The business' profits are subject to corporate taxes. After distributions have been made to the stockholders, these profits are again taxed as your personal income. Additionally, corporations must endure extensive regulation by federal, state and local governments.

You do not need an attorney to incorporate. Nevertheless, you would be wise to consult with an attorney and accountant if you plan to do so. They will help you draft the entity's articles of incorporation and assist you with other legal and tax matters. To incorporate, you must file with the appropriate state agency. You will need to pay the initial filing fee as well as an annual fee for as long as you stay in business. When filing, you must select a legal name, unused by any other in-state company, appoint your own board of directors and corporate officers (president, vice president, secretary and treasurer) and keep minutes of the required periodic meetings of the board.

A Subchapter S Corporation enjoys all of the benefits of a regular or C corporation except the owners or shareholders are taxed in the same way as owners of a sole proprietorship or partnership. Owners escape double taxation. As a flow through entity, profits and losses are reported on the shareholders' individual income tax returns. To form an S corporation, the following requirements must be met:

- The corporation must have fewer than 35 stockholders.
- All stockholders must be U.S. residents.
- All stockholders must be individuals, estates or certain trusts (no corporations or other entities).
- No more than one class of stock is allowed.
- The corporation must be domestic.

A new alternative to the aforementioned business entities is the Limited Liability Corporation (LLC). This new form of business entity combines the pass through tax treatment and operational flexibility of partnerships with the best feature of corporations, namely, limited liability protection. The LLC is really a hybrid business form combining the best features of corporate and partnership laws.

The owners (members) of the LLC are the equivalent of stockholders or shareholders in a corporation or the partners in a general partnership. Most states explicitly require more than one member in an LLC at all times. A few states will permit an LLC to have only one member.

An attorney, knowledgeable in LLCs, can set up your business this way by drawing up an operating agreement and articles of organization. The operating agreement delineates the rules for internal governance of the LLC entity. The articles of organization, filed with the secretary of state, provide the same function as the certificate of incorporation for a C corporation and a partnership's certificate of limited partnership.

The LLC as a business entity is becoming the premier choice for new businesses. Invariably, your attorney and accountant will guide you to this choice so you can exploit its numerous advantages.

To further research your choices among the various types of business entities, request IRS Publication 334, *Tax Guide for Small Business*.

Zoning, Licensing and Permit Requirements

Many individuals contemplating starting up a business wish to operate out of their own home. For some entrepreneurs, it is the ideal work arrangement. Benefits such as no commuting, low start-up costs, convenience and close proximity to family make home-based businesses attractive.

Whether your business is home-based or located in a commercial property, you must comply with your community's zoning laws. Before starting the business, conduct a thorough investigation of zoning regulations to determine how your business will be affected. Get a copy of the zoning regulations from your city hall, county zoning office or local branch of the library in the town or city you intend to locate your business. Comply with public health, public safety and environmental regulations. It's too easy for someone to drop a dime on you. Your business could face fines or even be closed down. Inquire with your local chamber of commerce if you need assistance in researching and understanding the local ordinances.

Your business must comply with permit and licensing requirements. The business permit may be obtained when you register your business at your city hall. Permit fees generally run only about $15 to $25. A license to conduct your business activity may be required by the local, state or federal government. Some licenses require your successful completion of a qualifying examination. Your attorney, accountant, chamber of commerce or local library can provide you with the essential advice on permits and licenses. Be cautious not to run afoul of these regulations. If you operate illegally, your business reputation will suffer and you'll lose precious time and money correcting the problem.

Employer and Tax Registrations

If you plan to hire employees you must register with your state's labor department. As an employer, you will be responsible for:

1. Withholding social security taxes (federal).
2. Withholding income taxes (federal).
3. Paying worker's compensation insurance.
4. Paying unemployment insurance.
5. Compliance with labor laws such as minimum wage statutes, employee health laws, OSHA, nondiscrimination and right-to-know laws.

The federal government requires businesses to have a taxpayer identification number in order to expedite IRS processing of business tax returns. Individuals have their own taxpayer identification numbers—their social security number (SSN). Likewise, businesses are awarded an Employer Identification Number (EIN) which must be used on all IRS returns. It is prudent to use an EIN to protect your own SSN. Employers, sole proprietors, corporations, partnerships, limited liability corporations, estates, trusts and other entities use the EIN to identify their tax accounts. You can apply for your own EIN by filling out IRS form SS-4, *Application for Employer Identification Number.* You can apply by mail or by phone. If you apply by mail, you may wait four to five weeks to get your EIN. If you call, you immediately receive your EIN when the IRS representative takes your information and establishes your account.

If your company will make taxable sales, makes taxable purchases or has employees and your state has a sales tax, then you must apply for a State Tax Identification Number. Contact your state's Department of Revenue Services to request the application form for your sales tax permit. Those companies planning to hire employees must obtain a State Unemployment Identification Number. Contact your state's Department of Labor for the application form and information on paying state unemployment taxes.

Developing Your Business Plan

Most inventors believe they can "wing it" when setting up a business. But they too—especially—need a business plan. Developing your business without a plan is like sailing from California to Hawaii without a map. You are bound to get lost along the way and not end up where you want to be. Proper planning is critical for your success. Attempting to navigate by the seat of your pants is a recipe for disaster in sailing and business. Business contains many rocky shoals through which you must navigate. A well-thought-out business plan will keep your company on course and help you avoid becoming a castaway.

Drawing up a comprehensive business plan will help you to understand your own business' goals and how your company operates. This document is your guide to starting up your business, managing it today and planning for its future growth. It should describe every aspect of your business. It summarizes your business opportunity and explains how you, as an entrepreneur, plan to seize and exploit this opportunity. The business plan is the preferred instrument to use when attempting to attract capital. The business plan must prove to potential investors you have identified an opportunity and possess adequate entrepreneurial and management skills to successfully take advantage of it. All this must be done within the confines of a financial blueprint that details income and expense goals for the first several years. A strategic marketing plan that evaluates the market, the competition and your product's potential is an essential element.

Use the following list as an outline of absolutely essential elements for your business plan:

1. Cover page.
2. Business description.
3. Marketing plan.

4. Operational plan.
5. Management plan.
6. Risks.
7. Financial plan.
8. Summary.
9. Appendix.

Cover page. The cover page should list your business name, address, telephone and fax numbers, email address and complete owner identification. Identify your primary business goals and objectives in a statement of purpose. The statement of purpose should summarize the essential components of the business. These should include your product's market potential, financial forecasts and an overview of your product's background.

Business description. This should convey to the reader the nature of your business, including a concise disclosure of your product(s) and/or service(s). Explain not only how you plan to start the business, but how you plan to attain your management objectives and plans for the future. Promote yourself and your product by stressing its unique features and describing how you will attain market share and exploit new technology to successfully meet the future. Define your proprietary position. Provide photographs or concept drawings of your product to better communicate your ideas. Be cautious, however; don't give away your trade secrets.

Marketing plan. This is your strategy for your venture's pricing, distribution and promotional policies. You must identify your market. Who are your customers? How to reach them? Identify the size of your potential market. Analyze your market potential by using market survey and test marketing results. Reveal your pricing policies, which will allow you to penetrate the market. Discuss your sales strategy. How will you deal with the competitors? Explain your proposed distribution methods. Identify your promotional policies such as price, service, and quality, which enhance customer acceptance. Identify the competition and how they do business. Compare your product with theirs. Is your product superior? Explain how you will successfully compete with them.

Operational plan. This should provide information on your company's production facilities. Include details of the physical site; zoning restrictions; intention to lease, build or buy a building; operating capacity; set-up costs; and advantages and disadvantages of the chosen location. Provide information on set-up and production requirements to generate a production schedule. List materials suppliers. Describe your workforce. Your personnel's skills and experience must be quantified. List the number of employees and future hiring plans, including how to train them to perform their jobs. Explain if unions or government regulations unduly affect your operation. Provide a full list of inventory and equipment needed. Discuss the company's research and development plans. Is your product ready for market or does more research need to be done? Explain how your research and development efforts will improve your products and create new ones for the marketplace.

Management plan. Present the backgrounds of key members of your management team. Detail each member's technical, scientific, educational and management experience. Include their full résumés in the business plan's appendix. Highlight each member's business experience and describe the skills needed for this venture. Show that this team can run the company successfully. Prior experience with your product line or similar products should be documented. Showcase your own background and experience and discuss your own strengths and weaknesses in starting up a business. If you plan to have a board of directors, name them, give a brief biography of each member and explain how they will contribute to the success of your company.

Risk. It is inherent in all business, and you must plan for and evaluate all identifiable problems and risks you might encounter. Planning at this stage will help you avoid or minimize problems when and if they occur. Your contingency plans should deal with risks because of problems such as legal actions stemming from patent, copyright or trademark violations; credit problems; cash flow problems; supply problems; and any other situation that could complicate your business. Prove that you have a plan to solve your potential problems. This is the second most important section of a business plan. Make certain you include it and it is comprehensive and fair.

A computer program such as @RISK for Microsoft Excel and Lotus 1-2-3 for Windows allows you to effectively evaluate risks using computer modeling. Best and worst case scenarios can be predicted based upon a host of variables. These variables can be sales, costs, revenues, profits and so forth. The program uses Monte Carlo simulation to perform the risk analysis. All possible outcomes are calculated based on numerous iterations of all valid combinations of input variable values. The computer runs every possible "what if" analysis to reveal all possible outcomes. Most importantly, the computer reveals not just the possible range of outcomes but also the probability distribution for the likelihood of occurrence of each possible outcome.

Financial plan. This will reveal whether or not your proposed business can make a profit. If your business is not yet operational and lacks hard financial data, you must use estimates to put together your financial statements. If your business is established you may wish to have your accountant prepare these statements using financial information from your records. Supply the following data:

- Start-up costs.
- Capital equipment list.
- Sources of capital and how it is used.

73

- Projected operating expenses.
- Break-even analysis.
- Cash flow projections.
- Profit-and-loss statements.
- Balance sheet.

Banks, venture capitalists and other financiers will look for a SWOT Analysis in which you identify strengths, weaknesses, opportunities and threats. As this analysis is standard in the industry today, you should consult a good business book to learn how to perform this matrix analysis.

Summary. This is your last chance to convince the reader your business will succeed. Clearly and concisely restate your business goals and objectives. Be sincere. Be convincing. Sell them on your proposal.

Appendix. Place all pertinent backup material referred to in the business plan in the appendix. Your supporting documents might include personal and management team resumes, engineering reports, laboratory tests, credit reports, patents, marketing reports, legal documentation, pictures of business location, products or equipment.

Business plans take time to write. It should take you several months to collect the required information and assemble it into a completed business plan. To assist you in this often confusing process, consider enrolling in a business plan writing course or seminar at your local college or university.

Your local Small Business Development Center (SBDC) offers a free or low cost consulting service to budding entrepreneurs. They will assist you in writing the business plan and critique it, offering feedback to effect positive changes in the document. With their assistance, your rough-around-the-edges business plan can be polished to perfection. See Appendix 2 for contact information for your state's SBDC.

Another intriguing option exists for getting your business plan critiqued. Many colleges and particularly business schools will be happy to offer a critique of your business plan. As part of a college business course, the students evaluate the plan and offer feedback on it. If there is a hidden flaw, they are bound to uncover it. It is rare for an entrepreneur to not have a powerful emotional attachment to their own project. You need an objective eye to provide careful scrutiny and generate constructive criticism.

Before you can begin to write you need to collect information to use in the plan. This is the most difficult and time-consuming part of the process. Knowing where to look for that required information makes the process much easier. The following is a presentation of some of the best sources of information for your business plan.

Indexes to books and periodical articles:

Applied Technology and Sciences Index
Bibliographic Guide to Business and Economics
Books in Print (R. R. Bowker Co.)
Business Periodicals Index
Computer Database Information Searches
Reader's Guide to Periodical Literature
Standard Periodical Directory
Standard Rate and Data Service
Subject Guide to Books in Print (R. R. Bowker Co.)
Ulrich's International Periodicals Directory (R. R. Bowker Co.)
Wall Street Journal Index

General data guides:

American Statistics Index
Business Information Sources
Consultants and Consulting Organizations Directory
Directories in Print (Gale Research Co.)
Directory of Industry Data Sources
Directory of On-Line Databases
Encyclopedia of Associations (Gale Research Co.)
Encyclopedia of Business Information Sources (Gale Research Co.)
Small Business Sourcebook
Statistical Reference Index
Trade Directories of the World

Local, state and federal government publications:

Bureau of Census Reports
County and City Data Book
County Business Patterns
Economic Indicators
Federal statistical services—all agencies
Guide to Industrial Statistics
U.S. Industrial Outlook

Organizations, networks and contacts:

Colleges and universities
Databases
Direct Marketing Association
Fellow entrepreneurs
Friends and family
Inventors associations and networks
Local Chamber of Commerce
Local, county, state and federal agencies
Local newspapers and regional magazines

Marketing Research Companies
Research librarians
Small Business Administration
Small Business Development Centers
Trade associations

Record Keeping

Good record keeping is a vital part of any business. It may not be interesting or fun, but it is crucial to your business success. There are plenty of good reasons to keep good records. You require complete and accurate records to prepare and file state and federal business tax and information returns. Potential investors need to see your records and financial statements if you seek loans. Good records allow you to control your business and plan for future growth. Records help you to control expenses, manage inventory size, track profits and losses, identify the source of receipts, enhance cash flow, record deductible expenses, provide information for annual reports and summaries, keep track of payroll requirements, carefully monitor your cash flow and evaluate your company's overall performance.

Accurate record keeping is the key to successfully managing your cash flow. One serious problem facing new entrepreneurs is underestimating the outflows of cash during the new business entity's start-up. This "burn rate," or rate at which cash is used, can be phenomenally excessive. If unplanned for, this hemorrhaging of cash can imperil your start-up. You must meticulously anticipate, plan and manage your cash flow with an unblinking eye on your spending. Failure to do so may mean bankruptcy.

Record-keeping systems range from the simple to the complex. Your goal as a business owner is to choose the simplest system that meets your objectives. Because businesses vary so much from one to the next, you must customize a record-keeping system to meet your needs. A very simple business may utilize a checkbook, bank statements and separate files for receipts, paid bills and unpaid bills. A more complex business may require more detail. These five basic business records may need to be kept:

1. Cash receipts journal.

2. Accounts receivable ledger.

3. Cash disbursements journal.

4. Accounts payable ledger.

5. Payroll journal.

Most small business owners are not well versed in accounting practices. Obtaining the services of an accountant before you start business is a wise decision. The best choice is a certified public accountant (CPA). Your accountant will assist you in designing a record-keeping system that is simple, easy to understand and able to provide information to draw up financial statements and tax returns. A properly designed system will pay for itself by enabling you to better control your business and reduce bookkeeping time and accounting fees. Alternatives to hiring an accountant are employing a part-time bookkeeper or a business service or doing the books yourself (if you have bookkeeping experience).

Part of responsible financial management of a business is fulfilling your tax obligation. The IRS provides assistance to small business owners by providing in-depth tax courses. The Small Business Tax Education Program educates small business owners and other self-employed individuals about their business tax responsibilities. This workshop provides training on starting a business, record keeping and preparing business tax returns. The workshop also identifies self-employment tax issues, explains quarterly tax returns and federal tax deposits and summarizes employment taxes. This free or low cost workshop supplies attendees with an assortment of IRS forms and publications in the Business Tax Kit. This kit contains many useful forms and publications for anyone planning to start a business. The Business Tax Kit contains the following forms:

SS-4, *Application for Employer Identification Number.*
1040-ES, *Estimated Tax for Individuals.*

It also contains the following publications:

334, *Tax Guide for Small Business.*
583, *Starting a Business and Keeping Records.*
594, *Understanding the Collection Process.*
910, *Guide to Free Tax Services.*
1057, *Small Business Tax Education Program Brochure.*
1544, *Reporting Cash Payments of Over $10,000 (Received in a Trade or Business).*
1779, *Employee or Independent Contractor.*

To order the Business Tax Kit, call 1-800-TAX-FORM (1-800-829-3676). To inquire further about the workshop, Small Business Tax Education Program, contact the IRS office nearest you or call (800) 829-1040.

The IRS publishes *Tax Tips*, a newsletter for new businesses. This newsletter is full of helpful tax tips and information on how to start and run your business. For a free subscription, courtesy of the Internal Revenue Service, write to:

Internal Revenue Service
M:C:DP Room 7018
1111 Constitution Avenue, N.W.
Washington, DC 20224-2686

The Community Outreach Tax Education Program, sponsored by the IRS, provides speakers to groups of small business owners. Through these talks, the IRS can bring the business community the information they need for compliance with their tax responsibilities.

Did you know your local Taxpayer Education Office maintains a collection of films and videotapes on a wide variety of subjects? The IRS lends these resources from their library for free. Call (800) 829-1040 to make requests from the Taxpayer Education Coordinator.

U.S. Small Business Administration (SBA)

The Small Business Administration offers a tremendous wealth of information to assist entrepreneurs in starting a business. This guidance, much of it free, includes offering training and educational programs, counseling services, financial programs, and contract assistance. Three organizations within the SBA are worth looking into:

1. Service Corps of Retired Executives (SCORE)—an arm of the SBA made up of retired corporate executives and small business owners who volunteer to counsel prospective and current business people. These volunteers share their years of acquired knowledge free of charge. Appointments are required. As well as offering free counseling on management practices, SCORE members provide seminars and workshops for a small fee.

2. Small Business Development Centers (SBDCs)—an alliance between the SBA, government, private sector and colleges supplying management assistance to individuals going into or currently involved in a small business. SBDC programs cover financing, marketing, production, organization, engineering and technical problems and feasibility studies. Attention inventors! Contact your local SBDC to inquire about programs and counseling specifically addressing patenting inventions.

3. Small Business Institutes (SBIs)—a program that links small business clients with qualified students and faculty of business schools. The business advisors provide counseling for management problems such as accounting system set-up and operation, and market research, while gaining experience in the business world.

To request further information about the SBA, SCORE, SBDCs or SBIs, call the Small Business Answer Desk at (800) 8-ASK-SBA (800-827-5722). Get access through the Internet to SBA OnLine (http://www.sba.gov). To make an inquiry with your local SBA office, consult the U.S. Government section (blue pages) in your telephone directory.

The SBA is a great source of information for anyone starting a business or learning how to better manage one. They offer numerous publications covering the following topics:

- Emerging business.
- Financial management.
- Management and planning.
- Marketing.
- Products/ideas/inventions.
- Personnel management.
- Procurement.

The publications are inexpensive, costing only $2 or $3. An SBA videotape series with workbooks is also available on such topics as marketing, business plans, promotional campaigns, exporting and home-based business. If you are interested in any of the publications or videotapes, request the *Resource Directory for Small Business Management*. Write for this catalog to SBA Publications, P.O. Box 46521, Denver, CO 80201.

The Service Corps of Retired Executives Association publishes the monthly newsletter, *Savant*. Be sure to check out this valuable and informative publication.

To end this chapter, let's summarize the important steps an entrepreneur must take to start a small business. Be advised, this is not a complete list and it is not necessarily the order in which you should carry out these steps. Many will be overlapping each other as you continue the process. Your business may require additional steps dependent upon your unique circumstances or nature of your business. Use our checklist as a guide for starting up your own business.

Business Start-up Checklist

- ❏ Choose the product(s) and/or service(s) you plan to offer.
- ❏ Obtain patents, copyrights and trademarks to secure proprietary rights.
- ❏ Consult an attorney.
- ❏ Consult an accountant (CPA).
- ❏ Obtain approval from zoning authorities.
- ❏ Decide on the type of business entity.
- ❏ Choose your business name.
- ❏ Write your business plan.
- ❏ Obtain all necessary business licenses and permits.
- ❏ Apply for your Employer Identification Number (EIN).
- ❏ Open a business checking account.
- ❏ Choose a business location. Set up office space.
- ❏ Set up a dedicated business phone system.

❏ Buy business insurance.

❏ Arrange financing.

❏ Apply for your state Sales Tax Identification Number.

❏ Apply for a state Unemployment Identification Number from your state's labor department.

❏ Learn the business laws that will apply to you.

❏ Set up a record-keeping system.

Business Start-up Resources

Tax Resources

The IRS provides business taxpayers with numerous ways to obtain tax forms, instructions, publications and other tax information. Call (800) TAX-FORM OR (800) 829-3676 for tax forms and publications. Call weekdays between 7:30 A.M. and 5:30 P.M.

- Call (800) 829-4477 for prerecorded tax information on the Tele-Tax system.
- Call (800) 829-1040 during regular business hours for personal assistance.
- Call (800) 829-4059 for users (hearing impaired) of TTY/TDD equipment.
- Dial (703) 487-4160 for copies of more than 100 of the most requested tax forms and instructions to be faxed directly to you. Service is available 24 hours a day, 7 days a week.

Contact the IRS via computer and modem:

Web	http://www.irs.ustreas.gov
FTP	ftp.irs.ustreas.gov
Telenet	iris.irs.ustreas.gov
Direct Dial	(703) 321-8020 (modem)

AT&T Home Business Resources (HBR) Web Site

This site provides home-based workers with a vast online library of business information. You can communicate online with home office experts and compare notes with other home-based business workers. Explore the numerous links to other connected Web sites. You can visit at http://www.att.com/hbr.

Government Printing Office (GPO)

The federal government prints more than 12,000 books, posters, pamphlets, as well as provides CD-ROMs and subscription services for sale. Contact the Superintendent of Documents for listings of titles of more than

150 free *Subject Bibliographies*. To receive a guide to this listing of *Subject Bibliographies*, write to:

Subject Bibliography Index
Stop: SSOP
Superintendent of Documents
U.S. Government Printing Office
Washington, DC 20402

From a touch-tone telephone or fax handset, dial:
U.S. Fax Watch
(202) 512-1716

You can also reach them via the Web at http://www.access.gpo.gov/su_docs.

To receive a business catalog featuring a plethora of useful resources for all types of businesses, write to:
Business Catalog
Superintendent of Documents
U.S. Government Printing Office
Stop: SM
Washington, DC 20401

Or you may fax your request for this catalog to (202) 512-1656.

Consumer Information Center (CIC)

The Consumer Information Center offers a catalog of free or low cost federal publications of business and consumer interest. The quarterly catalog offers more than 200 helpful titles. To order the catalog call (719) 948-4000 or write to:
Consumer Information Catalog
Pueblo, CO 81009

You can also access the CIC electronically on the Internet at http://www.pueblo.gsa.gov.

Business Assistance Service—Office of Business Liaison

This office of the Department of Commerce helps small businesses navigate through federal bureaucracy and publishes the *Business Services Directory*. They guide you to the appropriate federal agencies to help meet your business needs. Contact them at:
Business Assistance Service—Office of Business Liaison
U.S. Department of Commerce
14th and Constitution, Room 5062
Washington, DC 20230
(202) 482-3176

Chamber of Commerce Web Sites

The U.S. Chamber of Commerce Small Business Institute posts a Web site offering numerous resources to help small businesses compete in the marketplace. Their library of more than 200 books, audiotapes, videotapes and software is available at no charge. Look for their Small Business Resource Catalog at http://www.usccsbi.com. Other U.S. Chamber of Commerce resources useful to small business owners may be accessed at the Chamber of Commerce's Web site http://www.uschamber.org.

- ***Department of Labor***
  Office of Small Business and Minority Affairs
  200 Constitution Avenue, NW
  Room C-2318
  Washington, DC 20210
  (202) 219-9148

- ***Social Security Administration***
  6401 Security Boulevard
  Baltimore, MD 21235
  (800) 772-1213

The US Business Advisor

This Internet Web site provides a one-stop electronic link to government information and services available to businesses. Visit at http://www.business.gov.

"A man would do well to carry a pencil in his pocket, and write down the thoughts of the moment. Those that come unsought for are commonly the most valuable, and should be secured, because they seldom return."

—Francis Bacon

CHAPTER 6
Naked In the Marketplace

Invention Promotion Groups

Many people with ideas for inventions are unsure where to turn for patenting and marketing help. Some naive souls turn to invention promotion companies (also referred to as invention marketing firms) instead of a reputable patent attorney or agent. The aspiring inventor generally lacks business knowledge, marketing expertise and industry contacts. Invention promotion companies prey upon these poor souls, offering to evaluate, perform a patent search, develop, patent and market the invention. Aware of your limitations, these firms make many exaggerated or even false claims about your invention's prospects. These slick salespeople know your vulnerabilities. They know how desperately you want your idea to become a success. Knowing this, they often take advantage of you.

Some people distinguish between legitimate invention promotion companies and fraudulent ones. True, the fraudulent ones are out there, but even the legitimate firms can victimize you. *Be extremely cautious!* Contact your Better Business Bureau, the state Attorney General's office and local consumer protection agencies for your state and the state in which the invention promotion company is headquartered. Request a history of consumer complaints lodged against the company. For your convenience, we have included the addresses and telephone numbers of these agencies in this book's Appendices. We urge you to use them.

When considering whether or not to contract with an invention promotion company, ask the following questions and take the following steps:

1. How long has the company been in the invention promotion business under its current name?

2. Has the firm operated under another name in the past?

3. Obtain several references. Ask for the names and addresses of other local clients. Contact them and pick their brains.

4. What will the total cost of services be? Bottom line it and get it in writing.

5. What is the total number of inventions the firm represents? How many of its clients are making more money from their invention than they paid to the invention promotion company? Get this in writing.

6. Is there a large up-front fee? Those companies requesting such a fee make their money this way. This is usually the sign of a questionable company. A reputable licensing agent will make its money from the licensing of client inventions. Expect the company to be highly selective of the ideas they choose to represent. An above-board company will be willing to assist you with marketing your invention on a straight commission basis. These are the contingent-fee firms. If they truly believe in your invention, they won't ask for cash up-front.

7. Demand to study examples of the written market evaluation the company proposes. It must contain specific information, not vague or general statements. Beware of a tendency to throw an impressive set of statistics at you, for statistics can be made to lie. An above-board company will produce a detailed dollar analysis. You should expect no less, especially if you have paid for the report.

8. What are the company's rejection rates? What percentage of all ideas received were considered unacceptable for promotion by the company? Honest companies should have a rather high rate. Many submitted ideas may already be patented or not patentable ideas. Many others simply may be lousy ideas.

You need to protect yourself when dealing with any invention promotion company. Never allow your enthusiasm for your invention to overcome your common sense. Most inventors have such a powerful emotional attachment to their invention they fail to conduct their business with a clear head. Their perpetual optimism gets in the way. Get everything in writing and understand it completely before signing any contracts. It is advisable to see your attorney first. Your attorney must review the contract to protect you.

A few words about their fee structure: Their escalating fees will kill you. Make the company reveal all fees in writing before signing a contract. Some companies won't tell you what the final fee will be. Don't let them be coy and get away with socking it to you. Never pay more than $200 to a firm to perform a substantial evaluation of your invention. Exorbitant front-end fees are how many of these firms make their money. We consider these firms to be nothing more than con artists. They usually end up exposed on shows like *60 Minutes* or *Prime Time Live*, with the Federal Trade Commission breathing down their necks. The FTC suggests consumers follow this guideline: Reputable invention promotion firms derive their income from their share of royalties from inventions they have successfully licensed and marketed to industry. To make money, it is imperative they be incredibly selective when evaluating a submitted idea for an invention. The honest firms reject most submitted ideas. If you don't want to be ripped off, look for a firm with a high rejection rate.

Unscrupulous invention promotion companies may neglect to perform an adequate patent search. They may unwittingly or even willingly promote an idea that is already patented. Guess what? You just became the bad guy. It's called patent infringement and you will likely be sued. Expect your life to become a living hell if you are unfortunate enough to be sued by an individual or a company with deep pockets and the will to squash you.

If they perform a patent search, it should include an opinion of patentability by a registered patent attorney or agent. Be sure to obtain the name of the patent searcher and the name and registration number of the patent attorney or agent providing the opinion of patentability.

If we sound skeptical and pessimistic about dealing with invention promotion companies, it is with good reason. Roger, the co-author of this book, went that route once. He lost a lot of money without attaining satisfactory results dealing with an invention marketing organization in New York. The Multi-Scrub Power Cleaning Machine, patent 3,932,908, was developed by Roger and a partner back in the 1970s. See the accompanying Multi-Scrub patent we have presented for illustrative purposes.

Once the fees were paid, the company became very evasive when Roger and his partner tried to reach it. For all its purported marketing expertise, nothing happened. In our opinion, they were little more than a patent mill— an expensive one at that. Soon after, the U.S. government began investigating this invention marketing organization. Not surprisingly, the company soon closed shop. But don't think for a minute that this stopped them. Soon afterward, the company vice president opened a new patent development company. Back in the saddle again!

85

United States Patent [19]

Bitgood et al.

[11] **3,932,908**

[45] **Jan. 20, 1976**

[54] **PORTABLE SCRUBBING DEVICE**

[75] Inventors: **Andrew J. Bitgood; Roger T. Bellavance,** both of Moosup, Conn.

[73] Assignee: **The Raymond Lee Organization, Inc.,** New York, N.Y. ; a part interest

[22] Filed: **Mar. 20, 1974**

[21] Appl. No.: **452,965**

[52] **U.S. Cl.** **15/28; 132/73.6**
[51] **Int. Cl.²** **A46B 13/02**
[58] **Field of Search** .... 15/22 R, 22 A, 22 C, 23, 15/24, 28, 29, 34, 93, 97 R, 3.53; 132/73.6, 75.8; 51/170 R, 170 PT, 170 T; 173/170

[56] **References Cited**
UNITED STATES PATENTS

1,669,560	5/1928	Himes	15/28 X
2,008,920	7/1935	Moir	15/28 UX
2,917,023	12/1959	Cohen	15/3.53
3,183,891	5/1965	MacDonald	15/3.53
3,242,516	3/1966	Cantor	15/28
3,563,252	2/1971	Spohr et al.	132/73.6
3,715,770	2/1973	Gomez	15/28

FOREIGN PATENTS OR APPLICATIONS

1,267,147	6/1961	France	15/28

Primary Examiner—Edward L. Roberts
Attorney, Agent, or Firm—Howard I. Podell

[57] **ABSTRACT**

A portable scrubbing device incorporating a rotary scrubbing brush detachably mounted in a handle member powered by a flexible cable driven by a motor mounted in a housing unit. The housing unit is fitted with external recesses for storing the handle member and scrubbing brush.

1 Claim, 4 Drawing Figures

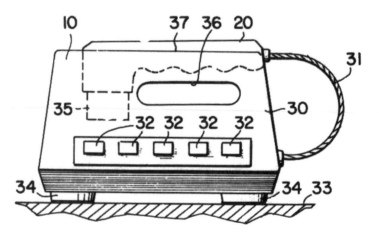

Multi-Scrub Patent, page 1.

86

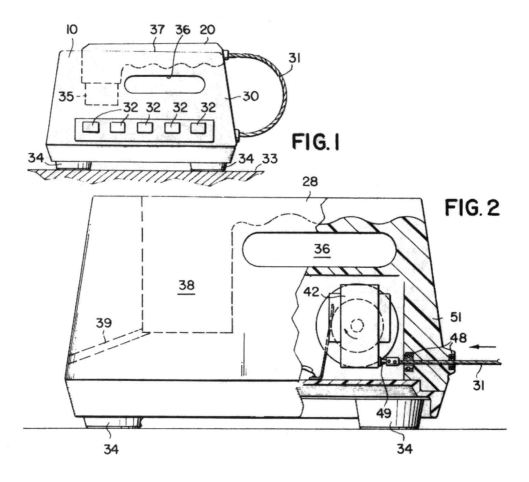

FIG.1

FIG.2

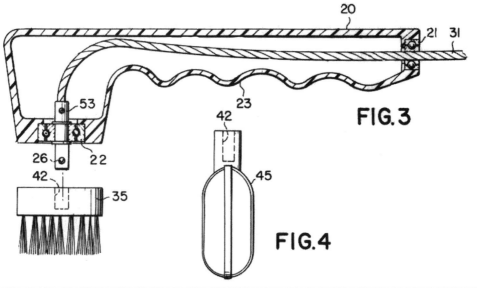

FIG.3

FIG.4

Multi-Scrub Patent, page 2.

1

PORTABLE SCRUBBING DEVICE

SUMMARY OF THE INVENTION:

Our invention relates to a portable scrubbing device and particularly to a scrubbing device in which a detachable rotary scrub brush is fitted to a handle member linked by a flexible drive cable to a motor in the housing of the device.

The housing unit is fitted with external recesses shaped to retain the handle member and scrub brush, when not in use.

BRIEF DESCRIPTION OF THE DRAWING:

The objects and features of the invention may be understood with reference to the following detailed description of an illustrative embodiment of the invention, taken together with the accompanying drawings in which:

FIG. 1 is a perspective view of the invention;

FIG. 2 is a sectional elevation view of the housing;

FIG. 3 is a sectional exploded view of the handle member and scrub brush; and

FIG. 4 is an elevation view of an optional stirrer attachment.

DESCRIPTION OF THE PREFERRED EMBODIMENT:

Turning now descriptively to the drawings, in which similar reference characters denote similar elements throughout the several views, FIG. 1 illustrates the appliance 10 in the stored position, with handle member 20 held in shaped recess 28 of the housing unit 30 and joined by flexible drive cable 31 to the motor and gear unit 42 located in the housing unit 30.

As shown in FIGS. 1–3, the housing unit 30 is mounted on fixed legs 34 so as to rest on a horizontal surface 33. Switch buttons 32 on the side of the housing unit permit the operator to turn the device ON or OFF, as well as select the desired speed of motor. A shaped recess 28 in the upper surface 37 of the housing unit 30 of a size to engage the handle member 20 is joined to a shaped recess well 38 of a size to fit about a rotary scrub brush 35 attached to the handle member 20. A drain hole 39 runs from the interior bottom of recess

2

well 38 to the exterior of the housing unit to permit water to drain from a stored brush 35 in the well 38.

Drive shaft 31 is joined in the housing unit to the output shaft 49 of the motor and gear unit and held by rotary bearings 48 in the housing wall 51. The drive shaft 31 is similarly mounted to rotary bearing 21 in the handle member 20 in which it joins the handle output shaft 53 which is mounted in a rotary bearing 22. Output shaft 53 terminates exterior of the handle 20 in a male plug 26 of a size to engage a female socket 42 of a rotary scrub brush 35, shown in FIG. 3 or in optional attachments, such as a stirrer 45 as shown in FIG. 4.

The underside 23 of the handle member 20 is shaped as a grip to fit the fingers of a user holding the handle member 20.

A through hole 36 is fitted in the housing 30 of a size to form a convenient hand grip for lifting the housing.

Since obvious changes may be made in the specific embodiment of the invention described herein, such modifications being within the spirit and scope of the invention claimed, it is indicated that all matter contained herein is intended as illustrative and not as limiting in scope.

Having thus described the invention, what I claim as new and desire to secure by Letters Patent of the United States is:

1. A compact portable scrubbing or stirring device comprising a housing member. a handle member and a detachable rotary tool,

said housing member incorporating a motor and gear unit linked to a flexible drive shaft which leads from the housing member into the handle member,

said handle member fitted with an output shaft rotatably mounted to said handle member, said output shaft linked inside the handle member to said flexible drive shaft, with said output shaft shaped, externally of the handle member, to engage a socket in said detachable rotary tool, in which a surface of the housing is formed with a recess of a shape to fit the handle member and an attached detachable rotary tool, with the bottom of said recess linked by a drain hole through the housing to the exterior of the housing, so as to drain excess water from the recess.

* * * * *

Product Packaging

The packaging design must appeal to the consumer. It doesn't have to look pretty, but it must reach out and grab them. It should scream out, "LOOK AT ME! PICK ME UP! BUY ME!" The worst packaging in the world is the kind that blends in with the other products on the shelf, like camouflage. If a shopper cannot see your product, it won't sell.

You must conform to government regulations and industry standards for your product packaging. Regulations exist regarding package design, package size and product claims. You should be cautious for there is some information you are required to print on the packaging as well as certain things from which you are prohibited. It is essential to consult with an industrial designer for help in planning the design and layout of your product's packaging.

A package's function is not only to hold a product for convenience in stacking and shipping. From the marketing perspective, a package must effectively project your product's positioning. You can choose to package your product similarly to your competitors or you can break the rules by choosing an innovative design. Doing the later can result in your penetration of a market niche, resulting in seizing a segment of market share.

A prime concern is how retailers view your packaging. Before you have your packaging designed, talk to retailers to find out what kind of packaging they prefer. A little research ahead of time can reveal lots of surprising feedback that can translate into better package designs (and more sales!). If it is too bulky, large, small, tall, lopsided, flimsy, heavy or just plain awkward, retailers will not be pleased. Displease a retailer and you can expect them to no longer carry your product. Instead, they will buy from someone else. Redesign that package or you won't keep it on store shelves. Remember the following hints for effective package design:

- Communicate a corporate or product identity to tie in with your product line.

- Approve designs that appeal to both customers and retailers.

- Employ company logos or slogans used in your advertising.

- Effective packaging should list instructions or visually display how to use the product. Sometimes plastic windows are used to show the contents.

- Design packaging to fit on/in standardized industry displays such as racks and shelving.

- Choose physical characteristics (size, weight, shape, colors, printing, etc.) that appeal to consumers.

- Use professionally written copy on the labeling to motivate the consumer to buy the product. Always sell the product's benefits and list the features.

- Your packaging should say "this is a quality product." Shoddy packaging will not help sell a quality product. Remember, quality and price are interlinked.

Exercise caution when dealing with packaging companies. Some of these companies will offer to package your product and warehouse your inventory. Some will offer to assist you in the marketing and sales of your product. The more product they package and warehouse, the more money they make. Roger dealt briefly with a New Jersey company that wanted to package and warehouse a large inventory of Hook Pens, promising the prospect of huge sales through their contacts. This company suggested mortgaging his home to help pay for the cost of packaging, warehousing and other services. An alarm went off in his head. Common sense overrode hope for large sales as he realized that he would probably lose out. Tying up cash in inventory is foolish. Roger learned the hard way, having made that mistake before. He still has 65,000 Emergency Call Police banners in storage. (You can see the banner in action in the accompanying photograph.)

Establish your market before you build up a reasonably sized inventory. What is a reasonably sized inventory? Small. Practice just-in-time (JIT) inventory management to minimize your costs. JIT is vital to your company's success and can be implemented on almost any scale. Practicing JIT is especially important now because of the very high inventory costs businesses face.

Keep just enough inventory on hand to meet your projected sales for the immediate future. A tightly controlled re-ordering program is necessary to maintain safe inventory levels. Seasonality of sales is a prime concern. Inventory must effectively track the inevitable seasonality in demand for your product. Don't worry too much if your stock runs out and you experience an occasional backlog of orders. This situation actually creates a favorable impression. Customers see the demand for your product, realize it is "hot" and they want it all that much more. If you offer an extensive catalogue of products backed up by a small inventory on hand but with a great network of JIT to quickly fulfill orders, you will make a powerful and favorable impression not only on your customers but your stockholders as well. To learn more about JIT, refer to the production and operations management section of any good business book.

In one respect, building a small business is like investing in the stock market. You never put at risk more money than you are willing to lose when playing the market. It is a prudent philosophy to do likewise when investing in a small business.

To locate a company that designs, manufactures the packaging and packages your products, refer to these sections of the *Yellow Pages*:

- Package Development
- Packaging Machinery
- Packaging Material
- Packaging Service

You can learn more about the packaging industry by utilizing the following resources:

- Industrial Designers Society of America
  1142 East Walker Road
  Great Falls, VA 22066
  (703) 759-0100
  Fax (703) 759-7679
  Email idsanhq@aol.com
  Professional society of industrial designers.

- Package Design Council International
  481 Carlisle Drive
  Herndon, VA 20170-4830
  (703) 318-7225
  Fax: (703) 318-0310
  Trade association for the packaging industry.

- *Packaging Marketplace*
  Gale Research, Inc.
  835 Penobscot Building
  Detroit, MI 48226
  (313) 961-2242
  Fax (313) 961-6083
  Directory offering a comprehensive listing of packaging manufacturers.

Dealing With Store Buyers

Salesmanship is similar to writing in that it's a combination of craft and talent. You can learn the craft, but the talent part is either innate or lacking. You can read books on sales, take courses and seminars—even apprentice. You will learn the craft. But do you possess that rare and special talent to induce another person to buy from you?

You need to be able to "read" people. You need to divine what they are thinking through their words, subtext and body language. Communicating directly, clearly and succinctly is essential. Learn to locate the locus of power within an organization. This is the person to whom you must direct your sales effort. Dealing with anyone else is usually a waste of time. Patience and courtesy must be your calling card.

This book is not meant to be a primer on sales techniques. Whole libraries exist on that topic alone. If you invent a product and intend to sell it, your sales technique most likely will be the deciding factor in the success or failure of your venture. Before you can sell your product, you must first learn to sell yourself. Go out and learn.

When dealing with store buyers, you may discover that they spend an awful lot of time out of the United States. To see why, just walk into any department store. All too often the shelves are lined with merchandise manufactured just about everywhere except in the U.S.A.

It almost seems many buyers are loath to deal with American companies. Roger tried to interest a buyer for a well known nationwide chain department store in purchasing the patented Hook Pen. Her reply was that they could just go around the patent and buy the pen from a company in Asia. Retail stores should keep in mind the following mantra: If you don't buy from U.S. companies, then don't expect U.S. companies (and their employees) to buy from you.

Why do so many buyers travel the world seeking out products instead of buying American-made merchandise? Some say there are certain "incentives" offered overseas that are not available here because of a few inconvenient laws to which we are all subject. Not being a store buyer, I cannot comment as to the validity of these rumors. But they certainly do persist. Many products can be bought cheaper overseas than in this country. However, in many cases, when you add the shipping and importation fees, duties, tariffs and so forth, the cost can be comparable if not higher. All too often, the imported products are of cheaper quality as well.

Blackmailing buyers to coerce them to place orders may not be common, but bribes, kickbacks and payoffs may be more so. Buyers as a group would probably be a very good target for intense IRS scrutiny. International business is a cutthroat world with a sordid underbelly.

An international code of business ethics simply does not exist. Ethical beliefs about what is right and wrong varies from country to country. In America, business ethics classes teach that offering or soliciting bribes is unethical. The U.S. government considers them illegal. Yet in the Middle East, bribery is a way of life. It is expected. It is business as usual. A bribe is considered nothing more than a tip. If a businessperson wishes to get anything done in the Middle East, bribery must become an essential business practice.

The rules, both written and unwritten vary widely from country to country. Outside of the United States, often the only rule is no rules.

Shelf Space and Slotting Fees

The next time a chain grocery store invites the public to its gala opening, go see it. Before you or any other customer walks through its front door, most likely that new store is entirely paid for. This money comes from the shelf space and slotting fees the grocery store demands from product manufacturers and distributors. These fees buy a space where the supplier stocks their product for display. The grocers make really big bucks selling shelf space. The demand for shelf space is so high that it has become an exorbitantly expensive and sought after commodity. Companies buy up other companies just to acquire the shelf space they are allotted. Suppliers routinely offer gifts, bonuses and trips to grocers as buying incentives. They have to do whatever it takes to get their products on the shelves.

If you have a product you wish to sell to chain grocery stores and others, your chances of getting it on store shelves in any quantity are slim to nonexistent unless you have shelf space or deal with a distributor with shelf space. You'll be swearing to yourself that "it's a closed market and they won't let me in."

Whoever owns the shelf space wins. Check out the bread display in the supermarket. A supplier comes in, pushes the competition's product out of his slot (squashing the loaves of bread in the process). He then stocks his company's product and leaves. The next supplier pushes the newly arrived stock aside, squashing it, then stacks his company's bread in the tight slot. The same process occurs in the potato chip section as well. Now you know why your bread is squashed and chips pulverized. Competitors routinely and knowingly damage each other's products.

Competitors continually scrap with each other under the watchful eye of the federal government. In spring 1996, the Justice Department's antitrust division initiated an investigation of Frito-Lay. The probe centered on Frito-Lay gaining unfair advantage by hogging shelf space in grocery stores. The Justice Department review explored the possibility of anti-competitive practices in the snack food industry. To date, Frito-Lay has gobbled up more than half of the $15 billion salty snack food market.

Small Entity Filers and the Specter of Infringement

As previously stated, a filer is entitled to claim small entity status if he or she is an independent inventor, a small business concern or a nonprofit organization. Small entity filers' fees are reduced by half as long as you file a verification statement with the Patent and Trademark Office.

Sounds like quite a deal. But filing as a small entity actually paints a big, fat target on your patent. A potential infringer who greedily eyes your patent can tell if you are vulnerable. As a general rule, most small entity filers have no resources to fight patent infringement. They have little time, less money and usually no legal expertise. In essence, the patent affords them no protection. They're babes in the woods. Easy pickings for the wolves.

On the date your patent is granted, your patent file, including specifications and engineered drawings, becomes available for public inspection. Any interested party can peruse your file to see if you are a small entity filer and if the patent has any assignees. If someone likes your invention, they can manufacture and sell the product with little or no fear that you can ever harm them. The FBI can't arrest them; neither can the state police. *You* must enforce the patent. The only way you can stop the blatant piracy is for your attorney to send a letter, full of decorum, telling them to please stop. It is customary to offer to license them and seek royalties from past sales, but that is really just a joke. An infringer has no intention of paying you your money. Expect their attorney to play a stalling game to run up your legal fees. You waste time, money and mental anguish.

Roger had the misfortune of experiencing just such a situation. The patented Hook Pen has been the subject of infringement. (See the accompanying photograph of the Hook Pen.) Early in the marketing of the patented Hook Pen, he discovered the very same Hook Pen for sale in an international

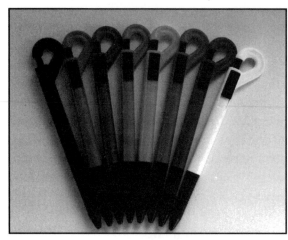

chain of toy stores. Roger didn't sell it to them. The search for the mystery supplier commenced. A New York–based distributor turned out to be the responsible party. Roger directed his patent attorney to fire off a registered letter to the distributor. The letter demanded they "cease and desist from any further activities relating to the manufacturing, importation, distribution and sales" of the Hook Pen. Additionally, a full accounting of Hook Pen sales was requested along with an offer of a willingness to settle this matter in an amicable and reasonable manner.

The first letter was never picked up from their post office box. With the assistance of the U.S. Postal Service, Roger tracked down another New York address to which the letter was again sent. Correspondence with the distributor's general counsel began. Roger's patent attorney told him to expect them to stall for time. Did they ever! First, they claimed a copy of the Hook Pen patent did not accompany the attorney's letter. Later, they claimed they had been selling the Hook Pen for five years. If true, this would have predated the patent and established prior art, which would seem to invalidate the Hook Pen patent. Naturally, Roger asked for proof of those sales in the form of invoices, documenting business they conducted with the Hook Pen. Not surprisingly, the distributor never sent an invoice to back up their claim. Nice bluff. Nice try.

The distributor further stalled by switching from an in-house counsel to an out-of-house legal counsel. One attorney claimed to have disassembled the Hook Pen and couldn't reassemble it. Consequently, he needed another Hook Pen sample sent to him. A delay of several more weeks ensued. Roger still laughs about this. Our six-year-old niece could strip and reassemble a Hook Pen in a few seconds. A grown man could not? (When we think of this lawyer, Jackie Mason's joke comes to mind: "Every Jewish mother wants her son to be a doctor . . . and if he's a little retarded . . . maybe a lawyer.") All these delays provided the distributor the opportunity to liquidate their stock of Hook Pens and pocket the profits. Eventually, they stopped selling the Hook Pen, although Roger never saw any money or accounting of their sales. The only thing this mess yielded was a large bill for attorney's fees.

In another example of infringement, we discovered a well-known non-profit organization was selling the Hook Pen in their catalog. Our first step was to contact the legal department at their national headquarters to determine their attitude toward intellectual property rights. We asked how they would feel if we used their trademark without permission. They warned us in the most strident terms the use of their intellectual property would be intolerable. Severe civil and criminal penalties existed and prosecution would be a certainty.

Having gauged their attitude toward infringement, we let the other shoe drop. We informed them we had no intention of using their intellectual property. We informed them Roger possessed the patent on the Hook Pen they were selling. We made it crystal clear we viewed their sales of the Hook Pen as infringement.

We were heartened by our conversation with their legal counsel. He indicated we should "do the sensible thing." We explained we had no wish to be adversarial. Our attitude was cordial, cheerful and positive. We offered to supply them with Hook Pens at a fair price, properly license them and settle up past accounts. Our attorney sent them a letter proposing the very same.

Sadly, a pattern emerged. Letters went unanswered. Phone calls were not returned. It was like walking around a corner and getting whacked in the face by a two-by-four.

We purchased a sample of their Hook Pens in an effort to collect evidence of their wrongdoing. Stunned is an understatement for how we felt when we saw "Made in USA" boldly emblazoned on their packaging. Pretty audacious we thought, since this pen was made in *Taiwan!* And although not visible on the pen's exterior, the Taiwan mark was nevertheless found molded onto the underside of the clip. As we understand the law, the bogus "Made in USA" claim on the package's header is a brazen violation of U.S. Customs law and also of interest to the Federal Trade Commission. The pen is required to be marked in a conspicuous manner with its country of origin; "TAIWAN R.O.C." molded into the underside of the clip would not appear to us (and the U.S. Customs Service) to be conspicuously marked.

Faced with competition from other companies who imported the Taiwanese Hook Pen, we decided to place an order for 12,000 pens. Trying to get molds made for U.S. production of the Hook Pens was proving daunting, time-consuming and expensive.

When the shipment arrived Customs seized the Hook Pens. This blew us away. Roger is the one with the patent, remember? According to Customs, the Hook Pens were not conspicuously marked with the country of origin. We were struck by the irony the infringers could get Hook Pens through Customs but we could not. Before liquidation of the shipment, all 12,000 pens had to be properly marked. Roger painstakingly labeled all 12,000 pens with "Made In Taiwan" stickers.

We fired off a certified letter to the chief executive officer of the infringing organization. In it, we stated our serious concerns regarding infringement, pen labeling and packaging. What do you suppose the response was? No response. Zilch. Zip.

This organization continued sales of the Hook Pens for several years despite our efforts. Would you be surprised to learn they continued to mark their Hook Pen packages "Made in USA"? U.S. Customs certainly was. Customs agents are now investigating this nonprofit organization.

Many companies have profited from piracy of the patented Hook Pen. A major pen manufacturer engaged Roger in negotiations to provide parts for 10 to 100 million pens to be assembled, marketed and sold. The deal fell through—presumably when this corporation discovered the extent of the pirating taking place.

No company would wish to license or adopt a new product when it is likely to require lengthy and expensive litigation to ensure an exclusive to that product. Many companies cannot commit to an expensive marketing effort for a new product if they cannot secure an exclusive in the marketplace against their competitors. Most companies feel that launching a new product should be done in secrecy. They don't want premature exposure of the new product, much less by the competition.

Numerous companies, some identified, some not yet identified, have engaged in manufacturing, importation, distribution and sales of our patented Hook Pen. In the authors' opinion, these companies have infringed upon a valid U.S. patent. None of these companies ever claimed or produced a patent providing proprietary rights for a Hook Pen. The patent holder never issued a license nor did he ever sell Hook Pens to any of these companies. Since Roger possesses a valid U.S. patent and the others do not, one would expect it be a simple matter for a court to decide indeed, they have infringed. Sadly, our court system doesn't work that way. The deck is stacked heavily against the independent inventor.

If you discover someone infringing on your patent, what are your options? Don't expect the PTO or any law enforcement agency to offer any assistance. By statute, the PTO cannot perform any function in patent infringement matters. Law enforcement has no jurisdiction in patent infringement matters. The patent holder has the responsibility for detecting and fighting patent infringement. You can choose from among some of the following options for courses of action:

1. Have your patent attorney send a letter to the infringer informing them they are infringing. Request they stop and ask for financial compensation for their past infringement activity.

2. Have your patent attorney send a letter to the infringer informing them they are infringing. Seek financial compensation for past infringement activity and seek to engage them in a licensing program for their future sales.

3. Initiate a patent infringement lawsuit in a federal court. Seek damages, including court costs and attorney's fees. Seek an injunction, barring use of your patented invention by the infringer. This option is expensive. Be certain the damages award will be sufficiently large to warrant spending a quarter to a half million dollars to prosecute the lawsuit. Additionally, be certain the infringer is financially solvent to be able to afford the payment of damages. All this is contingent on your winning the lawsuit, which is by no means certain. Realistically, it is likely you will lose.

4. Engage the infringer in arbitration, mediation or minitrials as an alternative to litigation. Arbitration has the advantages of low cost, speed, less formality and privacy for both parties. Alternative dispute resolution allows privacy to avoid public embarrassment, protect trade secrets and sensitive proprietary information, and keep the government's nose out of both party's business.

What if you don't have the financial resources to initiate and follow through with a lawsuit against an infringer? What if the damages you seek would be significantly less than the cost of the lawsuit (even if you were lucky enough to win the case)? What if the infringer is a greedy giant with deep pockets and a legal department that ties you in knots? Doing battle with them in a courtroom plays right into their hands. They control that turf with their unlimited money and sharp-as-a-tack legal talent. Seldom will you win there. The only chance you have is to control the battleground by waging your fight in the court of public opinion. Here you can win, especially if you are the David to their Goliath. The public and the news media love the underdog.

A wise entrepreneur will use media attention to publicize his or her plight and product. You have a golden marketing opportunity here. The publicity can help increase your market exposure and sales. The news media will be happy to be an unwitting co-conspirator as they spread the sad tale of how you've been put upon. They need a good story to sell ink. Be creative as you go on the attack and tell the world your story. Keep your sense of humor and inject wit into your story. If it is entertaining, the media is much more likely to pick up your story and run with it.

In this battle, we must use the strategy of taking your story to the public to embarrass, humiliate and otherwise expose the rats to the light of day. Your tactics should include the following:

- Create favorable publicity for yourself by sending news releases to the appropriate media outlets to get the word out. Target TV, radio, newspapers, magazines and get your story on the Internet. Organize boycotts and even picket outside their headquarters or one of their stores just before Christmas for maximum effect.

- Take your story to your customers. Mailings, fliers with your product or a sticker with a toll-free number on the product offering a free call for information on the infringement—all of these get the word out. Offer a "legal defense kit" containing preprinted complaint forms to be sent to the infringer as well as agencies such as the Federal Trade Commission, U.S. Customs Service, Better Business Bureau, Chamber of Commerce, and so forth, if applicable.

- Tell everyone you know and enlist their help in spreading the word.

- Employees especially should want to help because the infringer is threatening their job.

Bad publicity gives most companies a severe case of the willies. If you conduct your publicity campaign properly, you can significantly affect the infringer's bottom line. Their stockholders will not be pleased. Somebody will be held accountable for their decision to infringe on another company's patent. Be ruthless! Damage them as best you can! After all, they are seeking to destroy you, aren't they? It's the only way you'll be respected in the marketplace. As an added bonus, other potential infringers will think twice before tangling with you.

Finding a Manufacturer

Doing your own manufacturing requires a considerable investment of time, money and expertise. Many entrepreneurs contract with established manufacturers to produce their invention. Expect to encounter a considerable range in price quotes for work vended out. In Roger's case, molding his own pens was an option because of previous experience in molding technology. Seeking price quotes for pen molds was an eye-opening experience.

The immediate lesson is to not bother trying to do business with any company with a major portion of their business coming from government contracts. A nongovernment contractor quoted Roger a price of $98,000 for five molds to produce the Hook Pen. A government contractor quoted a price of $489,500. Another molding company with government contracts refused to even waste their time putting together a quote. The company representative said the company could make three to four times as much money performing government work than for the private sector.

Similarly, do not approach large corporations with sales in excess of $50 million. Good reasons exist for doing so. You will have to attempt to deal with a bloated, nonresponsive and inefficient bureaucracy. The NIH syndrome will be rampant in their corporate culture. Their waivers are much more intrusive and restrictive of your rights. With their power, they may even try to circumvent your patent. Most importantly, the decision makers will be more approachable in the smaller companies versus the large companies.

The best prospects are small to mid-sized manufacturing companies. Look for those in your vicinity so you can easily visit for negotiations, consultations, planning and monitoring the manufacture of your invention. The best prospects should have experience manufacturing products that are in the same product line or similar to your invention. They should be highly respected. Being known for having a quality line of products is essential. Look for a history of integrity and good customer service. Depth of experience and commercial success in marketing and sales is of paramount importance.

In discussing licensing your invention in Chapter 3, numerous resources were introduced for researching companies. The same strategies and publications are useful in finding a manufacturer to build and possibly distribute your invention. The *Thomas Register of Manufacturers* and *Dun's Million Dollar Directory* are indispensable for this research.

Additionally, network with other inventors, especially those who are members of Inventors Associations. We cannot stress enough how valuable this is. A good network of contacts will stretch far and wide. These contacts will be able to open doors for you that would be closed if you were on your own. Other search strategies include checking these resources:

- Small Business Development Centers at your local community colleges.
- Trade periodicals.
- Trade associations.
- Your state's Economic Development Commission.

- Local and state Chambers of Commerce.
- Invention magazines.
- Store shelves—contact companies who sell similar products.
- Distributors—find manufacturers of products similar to yours by back-tracking from retailer to distributor to supplier.
- The Internet—powerful search engines allow you to find almost anything here.

Let us emphasize if you don't know anything about the manufacture of your prospective invention, you are probably wasting your time with it. If you refuse to take the time to learn as much as you can, you are in big trouble. Better to get a real job and forget this particular dream. In this cutthroat world of business, it's highly doubtful there are many manufacturing companies out there that wouldn't take advantage of a naive inventor with a pocketful of money. You do yourself the greatest disservice by not obtaining the requisite education and experience with the manufacturing aspect of your invention. The opportunists will see you as a lamb willingly walking to its slaughter. They'll be thinking, "what a schnook!" as they pick your pockets clean.

"There is a better way to do it—find it."
—Thomas Edison

CHAPTER 7
Patents: The Joke Is on Us

A Patent's Real Worth

Everything you read in the chapters describing how to patent an idea . . . take it with a grain of salt. Too many people have discovered it is a waste of time. We guarantee you, no infringer is shaking in their boots at the thought of infringing on your proprietary rights. Even if caught, they laugh at how easy it is to get away with. If you want to have a U.S. patent to hang on your wall . . . fine . . . go ahead and patent your idea. It's worth the paper it's printed on. No more. And probably less.

We will repeat the following basic truth in this chapter in the hope the message will sink in. A patent is nothing more than a government-granted license to sue. You pay thousands of dollars to your patent attorney and the Patent and Trademark Office for the right to sue someone. That's all. Think about it. You pay all that money so you have the right to go out and hire a ridiculously expensive lawyer, just so you can fork over whatever money you have left to that lawyer for a guaranteed, definite, you can bank on it . . . maybe . . . to getting some small measure of satisfaction in a patent dispute (if you win—most do not). It will take years. The experience will suck your life dry. Forget justice—that only happens after you die.

Odds are, if you are a small entity filer, in one sense, your patent is next to worthless. It costs you money and lulls you into a false sense of security. Who has conspired against you to bring about this reprehensible state of affairs? Take your pick: the Patent and Trademark Office, big industry, the judicial system and lawyers.

To be perfectly fair, the PTO can be blamed only so much. The PTO doesn't make the rules under which they must operate. It would seem the only interests of concern to them are their own interests. The interests of inventors, particularly independent inventors, seem to be subverted by the interests of the PTO bureaucracy. Protecting and increasing the PTO's budget, jobs and prestige consume their advocacy efforts. These self-serving bureaucrats are no friend to the independent inventor.

Big industry has long had its boot on the neck of independent inventors. The rules under which the PTO operates did not come about by accident. The patent system has evolved, since the days of Thomas Jefferson, shaped by those wielding influence. Congress, hand in hand with big industry's lobbyists, have written the statutes and influenced the courts. Those with money have power and influence. Industry's lobbyists tailor made the law to favor just one group—big industry.

Most people react with disbelief when told that industry strongly desires weak patent laws. Wouldn't they wish to protect their own products with strong patent laws? Large corporations are not hindered by weak patent laws. They protect their products with their marketing strength and deep pockets. They patent their line of products to have the legal device to go after any small guy who dares infringe. Be assured, they have the legal staff and bankroll ready for just such a contingency. When they go after someone, they hammer him. There is no mercy!

A large number of history's most valuable and groundbreaking inventions owe their genesis to independent inventors. If patent protection is deliberately weak and expensive to prosecute then big corporations can swoop down and steal the ideas with impunity. It's no surprise that they do precisely that.

This country's courts are no friend to independent inventors. Sadly, 80 percent of patents brought into the courts end up overturned or held invalid. One has to wonder just how good a job the PTO does when considering an application for a patent. If so many patents end up invalid, something is seriously wrong in the PTO. Reasonable people might begin to think of it as nothing more than a patent mill!

If you are unfortunate enough to have to suffer through a patent validity suit, expect it to cost you about $250,000 to $500,000. Most of us don't have that kind of spare change lying around, which means you've already lost. Until a court has declared your patent to be valid and that the patent belongs to you, it's not really your invention. Since the courts and especially judges are ignorant for the most part about patents and modern technology, one should question how qualified they are to pass judgment on such issues. There's an old rule of thumb: The legal team that dumps the greatest volume of briefs and information on the court wins. It is impossible to believe the judge can digest all of this information to be able to render a just verdict. It takes time and massive amounts of money to generate the mountain of information needed to protect your patent in a lawsuit. Patent attorneys regard infringement cases as cash cows, many charging up to $250 per hour. It is not uncommon for the best, most in-demand legal talent to charge even more.

When faced with the prospect of any kind of patent lawsuit, inventors must necessarily drop whatever they are working on to devote themselves fully to preparation for the suit. Lives are put on hold. Work essentially stops. Health and family life suffer. Bank accounts shrink. Many inventors who have gone through this turmoil have vowed, never again! Their attitude becomes don't even bother patenting your ideas. Make and sell your product for as long as you can and still make profit. If others copy your product and your market shrinks resulting in dwindling sales, walk away from the product and move on to something else. It is said copying or infringing on your invention is akin to paying you a compliment. Some people in the industry have this strange idea. The thinking is that it must be a great invention if it is good enough for someone to go to the trouble to steal. Too many inventors have suffered too long from too many of these "compliments."

Patents should be granted the identical protection offered to copyrights by the U.S. government. Protection is granted for life plus 50 years for a copyright. Even better, legislation is pending that extends the coverage to life plus 70 years. Passage looks very promising.

The FBI should be empowered to investigate allegations of criminal patent infringement. According to Title 17 of U.S. Code, federal law provides severe civil and criminal penalties for the unauthorized use of copyrighted material. Patents should be similarly and vigorously protected with the Attorney General and Justice Department squarely behind the inventor. If the PTO cannot or will not issue valid patents and back them up against infringers, then patents are worthless and the PTO should be abolished. We can eliminate this section of the Commerce Department. This will never happen because the PTO is a profit-making enterprise for the government. Approximately $100,000,000 per year is taken from the PTO's operational proceeds and diverted into the General Fund. If run more as a quasi-governmental agency such as the U.S. Postal Service is, the PTO would be more effective and responsive to the needs of its constituents—inventors, applicants, and patent attorneys and agents.

Most people pay less than $100 to register an automobile. If it is stolen and transported across state lines, the FBI can step in with all its vast manpower and expertise to seek out, arrest and, in concert with the Justice Department, prosecute the perpetrator. They will do this even if the car is a $200 hunk of junk.

An inventor must pay thousands of dollars for what he or she thinks is a valid U.S. patent. When infringed upon, the FBI or any other law enforcement agency cannot help you. No government agency can stop the piracy for you. You will be told you must "enforce the patent on your own." Unless you have money to feed your lawyers, you are not stopping the piracy. Folks, you truly are on your own.

Patent and Trademark Office Scandals

Thomas Jefferson described the Patent and Trademark Office as "the locomotive that runs industry." As the PTO's first administrator, he oversaw the development of a filing system requiring floor to ceiling catalogs of shoe boxes. Only recently, with the advent of computerized inventories, which bring the PTO into the twentieth century, has this unwieldy and antiquated system begun to be phased out. Jefferson intended patents be filed in such a manner that examiners could easily research them. It hasn't worked out that way.

In 1989, 1,600 patent examiners were responsible for evaluating 165,000 new patent applications. Almost a million supporting documents accompanied those applications. According to the *Wall Street Journal*, in 1990, almost 2 million of the PTO's 30 million documents were lost. One out of every 15 documents lost is a national disgrace and a tragedy. That's not much of a filing system. One has to wonder, where did all those documents go?

A story circulated in the news media that may be disputed—and then again may not—of a patent examiner's office ceiling collapsing. Evidently the excessive weight of "lost" patent applications packed in the space above the soundproofing caused the structural failure. This is an odd place to be storing patent applications.

Another horror story the patent examiners tell is of the elevator shaft that ate hundreds of patent applications. Somehow, these documents had fallen through a crack down to the bottom of the elevator shaft's gaping maw. It was only when the pile of applications stopped the elevator that they were discovered.

A patent examiner, wishing to remain anonymous, complained of not being able to locate a particular reference book in the Patent Office library. It was a rare and valuable book published in the mid-nineteenth century. Other texts on the same subject were similarly missing. The examiner queried the library staff and was given the name of another patent examiner who checked those books out years earlier. Strangely, repeated attempts to contact this other examiner by phone were unsuccessful. The patent examiner finally found out from a colleague of the borrower that the borrower sold all those books some years back. Trafficking in stolen government property is a felony, but no one seems to care in this case.

The PTO is just like every other federal agency in Washington, DC. The "revolving door" policy sees patent examiners at the PTO quickly moving on to practice patent law in private practice. A patent examiner must possess highly technical qualifications. This degreed individual must possess a specialization in a particular discipline. The PTO's Patent Academy instills further training in the legal aspects of patenting during the examiner's first year. In four or five years the examiners are able to complete their federally subsidized patent law studies at local law schools. Most quit government work at this time to go on to private practice where a successful patent attorney can earn up to $500,000 or even more each year. No one seems too concerned about the potential conflicts of interest that inevitably arise from this incestuous situation.

The Maintenance Fee Trap

Not one to pass up another way of making a buck, Congress mandated the imposition of maintenance fees for all utility patents that issue from applications filed with the PTO on and after December 12, 1980. These fees must be paid to keep your patent in force for the full 20-year term. Three payments are required, each markedly higher than the previous payment. These maintenance fees are due at 3.5, 7.5 and 11.5 years from the date of issue of a patent. The current fee structure requires a first payment of $1,050, a second payment of $2,100 and the third and final payment of $3,160.

The maintenance fee must be paid during the six-month period preceding each due date. No surcharge is applicable during this "window period." If you fail to pay the correct maintenance fee within the specified time, you may face termination of your patent rights. The PTO provides a six-month grace period during which you may submit the maintenance fee along with a surcharge. The PTO *may* send you a reminder to pay the maintenance fee if they have not received it at the completion of the normal six-month payment period. If by the end of the grace period, you still have not paid the maintenance fee, your patent will expire. At this point the PTO *may* send you a Notice of Patent Expiration. (According to the PTO, sending patent holders a notice is considered a "courtesy.") The PTO immediately prints an announcement in the *Official Gazette*, stating your patent has lapsed.

In rare cases, you may be able to revive your expired patent if you successfully petition to show by declaration the delay in payment was "unavoidable." A stiff surcharge accompanies the petition.

When paying maintenance fees, make sure you fill out every blank on the form. You must include the serial number from your patent application. The tiniest mistake gives the PTO the excuse to apply a surcharge if the resulting delay in processing carries you into the grace period. You will receive a maintenance fee statement when the PTO accepts your maintenance fee with all paperwork in order. Strangely enough, the PTO will not accept payment of the maintenance fee at any time before the due period.

Nowadays, when a U.S. patent is issued, printed on the inside front cover is a notation that maintenance fees are due at 3.5 years, 7.5 years and 11.5 years. When you first receive your patent, one of the first things you should do is to calculate the three future dates upon which the maintenance fees are due. Staple a note with this information to the end of your calendar. Carry this note forward each year to the new calendar. Mark the due date.

Boldly highlight it. If you value your patent, you do not want to make the grave mistake of forgetting to pay your maintenance fee.

We feel that patents should be marked with the actual dates the maintenance fees are due. This would help to alleviate any confusion that may result from a vague reference to fee due dates. Additionally, notices should be sent out to the patent holder before the six month window preceding the due date. This gentle reminder that the fee is due would go a long way toward reducing the number of patents inadvertently lost due to a missed maintenance fee payment.

When considering senate passage of the bill (H.R. 6933) requiring maintenance fees be paid on patents, Senator Birch Bayh stated in remarks "on the floor" the bill be so amended to provide "that patent holders be personally notified through the mail shortly before the payments are due." Regrettably, this suggestion did not make it into the law as finally drafted as 35 USC 41 (b). Many inventors consider this section of the law to be defective and in need of legislative remedy.

Roger suffered the misfortune of having one of his patents inadvertently expire because of a missed maintenance fee payment. The switch from a patent agent to a new patent attorney contributed to a bit of confusion about who was responsible to notify the patent holder about the maintenance fee coming due. The next thing he knew, Roger was notified his patent had expired. He immediately began the arduous task of getting his patent reinstated. A conversation with a representative in the maintenance fee department of the PTO revealed that between 5,000 and 10,000 patents expire each year due to nonpayment of maintenance fees. This individual was somewhat elusive about exactly how many. These lapsed patents include those of not just small entities but those of large corporations as well.

The PTO makes it unbelievably difficult to reinstate a patent. Roger begged and pleaded. Roger and his patent attorney jumped through all the PTO's hoops in petitioning for the revival of the patent. The PTO denied the petition.

When a patent lapses or expires due to nonpayment of a maintenance fee, anyone may make, use or sell the invention. No permission is required from the patentee. The PTO certainly doesn't need the periodic maintenance fees to keep its budget afloat. These fees are meant to impose a financial burden on the inventor. If an inventor can be manipulated into not paying the fee, his constitutional right of monopoly is lost. The technology becomes available to industry, both foreign and domestic, for free. Remember, industry lobbies to manipulate patent law to its advantage. Industry wants only those with money to have patent rights. Furthermore, if you don't have money, they want your technology. Don't expect them to pay for it when they can manipulate the system and get it for free.

The PTO's dismissal of the petition for reinstatement of Roger's patent left him with no alternative. Roger brought a civil action against Harry F.

Manbeck, Jr., Commissioner of the Patent and Trademark Office. The civil action for mandamus and injunctive relief was filed in the U.S. District Court for the District of Connecticut. The reason for this choice of venue was to force the commissioner to come to Roger's home state. Sadly, the U.S. Attorney granted summary judgment to the commissioner of the PTO.

According to 35 USC 41 (c) (1), the law stipulates petitions for reinstatement of patents lapsed due to nonpayment of maintenance fees can be granted only if the delay in payment was "unavoidable." Many patent holders (Roger included) have lost patents due to this too stringent requirement. Many lawsuits against the PTO have resulted.

Legislation introduced (H.R. 5328) by Representative Bill McCollum (R–Fla.) sought to amend the code to replace the "unavoidable" standard with an "unintentional" standard. This legislation sought to change the language of 35 USC 41 (c) (1). The first sentence would now read, "The Commissioner may accept the payment of any maintenance fee required by subsection (b) of this section which is made within twenty-four months after the six month grace period if the delay is shown to the satisfaction of the Commissioner to have been unintentional, or at any time."

The house of representatives passed H.R. 5328 on October 3, and the senate did likewise on October 7, 1992. Shortly thereafter, President George Bush signed H.R. 5328, thus enacting it into law.

We are happy to report Roger's patent was reinstated, squeaking in under the 24-month time limit. It's sad to note the change of this bad law did not come from within the PTO. Those people working for the PTO are experts in how the patent system works. Who better than they to tell when the system has a flaw that needs correcting? A case such as Roger's reveals the vacuous bureaucratic mindset that pervades too many of our government institutions. A woman who works in a patent attorney's office in private practice shared her concerns regarding this problem with her Congressman. The law changed for the better as a result of her involvement, and in spite of the PTO rather than with the help of the PTO.

"Imagination is more important than knowledge."
—Albert Einstein

CHAPTER 8
Spies, Lies and Industrial Espionage

Piracy of Intellectual Property

As long as there have been secrets, there have been spies who seek to steal them. Many businesses and governments rely upon theft of intellectual property to give them an edge in the dog-eat-dog world of business. Too many people remain naive about the common practice of trafficking in stolen ideas. In 1987, this sort of "piracy" cost the United States $20 billion.

A Richard Reeves op-ed piece from 1987 illustrates the danger. It tells the story of Stephen King, who suffers several burglaries each year. This is not the famous writer of horror stories but a London clothing designer. Nevertheless, what happens to him is a horror. His designs end up on the Hong Kong or Taiwan fashion market shortly after each burglary. Cheap "knockoffs" are big business for newly industrialized countries. The originators of the ideas or intellectual property are the big losers. Taiwan and China are well known for turning a deaf ear and a blind eye toward patent, copyright and trademark piracy. Their governments excel at fighting piracy by words but not deeds.

Close allies such as Germany and Japan have not been immune to the greed for pilfered intellectual property. America is full of people whose loyalties lie outside this country. We can count on not only our enemies to spy

109

on us but our friends as well. Intellectual property is a valuable and heavily trafficked commodity.

Potential Targets

We have talked at length about theft of intellectual property after an idea has received patent protection. Theft of ideas before you can obtain patent, copyright or trademark protection is not uncommon.

An ideal, high-value target for industrial espionage is a patent agent or attorney. Very often, patent agents perform consulting work for major corporations, commonly in the high technology and defense sectors. Phone taps and break-ins can net the unprotected proprietary information of an independent inventor or of the largest corporations. Security for a patent attorney's or agent's office is usually poor to nonexistent, especially for those working out of their home. Too often, these professionals underestimate the value others might place on this proprietary information and the steps they might be willing to take to acquire this commodity.

Another ideal place to pilfer technology is in the Patent and Trademark Office itself. An examiner in the PTO is in an ideal situation to peruse unprotected technology. How quickly and easily it could be copied or faxed outside. This really is the perfect position for anyone willing to engage in industrial espionage. The information comes to you. No wiretapping. No break-ins. No need to bribe an employee for information or blackmail them. It is almost too easy.

Illegal Wiretapping as a Proprietary Venture

Should you be paranoid about secrecy? Of course not, but some inventors are. We try to strike a balance between secrecy and trust. We believe anything of value should be treated like a hand of cards—kept close to the vest. If you think it's just a fantasy that some renegade group is out there illegally tapping phones and selling the sensitive information they monitor, you would be dead wrong. It happens.

Gregory Flannery, who reports for the *Mt. Washington Press* in Cincinnati, exposed a scandal in which employees of Cincinnati Bell Telephone Company blanketed the city with a network of illegal wiretaps. From 1972 to 1984, these two employees, Robert Draise and Leonard Gates, installed more than 1,200 wiretaps. They claimed they were directed to do so by phone company security officers and undercover police officers. What was intended to be a crackdown on organized crime and student radicals evolved into a shadowy conspiracy of political and industrial espionage.

The alleged victims included Ohio Senator Howard Metzenbaum, three federal judges and local politicians. Lawyers, journalists, union groups as well as radicals such as Black Muslims and the Weathermen had their privacy invaded. Local businesses such as Procter & Gamble, the American

Financial Corporation and the Cincinnati Stock Exchange were tapped. The lines to the vote-counting computers at the Hamilton County Board of Elections were tapped and made capable of altering votes. Even President Gerald Ford's phone was tapped when he stayed at the Stouffer Inn during a presidential visit.

When exposed, Cincinnati Bell found itself accused in a $112 million class-action lawsuit of conducting illegal wiretapping and selling private information.

In accordance with federal law, a court order is required along with approval from the office of the U.S. Attorney General to sanction the use of a wiretap. The legal use of wiretaps and electronic monitoring by federal agents increased 32.4 percent in 1993 to a total of only 450 federal surveillance orders, mostly against suspected drug traffickers. Leonard Gates, who was a former installer and supervisor for Cincinnati Bell, testified he was told the FBI relied upon phone companies for "extralegal" help. He claims this information came from Richard Dugan, the former president of Cincinnati Bell. Sgt. Howard Cade, a former member of the police intelligence unit, testified under a grant of immunity from prosecution that information developed from these wiretaps was shared with the FBI, IRS and Bureau of Narcotics and Dangerous Drugs.

Gates and Draise claimed after 1975 the majority of the wiretaps were solely to gather information for the phone company to sell as a proprietary venture.

We believe where there is smoke there is fire. One has to wonder how many other phone companies (or at the very least a few rogue employees) all across this country illegally wiretap and traffic in information?

Busted! Spy Chain Indictments

In August 1995 in an unrelated development, U.S. Attorney Mary Jo White announced indictments against Spy Factory, Inc. on charges the spy shop smuggled illegal bugging and wiretapping devices into the United States and sold them.

Spy Factory, Inc. bases its operations in San Antonio, Texas. Its satellite stores include Tucson; Denver; Atlanta; Chicago; St. Louis; Seattle; Salt Lake City; San Diego; San Francisco; West Hollywood and Costa Mesa, California; Dallas; Houston; and El Paso, Texas.

The import, sale or advertising of eavesdropping devices is prohibited by federal law. Items sold ranged from pens, calculators and power strips with hidden bugs to wiretapping equipment capable of intercepting both sides of a phone conversation and transmitting it to a receiver in another location. An undercover U.S. Customs Service agent discovered most of this illegal equipment was sold to private investigators and local attorneys.

The indictment accuses the defendants of selling more than $1.5 million of espionage equipment over the last five years. An executive at the Japanese manufacturer of the devices, Micro Electronics Industries Co., LTD., of Tokyo, pleaded guilty in federal court on July 11, 1995, to conspire to manufacture illegal wiretapping and bugging equipment and to smuggle and sell the devices in the U.S.

Personal Privacy Issues

Loss of privacy is a hot issue in the 1990s. Employers routinely conduct legal electronic monitoring of their employees. Audio and video surveillance as well as telephone and computer monitoring is used to allow the boss to keep his or her finger on the pulse of the workplace. Illegal monitoring of the employees in restrooms, locker rooms and dressing rooms is not uncommon in the state of Connecticut. Connecticut is the first state to prohibit electronic monitoring of locker rooms, restrooms and contract negotiations. The rest of the states still allow this intrusive practice. Occasionally an employer is caught in this illegality and lawsuits usually result.

The federal government has a powerful desire to intrude into your life through expanding use of electronic surveillance. Law enforcement considers wiretapping a critical investigative tool. We should be concerned if the overzealous Feds utilize illegal wiretaps to monitor us when the courts refuse them authorization to tap. Such extralegal eavesdropping is antithetical to freedom and democracy.

Twice, Roger found it necessary to contact his local phone company to check his line for wiretaps. Immediately after a series of calls to Washington to complain about patent infringement on the Hook Pen, his phone line developed problems. He heard loud clicks on the phone lines and had difficulty hearing the other person on the line. We've learned clicking noises on your phone line is often an indication the line is compromised and being monitored. After the phone company cleared the line, Roger inquired if they found any sign of wiretapping. The phone company indicated company policy is to not divulge this information to a potential victim. A conspiracy of silence exists and we are all victimized by it.

Did you know when you browse many Web sites, the owners can collect personal information about you, then sell that information to advertisers or anyone else who is interested without your knowledge or consent? They can track your recently visited Web sites. They can detect which Web pages you browsed. They can determine your hobbies and other very personal information. All this information can be linked to your name and address. Count on them to use it.

Here are a few snippets of information about phones and privacy issues:

- Not long ago, an electronic kit was advertised for sale that could be used to secretly monitor a remote location with only a phone call. A device could be installed in the "target" phone that allowed a person to call that phone without the target phone ringing. Using the receiver to amplify sounds, one could hear any conversation in the vicinity of the target phone. Tens of thousands of this insidious product sold before the government cracked down on it.

- All 800 and 900 number callers are identified by the ANI (Automatic Number Identification). Each phone number possesses its own signature voltage, which tells a subscriber your telephone number, address and the name of the individual the phone service is in. This information is available to the subscriber of the 800 or 900 number before they even answer your call. It may also be linked with a computer file containing information about your past purchases, personal demographics and credit report. All this information is instantly available as they answer the phone. We laugh every time we see a TV commercial for a new, at-home HIV test kit. One is supposed to take a sample of one's own blood and mail it anonymously to the testing laboratory where the test is performed. They instruct the patient to call their 800 number, give an anonymous code number from the test kit, and get the HIV test results. Supposedly, this protects your identity and privacy. What a joke! The pharmaceutical company marketing the kit knows exactly who you are. The million-dollar question is what do they do with this information?

- Businesses, government and other organizations can now utilize pest elimination software to avoid receiving phone calls from those they consider to be cranks, gadflies, etc. Since phone systems can now identify the caller using the ANI or Caller ID, software assigns call-answering priority based on past history of dealing with an individual. Those who are customers or are otherwise held in high regard have their phone calls answered promptly. The unfortunate callers who are problems to the organization cannot reach an operator.

Safeguarding Your Intellectual Property

What is the likelihood a novice inventor would be victimized by industrial espionage? In truth, practically nil. After all, a novice is essentially anonymous. How can you be targeted if they don't know you exist? Be realistic and don't get paranoid.

Is it possible a friend or acquaintance could rip off your idea? It can happen but it is very rare. We've already discussed how extraordinarily difficult it is to conceive of an idea and bring it all the way to market. The commitment of time, money, experience, contacts, talent, persistence and luck required to be successful make it unlikely anyone will purloin your idea

113

for their own profit. They would have to be a little crazy to do so. You can easily protect yourself by taking a few basic precautions.

If you are an experienced inventor with a track record of success and well known as a result, this may be a very different story. Other businesses may be intent upon collecting competitor intelligence to gain business advantage. You could be the victim of computer hackers, probably not malevolent but curious about inventions you are working on.

Whether you are a novice or an experienced inventor, you should take certain basic precautions to safeguard your intellectual property.

Always remember LLSS (loose lips sink ships). Don't be a blabbermouth about what you are working on. Use discretion regarding to whom you disclose your inventions while they are unprotected. The fewer the people who know the better.

Be especially discriminating regarding sharing trade secrets. These should almost never be disclosed to anyone. You may need to disclose the trade secret to business partners or key employees in order to manufacture and sell the product. Make certain they are trustworthy and that they sign a confidentiality or nondisclosure agreement.

Before you disclose your ideas to people, insist they sign a confidentiality or nondisclosure agreement. Circumstances differ, so your attorney should draw up this document specifically for you. It must be worded just so in order to protect you and your intellectual property. A generic form may not adequately protect you. The witnesses to your invention should sign this agreement.

When bringing documentation of your intellectual property to fax, photocopy or other commercial services, be certain to secure all your information. Always leave explicit instructions on how to handle your material. It is best to never leave it with them while they do the job. Wait there while the work is done. Don't leave any junk copies. Always take them with you or insist they be shredded immediately. Let's face it, people are naturally curious. If you can avoid situations in which they see the information and can ask what it is all about, all the better. You do not owe them an explanation.

Do not discuss sensitive information over the telephone. Wiretapping may be rare, but industrial espionage is a real threat. Some companies do go beyond legal methods of collecting competitor intelligence.

It is not an uncommon experience to pick up the telephone and hear a faint conversation. Their signal somehow crossed onto your line. You hear them but they don't hear you. Be cautious of what you discuss on the phone because you never know if someone else will hear. Be aware of how you use speakerphones and intercoms. Who knows who may be within earshot of a speakerphone? Install a private telephone line and connect a single-line telephone to it. Use this phone for confidential conversations. Keep this telephone number private and be very discriminating about to whom you reveal this number.

Providing for the safety and security of computer files challenges many companies. Preventing unsophisticated and unauthorized users from accessing your files is easily accomplished with the use of passwords and locking keyboards. Provide a secure storage area for your computer disks. Use several levels of access codes and change them often. It is harder to deal with the more sophisticated threats such as computer hackers and cyber-anarchists. Most inventors can eliminate this threat by simply not storing sensitive information in computer files within computers connected to the outside world. Every computer user should utilize powerful anti-virus software to protect and preserve their files from outside threats. Use surge protectors or an uninterruptible power supply to protect the computer from power surges or outages. Open or unsaved files run the risk of being lost if power is interrupted.

Secure your sensitive information in a locked file cabinet. Even better, store this information in a locked, fireproof safe. Don't get sloppy about leaving keys lying around and control access to these keys if you have employees. Always protect your most sensitive documents by keeping copies off-site in a bank safe deposit box. Should a natural calamity occur, such as fire, flood or severe storm, your information is preserved.

Install an alarm system to protect against break-ins. Alarm systems can protect personal property and people as well as intellectual property. Commercial offices, home-based businesses and private homes alike benefit from being wired. Numerous options exist. One of the best systems turns on lights and sounds an audible alarm both inside and outside the building while transmitting an alarm message to the security company's headquarters. It should include a cellular backup in case the telephone line has been compromised by more sophisticated criminals who commonly cut lines or tie up the phone line. How do you decide what security you need? Consult with security specialists who can evaluate your situation and recommend solutions.

*"There are no foolish questions and no man becomes
a fool until he has stopped asking questions."*

—Charles Steinmetz

CHAPTER 9

How to Direct Market your Inventions

Choosing an Ideal Marketing Strategy

Many inventors come up with an idea for a product then get it patented and manufactured. At this point the really hard work begins. Selling the product is the real challenge. Most often, when conceptualizing the product, little or no attention is paid to how to market it. It may well be something that is simply hard to market or won't turn a good enough profit. In short, you've come up with an idea for a product, now you must determine a marketing strategy, which is, of course, dependent on the nature of the product.

Look at the example of the Hook Pen. It is not an easy product to market. Your markets are retail stores and sales as premiums or promotions. Each sale yields a tiny profit of only cents per pen. Had we considered the marketing aspect of the invention early in the invention process, we may well have never patented the pen and not wasted another minute on it. We would have considered patenting some other invention and better invested our energy, time and money.

Let us present you with an exercise. Instead of inventing a product then trying to market it . . . turn it around . . . first identify a successful marketing technique and then find a product that fits it. Consider the following ideal marketing criteria:

1. Product pricing allows $50 to $150 profit per sale. Of course, more is even better. Look for substantial profits from relatively few sales.

2. Product generates great excitement or buzz. Customers seek you out.

3. Product generates reorders.

4. Product lends itself to promotion by word of mouth and publicity stunts.

5. Product can be intensely marketed in your local geographic area.

6. Can be patent, copyright or trademark protected if it's a hit. Licensing possible.

7. Product can be franchised.

8. Product can be sold by flea markets, cable television shopping channels, TV and radio ads, classified and display advertising with direct response mail order, and direct mail.

9. Product must be priced cheaply enough so customers can purchase it without feeling guilty about spending a lot of money, and not so expensive as to hinder impulse buying: $20 to $200 is a good range but $50 to $150 is best.

10. Shipping and handling must be reasonably priced. Never abuse this as a profit center. Offer shipping and handling at cost as a convenience and incentive to the shopper. They get very irritated when they see this as a blatant ploy to increase profits.

11. Product should have little or no competition.

12. Product satisfies a variety of needs for people.

13. People feel like they are getting a bargain.

14. Product can be used by many people.

15. Product should be easy to manufacture.

Whether you invent first then plan your marketing strategy later or choose a product based upon an ideal set of marketing criteria, you need to know the many options available to get your product sold. One of the best ways to do this is to use direct marketing techniques to bring your product to the consumer.

Direct Mail

What Is Direct Mail?

A direct marketing program can bring your product directly to the consumer in a manner unlike most other sales outlets. Also referred to as direct mail or mail order, this marketing technique is powerful, profitable and proven. You deal with one highly targeted prospect at a time. You contact the potential customer, give them your sales pitch and take the order. All by mail. Big corporations have to rely on mass marketing. You rely on micro-marketing.

The marketing effort is personalized, concentrating only on carefully chosen prospects who are most likely to buy. Statistics show that approximately 20 percent of all products are sold through direct marketing. The growth of direct marketing is leaving retail store sales in the dust.

Advantages of Direct Mail

Direct mail offers numerous advantages over other marketing techniques. Every business should give serious consideration to implementing a direct mail campaign for many of these reasons:

- Direct mail allows you to select a highly targeted group of prospects. You don't waste marketing effort and money on those who are unlikely to buy.

- Direct mail allows you to constantly test your offer. You fine tune your marketing materials until you get a successful response.

- Direct mail literature is easily kept, allowing a prospect to mull over the offer. It allows the consumer to respond via an order form and return envelope. More details about the offer are available for consideration, unlike other media such as radio or TV, newspaper or magazine ads.

- Direct mail can be fast and cheap. Design of the direct mail package is much simpler than preparation of radio and TV ads or even magazine ads inviting a direct response. Small test mailings can be prepared on your business computer with inexpensive publishing software for surprisingly small amounts of money. You can test the offer quickly and cheaply.

- Direct mail allows you to personalize your marketing plan to become more responsive to your customers' needs. You can concentrate on keeping valued customers and enjoying repeat business from them in the future.

- Direct mail allows you to quickly measure the effectiveness of your marketing campaign. You can expect 90 percent of your orders to come within four weeks of your promotional mailing.

Product Selection

What do you have to offer that is different from what is already on the market? As a business operator you must offer a product that fills definite needs. If it is a unique product—all the better. Customers will not buy from you unless they perceive a need for your product. This rule applies to impulse buying as well. Even with an impulse purchase the buyer responds to some underlying need of which he or she may or may not be aware. The need your prospect perceives may be natural or artificial. If artificial, your marketing savvy invents a need where none would ordinarily exist. How do you think pet rocks became such a success?

Successful entrepreneurs must offer products that provide tangible benefits to their customers. Products should stand out from the rest of the competition. Your product may be smaller, lighter, stronger, more powerful, cheaper, more attractive or possess any other quality which your customers see as beneficial. A product offering no new or distinct benefits is a product that won't sell. If you've patented an invention that by definition should be novel and new, it should provide a benefit to consumers. Your success or failure will likely depend on just how much of a benefit consumers perceive your product to present. Publicity and promotion of these benefits are vital to your venture's success.

Whether you invent something or not, how do you select an appropriate product for mail order? Ask yourself what people want. What problems need solutions? How can you improve on what is out there? When considering what consumes people, use the four F guidelines. People want:

- Fortune
- Fame
- Food
- Fun

When you engage in product selection research you must cast out your idea net. Pick peoples' brains. Read magazines and trade publications. Attend seminars, conventions and product shows. Talk to manufacturers and suppliers. Spy on the competition. Scrutinize ads for products. Get to know your retailers and find out what they want. Schmooze with club members and hobbyists. (Here's a hint: Talk to anyone working in a product complaint or consumer complaint capacity who is willing to spill their guts. You can get the inside scoop on product problems or deficiencies. With this knowledge you may be able to improve on the product and outmaneuver the sluggish competition.)

Through your research and creative efforts you will come up with one or several products deserving of evaluation. You must evaluate the use of direct mail to market this product. Remember, direct mail is only one potential way to market the product. You may find other marketing techniques more appropriate for bringing your product to the consumer. The following criteria need to be considered to evaluate your product's prospects in a direct mail campaign:

- Does the product fill a consumer need?
- Is the projected profit margin high enough?
- Consider the market size. Is there enough demand?
- Will the competition be too great?
- Can you target your marketing effort to the best prospects?

- Is the product easily manufactured or obtained?
- Is the product easy and inexpensive to ship?
- Is the product unavailable in stores?
- What is the potential for repeat business?
- Will the investment in this product line be within your means?

Product Pricing

The first step in knowing what to charge for your product is to determine the total cost to manufacture or otherwise obtain the product. Include every expense for an accurate appraisal. Once you calculate this figure you will use it to determine your break-even point for your direct mail promotion. The break-even point will tell you at which point your direct mail campaign's responses begin to show a profit. Most direct marketing products must sell at 300 or 400 percent of their cost to make a profit. You should examine your competitors' pricing and attempt to price your own product similarly. If you price too high you may lose significant numbers of sales. Paradoxically, you may induce a higher perceived value for your product and customers may be willing to pay the higher price thinking the product is superior to others. If you set your price too low, you may not be able to make enough profit to warrant continuation of the offer. Remember, you're in the business to make money. If you lowball the price your prospects may decide your product is inferior in some way to that of your competition. You will lose orders. In certain cases you may ignite a price war that benefits no one.

When testing your direct mail offer you will test the price. You may raise or lower it. Monitor your responses to determine optimum pricing. Many mail order promoters don't mind breaking even or even losing a little money on an initial order. They plan to reap their profits on repeat business with that customer. It costs money to gain a new customer. But once you have them, you can sell your complete product line to them. This is why your product should lend itself toward repeat sales. That's where the bucks are.

All savvy mail order businesses know their most valuable asset is their customer list. Not only do they enjoy future business from these people, but they can rent or sell the lists. A significant portion of a company's income can come from the list rentals. Companies with similar and related product lines will show interest in renting your in-house customer list. You should be careful not to rent to a competitor with a product line that competes with your own. The rental fee is unlikely to exceed the product revenue of lost customers. You can avoid self-sabotage by always evaluating the list renter's product before approving release of the list.

Direct Mail Package Design

To conduct a successful direct mail promotion, the following three variables must be optimally designed. The offer, package and list. These three essential components require care, diligence and creativity as you decide their makeup.

The offer: The product itself is the key element in the offer. Is it irresistible to your customers? Do they feel the need to place an order for it? Will the benefits entice them to buy? If your offer isn't appealing enough, the prospect is not likely to buy. Smart direct marketers continually test the offer to entice the customer to buy. Consider some of the following methods of testing:

- Offer a free gift with purchase.
- Offer a discount or rebate with a high volume sale.
- Buy one, get one free or buy one, get the second for a penny.
- Offer your product for higher or lower than retail price.
- Allow flexibility in payment options.
- Give your customers a finder's fee for bringing new customers to you.
- Make ordering options easy. Use toll-free numbers and business reply envelopes (BREs).
- Give your customers an iron-clad guarantee.
- Give your customers shipping options including rush service.
- Bundling is a popular and effective method of selling. This is the practice of offering additional items as bonuses to go along with a main product selection. Bundling enhances the perceived value of the total package. The customer feels that they received more for their money. Look at the example of the amazing Ginsu knife. Not only do you receive the Ginsu knife but also the Ginsu steak knife set and potato peeler for the same low, low price. Wow! What a deal!

The package: Writing effective advertising copy is the key to getting positive responses culminating in orders. You must take into account the appearance, layout, paper and creativity of the ad copy when assembling your direct mail package. What will your package consist of? The classic direct mail package consists of the outer envelope, sales letter, brochure, order form and a business reply envelope. The writing needs to be strictly top-shelf. If you have any doubts about your ability you should hire a professional copywriter experienced in direct mail.

When considering the design of the outer envelope, keep in mind what your goal is. Get them to open the envelope! If the prospect doesn't open the letter—it goes in the trash. It's garbage. You've wasted your time and money. Use an envelope teaser to get them inside. For example:

- "Free gift inside."
- "Open immediately for exciting details about _____."

- "Inside—Details your competitors would kill for."
- "Double your profits for a dime a day."
- "Personal and confidential."

The ad copy in the sales letter and brochure needs to grab the reader's attention. The headline must stress the most important benefit your product offers. Appeal to your prospects' self interest. Get them curious about what you have to offer. Keep them reading. Be positive, believable and take advantage of these psychologically persuasive words in your sales pitch:

AMAZING	AT LAST	BARGAIN
CHALLENGE	DISCOVER	EASY
GUARANTEE	HEALTH	HOW TO
HURRY	IMPORTANT	JUST ARRIVED
LAST CHANCE	LOVE	MIRACLE
MONEY	NEW	POWER
PROVEN	REMARKABLE	RESULTS
REVOLUTIONARY	SAFETY	SAVE
SECRETS	SENSATIONAL	SUCCESS
WANT	WHY	YOU

The most persuasive word in the English language, which you can use in sales literature is this magic word: free. It attracts attention like no other.

In an effective sales letter, stress the benefits of buying your product. You must overcome the prospects' natural inertia and convince them to buy. Don't try to sell the features of your product, sell the benefits. Sizzle sells. Make no mistake, do list the product's features. Emphasize the uniqueness.

If there's one thing you must deliver on, it's credibility. If you lack it, you lose the sale. You should offer an unconditional guarantee written in clear terms—no legalese. Let the language in your guarantee reflect the confidence in your product or service. Offer customer testimonials touting the excellence of your product. You may use a testimonial from your banker or accountant to help establish credibility. Product reviews in the media or trade literature go a long way to reassuring a skeptical public your company is no fly-by-night operation.

Okay, you've given your prospect all the information they need to make a buying decision. You've dangled the benefits before them. It's time to close the sale. You must deliver a call to immediate action. Ask for an order. If your customer deliberates, dawdles or procrastinates, your likelihood of a positive response plummets. Heed the following tips:

- Continue selling on the order form headline.
- No confusion. State the directions and terms clearly.
- Enclose a self-addressed business reply envelope. Use pre-paid postage.
- Print the guarantee on the order form.

- Give the option of calling in the order rather than mailing it. Customers love toll-free numbers.
- Use customer involvement devices such as check boxes or stickers.
- Restate your offer on the order form.
- Preprint the prospects' name and address on the order form.
- Code your order forms to allow you to track results of testing.
- Print your company's name and address in numerous places in the direct mail package, including the order form.
- Use symbols like asterisks and arrows to call attention to key ad copy.

As a direct mail marketer you can get as creative as you want and test all you want to search for success. However, never forget this basic and widely used copy structure we've just discussed:

- Seize the prospect's attention.
- Get them interested. Show benefits.
- Establish credibility.
- Deliver your call to action.

The list: According to industry figures, 60 percent of direct mail success can be attributed to appropriate list selection. Choosing the right list for your promotion is so vital the list business has become highly targeted and scientific.

There are three kinds of lists: the occupant list, which is a collection of all residences in a geographic area; the compiled list, which includes names gleaned from directories and phone books; and the response list, which gives names of people who have responded to offers for related goods. You will find the response list to be the most useful list and therefore, the most expensive because they are so highly targeted. Expect to pay $60 to $120 per thousand. Remember, the name of the game in direct mail is targeting.

How do you go about selecting the right list? If you've been established for some time, you will, of course, have your own customer list, which you should keep updated given 25 percent of the people on your list may have moved during a given year. Clean your list every six months. Your own customer list is one of your company's most valuable assets. These are people who have ordered and are likely to continue to do business with you. You can expect the best return on any mailing from them.

If you're just starting out, you'll have to rent your lists. The type of list you will rent depends on your product. Consider renting lists of people who have bought similar products or related products. Also consider renting compiled lists from directories or membership lists of related organizations. Subscribers of magazines and newsletters may be more likely to buy from a direct mail package than from a classified or display ad in the publication.

The best list resource to consult is the *Standard Rate and Data Service (SRDS)* direct mail catalog found in most major libraries. This indispensable source of direct mail information contains more than 12,000 mailing lists. The *SRDS* volume entitled *Direct Mail List Rates and Data* will catalog the numerous list brokers who rent lists for just about any category imaginable. They will help you to carefully select the exact demographic groups for your marketing plan. Be aware that when renting a list you are allowed a one-time use only. If the prospect responds, you now own that name and can add it to your own in-house list. You are free to continue mailing to that person. Don't try to cheat on the one-use only rule. Lists are always seeded with decoy names. This policy allows list owners to verify renters use the list once only. One or more direct mail packages you send out are coded to go to the list owner. They're checking up on you. Dishonesty doesn't pay.

You can expect seasonal variations in responses for nonseasonal, general direct mail products. Exceptions to this rule are gardening supplies, Christmas-themed products and other seasonal products. What this means is that mail order entrepreneurs are wise to time their offers to coincide with periods of highest interest in a product line. Summer is generally a bad time for mail order. The mail order months, from best to worst, are: January, February, October, August, November, December, September, July, April, May, March and June. June's responses can be as much as 25 percent less than the yearly average. Successful direct marketers must be aware of these seasonal variations in response. You should carefully track the results of previous offers for similar products to make accurate projections to draw up your own seasonal response chart. Proper timing of your direct mail offers can make the difference between success and failure.

Additional Tips for Direct Mail Success
- Get merchant status for accepting VISA and MasterCard payments. Accepting charge cards for payment will increase your returns significantly.
- Offer your customers toll-free ordering convenience. The use of 800 or 888 numbers gives you significant leverage and groups you with the big guys.
- Seek to generate repeat business with your established customers.
- Keep excellent records. Computerization allows accurate record keeping and higher productivity. Use computer software for your database, desktop publishing and business letters as well as forms and spreadsheets.

If you start a small business and begin selling via direct marketing, it is unlikely your bank will extend credit card merchant status to you. You can expect to be almost universally denied this necessary status. Because the ordering convenience of toll-free numbers and credit cards translates into significantly increased sales responses, you need merchant status.

Accepting electronic payments for the purchase of goods and services is not a right; it is a privilege. You must pay for this privilege. You will be required to purchase or lease credit card payment equipment and pay processing fees of between 1 and 7 percent per transaction. The processing fee will depend on risk factors for your business and volume of transactions.

Some companies provide merchant accounts for direct marketing companies. Here are a few to contact with inquiries:

- CardService International
  501 Worcester Road
  Framingham, MA 01701
  (800) 370-4549

- Direct Marketing Guarantee Trust
  141 Canal Street
  Nashua, NH 03061
  (603) 882-9500

- Professional Marketing Associates
  903 South Hohokam Drive
  Tempe, AZ 85281
  (602) 829-0131

Direct Mail List Resources
- *Standard Rate and Data Service (SRDS)*
  1700 Higgins Road
  Des Plains, IL 60018
  (800) 851-SRDS

- *The Direct Marketing Market Place*
  5201 Old Orchard Road
  Skokie, IL 60077
  (708) 256-6067
  A direct marketing reference book published by SRDS.

- *Direct Mail List Rates and Data*
  5201 Old Orchard Road
  Skokie, IL 60077
  (708) 256-6067
  Offers more than 12,000 mailing lists to rent.

Direct Marketing Publications and Resources
- *Advertising Age*
  Crain Communications
  740 Rush Street North
  Chicago, IL 60611
  (312) 649-5200

- Direct Marketing Association, Inc. (DMA)
  1120 Avenue of the Americas
  New York, NY 10036-6700
  (212) 768-7277
  Fax (212) 768-4546
  Web site http://www.the-dma.org
  Trade association for direct marketers. Membership dues start at $560 per year. Ask for the DMA's free publications catalog of direct marketing publications. Nonmembers can order from an extensive list of trade publications.

- *Direct Marketing*
  Hoke Communications
  224 Seventh Avenue
  Garden City, NY 11530
  (516) 746-6700

- *DM News*
  Mill Hollow Corporation
  100 Avenue of the Americas
  New York, NY 10013
  (212) 741-2095
  DM News online Web site http://www.dmnews.com
  If you are involved with direct marketing, send a request on your company letterhead for a complementary subscription to:

  DM News
  Subscription Department
  P.O. Box 10552
  Riverton, NJ 08076-0552
  (609) 786-4780/4781

- *Target Marketing*
  North American Publishing Company
  401 North Broad Street
  Philadelphia, PA 19108
  (215) 238-5300

- *Direct Magazine*
  Cowles Business Media, Inc.
  Six River Bend Center
  Stamford, CT 06907
  (203) 358-9900

- *How to Compile and Maintain a Mailing List*
  Quill Corporation
  100 S. Schlelter Road
  Lincolnshire, IL 60069

Direct Response Mail Order

The previous section introduced direct mail, or mail order as it is also known. This section concerns itself with a similar and equally valuable marketing technique known as direct response mail order. Some people confuse the two but direct response mail order is different. Instead of sending a direct mail package to a targeted list of prospects, media advertising is used to reach them. Obviously, to be successful we must endeavor to advertise only in media outlets that our targeted demographic and psychographic population of prospects read, view or listen to. Direct response utilizes media outlets such as magazines, newspapers, newsletters, TV, radio, card packs, the Internet and others. This section will concern itself primarily with magazines, newspapers and card packs. The other media outlets will be discussed elsewhere.

How can direct response mail order benefit the entrepreneur? To start, you can target your prospects with magazines and card packs fairly well. Other media such as newspapers, TV and radio are much less successful at targeting prospects. Start-up costs for direct response can be inexpensive. Classified ads are cheap, and many bargains exist for small display ads. Just as in direct mail, the name of the game in direct response is testing. Start with a small outlay of money and test the ad, the price and the offer. When you get a positive response you can expand your ad campaign to build your business.

Another benefit of direct response is the strong, personal relationship you can establish with your customers. This beneficial relationship can generate many repeat orders as well as provide the business owner with a hot response list for rent. Remember, a substantial portion of a company's income may be derived from in-house list rentals.

Nothing determines direct response success more than the quality and effectiveness of your advertising. The ad is the key. If you write the ad copy yourself, be sure to make it the best writing you are capable of. It must be clear, concise and persuasive. Every word counts. By all means, do try to write your own ads. But if it isn't quite good enough you may not make the sale. You may find it in your best interest to hire a professional ad copywriter.

Matching your product with prospects is an essential first step in a direct response feasibility study. Does your product have the four F appeal? Does it help your customer attain fortune? Fame? Food? Fun? Evaluate the product's benefits and decide if they are enough to make people want to buy it.

Pricing is another consideration. To be successful, a direct response mail order product should sell for at least three times its cost. If it fails this test, at worst you will lose money, at best, you will break even. Don't forget you're in business to make a buck. If you can't price the product to allow a reasonable profit for yourself, then dump the product. Choose something else to sell.

Who are your prospects? What kind of people are most likely to buy your product? Carefully consider to whom your products would appeal. List their characteristics. Draw up a customer profile using demographics and psychographics. You must evaluate what magazines or newspapers and which sections of those publications your prospects are most likely to read. Place your advertisements there to target your prospects. You know you've chosen well if other similar products are advertised there. If their ads continue to run then you know they are successful. No sane entrepreneur continues to run an ad if it fails to get results. They are making money here and so can you!

To fully research all the publications you deem appropriate for your advertising, consult the *SRDS* in your library. Not all libraries stock this directory, so give them a call to inquire if they have it available. If not, look for the *Standard Periodical Directory, Gale's Directory of Publications and Broadcast Media* or *Ulrich's International Periodicals Directory*. Any of these directories will give you the information you need to begin querying the publications in which you wish to advertise.

If you use the *SRDS*, consult the volume entitled *Consumer Magazine and Agri-Media Rates and Data* to research magazines. Consult *SRDS's Newspaper Rates and Data* for advertising in newspapers.

The next step in planning your advertising campaign involves contacting publications to obtain vital information. Request their media kit. It should include their advertising rate card specifying both classified and display ad rates. It should also include their customer demographics and audited circulation figures (number of actual subscribers). This information is useful for calculating and comparing the ad costs for various publications. This is expressed as cost per thousands of readers. Other information commonly requested would be the availability of special discounts and negotiating possibilities which we will cover shortly. Ask about special upcoming issues of the publication. Request they put you on file so you can be updated regularly with any changes. Ask for several sample copies of their publication. Use these to familiarize yourself with the publication. Study the ads.

Okay, you've chosen a product, identified your prospects and researched publications and selected what you hope will be an appropriate media outlet for your ad. Now it's time to write the ad. You can choose to use classified or display ads to reach your prospects.

Writing ad copy for direct response follows the same copy structure as direct mail:

- Seize the prospect's attention.
- Get them interested. Show benefits.
- Establish credibility.
- Deliver your call to action.

Classified ads can be an effective sales tool for rolling out a new product. Short and sweet, these ads have pulling power. Classifieds can also support sales of a mature product as well. If you research magazine classifieds you will discover ads that have run literally for decades. These ads are proven winners that make money. Their owners tested and fine-tuned their ads over time until they found a winner and stuck with it. Why tamper with success?

Ad copy for classifieds should be spare but highly descriptive. Use psychologically persuasive words and the power of action verbs to energize your ad copy. Make every word count. Remember, every word costs you money.

Hints for Powerful Classified Ads

- Seize the reader's attention with a dynamic headline printed in capitals and bold print.

- Use short, clear copy. Use the power of words to persuade.

- Don't be cheap. If the ad is too short and ineffective it won't pull.

- If your product costs more than $10 don't ask for a sale. Instead offer free details or a free brochure. Seek an inquiry, then send a direct mail package.

- Always tell them it's guaranteed . . . and always make good on it.

- Avoid the hard sell. It seldom works. Treat them as you would like to be treated.

- Call for action. Provide a toll-free number for inquiries or ordering. Customers love them. The ad will also cost you less since a telephone number is shorter than your address.

- Highlight the product's benefits in bold letters. It's cheap to do so and the benefits jump out at the reader.

- Test your ads. Mimic other ads if they are long running and successful. They must be doing something right.

Graduating up to display ads is a natural and logical progression for your marketing plan. After proving your product's consumer appeal with successful classified ads, it's time to think bigger. Classifieds can do only so much. You want greater exposure and more ad frequency to expand your business. You want to project the air of legitimacy that goes with a display ad. You'll be taken more seriously by the consumer.

When moving up to display ads, however, do not jump to half page or full page ads. Start small and take it slow. Test your ads. Start with an ad as small as a twelfth of a page. Go for frequency. Numerous small ads in the same issue of a magazine or newspaper will pull better than one large ad. When prospects notice these ads again and again, they perceive you as an established business, doing well and moving an appealing product.

Thoughtful and effective display ad layout is crucial to success. Though you have more space than a classified ad, you are still tightly constrained by this concern. Every word, picture or diagram counts. Seizing the reader's attention is of paramount importance. If your ad blends into the rest of the page like camouflage, it won't get read. You won't get orders. It's that simple. Several techniques for making your ad standout are reverse printing, uncommon display typefaces and borders. The use of a second color in printing is also effective in getting your ad noticed and can significantly increase orders.

Hints for Powerful Display Ads

- Your headline will make or break you. Seize the reader immediately. Emphasize your major benefit.

- A picture or illustration captures reader interest. Show your product in use.

- Design your ad copy to look like editorial copy. Mark "advertisement" in small print at the top or bottom of the ad.

- Testimonials work to make your ad believable. This allows customer word-of-mouth to influence others. Reassure your prospects to get more sales.

- Design your ad with an order coupon on the lower outside corner for easy clipping. Make the coupon easily readable and allow enough space for your customer to fill in information.

- Positioning of your ad affects results. Negotiate for your ad to appear on the outside of a right-hand page. An ad in the front of a magazine gets better results.

- Start a swipe file. Clip ads that work. Use the best parts of their copy in your own ad.

- Offer a money-back guarantee to help reassure the skeptical.

Proper scheduling of when your ads run must take into account when your customers are likely to buy the advertised products. Seasonal tie-ins often exist. If your product line consists of items with a Christmas theme, you would expect the best responses to your ads to be in October, November and December. Don't expect April or May ads to pull very well. Books generally do poorly in the summer because people spend more time out-of-doors instead of reading. Surprisingly enough, gardening items including plants and seeds are best advertised in the dead of winter. Gardeners are getting a bit stir crazy and start dreaming about planting in the warm spring. Ads and catalogs do well in January and February based upon the gardeners' psychological need for winter's end. Fortunately for the gardening businesses using direct mail or direct response, this period coincides with the season producing highest direct marketing responses in general.

Timing ads to coincide with periods of greatest interest in a product is only one aspect of ad scheduling. Drawing up an advertising schedule will help your business avoid overspending on your ad budget. You should lay out a schedule of advertising to plan when to make your ad placements. Don't forget to pay close attention to the medium's lead time requirements and deadlines for ad submission. You must be very cautious not to overextend yourself and cripple your cash flow. Your business may not survive.

A more enviable problem is responding to greater-than-projected success. In this case you will probably want to increase spending and expand your advertising campaign with more frequency or into other media. The goal is to increase sales and make your business grow at a controlled rate.

It is vital to track responses to your ad to determine whether it pulls enough to be profitable. As you test different ads and vary the offer or copy or media placement, you need to be able to keep an accurate record of responses to each. You accomplish this by keying or coding your ads. Every variation of your ad has its own unique code. You indicate this by inserting your code in your return address in the ad. For example, you may use a code of Suite or Dept. PS028C. The "PS" refers to *Popular Science* magazine. The "02" refers to the second month, or February issue. The "8" means a 1998 volume. Finally, "C" means you used a classified ad. Keep track of the source codes you use either in your computer database or on three-by-five file cards. When you prove to yourself your ads are profitable, you can build in frequency or increase ad size (or both). When unprofitable ads are revealed by your analysis, kill them. You're not in business to lose money.

Magazine advertising offers you numerous benefits compared to other media outlets. Most magazines have targeted audiences and well-defined demographic and psychographic readership, allowing an advertiser to choose the best publication to carry his or her message to the consumer. Numerous response options can be offered with those responses easily measured. The high reproductive quality of your ad better illustrates your product. You have plenty of creative flexibility in ad design. The life span of your ad is typically very long with orders coming in for months and even years later from a particular ad. Magazines tend to get passed along from one person to the next allowing many potential prospects to see your ad. The high pass-along rate means the opportunity for many more orders.

Newspaper advertising is quite different from magazine advertising. By nature of their local coverage, newspapers have high geographic selectivity. Newspaper ads can be quite inexpensive to produce. Often, the paper's staff will help set up your ad. The simplicity of producing a newspaper ad allows a short lead time and great flexibility in timing your ads. An important benefit of newspapers is the lightning-fast response time to your ads. Up to 95 percent of your expected responses are received within two weeks.

Money-Saving Advertising Secrets

1. Form your own *in-house ad agency* to qualify for a 15 percent discount on advertising fees. Any approved ad agency gets this automatic discount as part of its compensation. Media outlets pay the 15 percent commission to ad agencies for bringing them business. If you form your own ad agency, you get the money.

   Caution is called for because many media outlets will not extend this discount to an in-house ad agency. To get the discount you must be coy about it. You make your in-house ad agency appear to be a separate business entity. These steps are not particularly onerous when you consider the return on your investment. You can form your own in-house ad agency for a very modest cost. If you do $50,000 worth of advertising per year, your discount will allow you to keep $7,500 of it. Not a bad chunk of change for a little extra effort. Take these simple steps:

   - Choose a separate business name indicating the nature of the business . . . an ad agency.
   - File a dba (doing business as) fictitious name and obtain any necessary permits or licenses.
   - Use a different address from that of your home or business.
   - Set up a separate phone line for the ad agency.
   - Set up a separate business checking account for paying advertising bills.
   - Print ad agency stationery for ad related correspondence.
   - You may wish to choose an AKA (also known as) fictitious name for yourself to conduct advertising agency business.

2. Qualify for a *2 percent cash discount* if you pay your bill within 10 days. Not all media outlets offer this discount, so be sure to check rate cards. This can be quite a savings. For example, in a hypothetical ad budget of $50,000, the 2 percent cash discount amounts to $1,000.

3. Numerous magazines offer *mail order discounts* to direct marketing advertisers. Rates vary but you may be able to obtain up to 40 percent off your advertising costs. Why the steep discount? Magazines recognize mail order advertisers must make a profit from their ads to stay in business and keep advertising with them. This is a big, big discount you cannot afford to pass up. A $1,000 ad for $600 is a superb bargain. Be sure to ask about it.

4. *PI (per inquiry) or PO (per order) deals* allow you to advertise for free in exchange for payment of about 50 percent of the selling price to the media outlet. It's difficult to find a deal like this because media outlets don't want their regular advertisers to find out about it. Magazines as

133

well as TV and radio are your best bets for PI deals. Inquire with the media sales representative about the availability of such deals.

5. It is standard operating procedure for media outlets to offer *frequency discounts*. They knock off a certain percentage of the cost of the ad if you commit to buying a certain number of ads. Don't commit to a long-term placement of the ad until you are sure it pulls.

6. *Remnant space* may be available at deep discounts of up to 50 percent. Leftover, unsold space must be filled, often at the last minute. If you have several, different-sized ads ready to go at a moment's notice, you may be able to scoop up the ad space for bargain-basement prices. Regional editions of national magazines are especially good prospects. Often the regional editions fail to sell all their ad space. Check with the media sales representative on their policies and requirements for setting up remnant space deals. Though you cannot control your ad placement, the deal is too good to pass up.

7. *Barter* for services. The media outlet has advertising space. You have a product or service. Why not an exchange in lieu of payment? You both win this way.

See Direct Marketing Publications and Resources in the section on direct mail for a list of direct response mail order resources. Also consult the Bibliography for a list of titles of interest to direct marketers.

Card Packs

These are one of the best tools a direct marketing entrepreneur can use for creating inquiries. Card packs consist of anywhere between 10 and 150 business reply postcards. The card pack publishers polyseal the postcards then mail them to a carefully targeted group of prospects. Card packs can be used to reach almost any audience, from consumers to professionals. Professionals are the better prospects, as they more often become buyers.

The chief benefit of card packs is their excellence in generating leads. It's easy to send out a direct mail package or use telemarketing to follow up on your inquiries. The cost per thousand is so low it's almost irresistible. Use of a card pack can cost you less than 10 percent of a direct mail package. Additionally, many card packs offer per-inquiry deals, which cost you nothing up front for your advertising. It's not uncommon for you to receive free layout and design help with your card from the card pack company. Use of card packs is fast and easy with nearly half your projected responses received in the first two weeks.

Several card pack disadvantages should be considered, however. You can expect a rather low response rate. The average industry response rate varies from 0.1 to 1.0 percent. But given the incredibly low cost, you still get a good deal. In order to be profitable, we recommend a minimum price for your product of no less than $50. Because of space limitations inherent in the size of the post card, you have a very small area in which to describe your product. This naturally restricts your ability to convince the prospect to inquire or order. You must make the best use of the finite space to attract attention, generate interest and induce the prospect to act.

Advice for Effective Card Pack Use
1. Design a headline that grabs the reader's attention. Readers will glance at each card for only about one second before moving on to the next.
2. Always use a recently cleaned response list instead of compiled lists.
3. Include a photograph or illustration of your product on the card.
4. Multiple colors attract attention and pull more than black and white.
5. Insist your card be positioned in the first half of the pack. You'll get twice the number of responses.
6. Seek out remnant space deals and ask about first placement discounts and 15 percent agency discounts.

To research media outlets using card packs to promote products or services, refer to the *SRDS Card Pack Rates and Data Directory.*

Catalog Sales

Planning on branching into catalog sales? You won't be alone. Blockbuster corporations such as J.C. Penney, Sears and L. L. Bean dominate a crowded field. Other catalogs struggle to compete. The secret is to offer a product or service that distinguishes you from the competition.

If you are considering catalog sales, your first step is to do your research. This specialized field of marketing requires the right products, in-house and out-of-house expertise and adequate money to invest in this venture to see you through several years of hard work. Failure rates for new catalogs run 50 to 80 percent within three years of launch. To avoid inclusion in this unfortunate group, start small and exploit a market niche left untapped by the big guys. You can dominate a specialty market by offering the kind of intensely personal service large companies cannot match.

Start small with a catalog of only several pages and grow as you service each and every individual customer. Your business will build as long as you target your mailings to the best prospects. Choose your lists with great care to maximize your response rates. Your best prospects are your previous customers. In time, your catalog can grow to be an extensive offering, especially if supported with an efficient JIT inventory system. Just as in other direct marketing methods, you must test continually. Test your pricing, lists and offers until you discover what works best.

Strive to give your catalog a personality that is distinctive and reflects your company's philosophy. Remember . . . personalize it!

The same rules of direct marketing apply to catalog sales. Attract your reader's attention with effective headlines. Make your copy clear and concise. Sell the benefits. Offer testimonials to spread good customer word-of-mouth. Give them an iron-clad guarantee. Make ordering as painless as possible with credit cards and toll-free numbers and other options which make shopping convenient. Always remember, the major reason customers like shopping by catalog is the convenience it offers them.

Hints for Boosting Catalog Sales

- Use powerful, compelling ad copy sprinkled with action verbs.

- Seize the reader's attention with knockout headlines.

- The more product information you can offer the better.

- Provide your customers with an easy-as-pie order form to make ordering a breeze.

- Zero in on the benefits. Remind your customers several times.

- Target your list like a laser.

- Consult with a marketing expert with experience in catalog design and sales.

- Draw up a comprehensive marketing plan including detailed specifications for your catalog design.

- Offer specials on high priced items to boost average sale dollar value. For example, buy three items and get one free. Build higher profits this way.

- Train your order takers to be order makers. Employees taking phone orders should suggest items that complement a customer's order.

- Always pack a current catalog in every order you send out. These customers are most likely to order again in the near future.

- Always analyze every product you offer in your catalog for profitability. If it does well, give it more space to promote it better. If it fares poorly, either reduce the allotted space or dump the item.

Because of the substantial risk and fierce competition in catalog sales, you may find it prudent to sell your product or products to other catalogs in addition to your own. This approach may complement your catalog sales efforts because their catalog may penetrate markets yours does not. Sales increase and everybody wins. Another option is to sell to another catalog and simply avoid creating your own. You may find it prudent to avoid the financial risk and difficult competitive atmosphere and concentrate your marketing efforts elsewhere.

The catalog buyer will need a merchandise data sheet from you. This document provides a listing of your product's specifications, pricing, shipping details, discount schedule, terms and other product information. A catalog retailer will expect a product sample, artwork or photographs and product literature such as brochures or fact sheets. The catalog company subjects this information to their product screening process. If all goes well you may soon have orders. Some people use catalog product brokers to match the right catalog with your product. The best way to pay for their expertise is on a commission basis. Their pay comes from orders you receive.

To further research catalog marketing consult the Direct Marketing Association's *Catalog Start-Up Resource Guide*. This comprehensive volume covers catalog company formation from A-to-Z. This volume is available at DMA, 1120 Avenue of the Americas, New York, NY 10036-6700, (212) 768-7277.

The *Catalog of Catalogs* offers a comprehensive directory for obtaining catalogs for almost every subject imaginable. Use this resource whenever you need information on mail-order catalogs.

One of the best trade publications in the industry is *Catalog Age*, 911 Hope Street, Six River Bend Center, Stamford, CT 06907, (203) 358-9900.

"Facts which at first seem improbable will, even on scant explanation, drop the cloak which has hidden them and stand forth in naked and simple beauty."

—Galileo Galilei

CHAPTER 10

More Marketing Options for Your Inventions

Web Sites: The Electronic Frontier

Internet. Information Superhighway. World Wide Web. You've heard the optimistic and idealistic predictions for a globally linked information society. Despite all the hype, it really is a brave new world. The electronic age is now our latest, greatest frontier. Exploitation of a rich medley of business applications can provide a treasure trove for your company if you are willing to engage the future.

High tech, leading-edge organizations blaze the way as the Internet evolves. The World Wide Web is developing into the hottest if not trendiest mass communication medium. Setting up your own Web site has become an essential activity for entrepreneurs.

What is a Web site? The Web combines text, pictures, sound and occasionally animation to present information. This multimedia hyperlinked database spans the entire globe. Any Internet user can access your Web site, or home page, to learn about your company. You can use your Web site to expand into a new channel of distribution for your products or services. The multimedia extravaganza you post on your Web site enhances your business with unique advertising capabilities.

139

Numerous tangible benefits exist for Internet entrepreneurs. The Web offers a unique forum for your advertising. Because of this increased exposure you will realize increased sales. It is important to note that to attract attention to your advertising, you must offer useful information or entertainment on your Web site. This strategy will draw your prospects to you. Fail to do this and your Web site will be a lonely place.

Advertising costs are inexpensive as compared to a direct mail campaign. Where it may cost several thousands of dollars to reach 10,000 direct mail prospects, a Web advertising campaign will cost less than $30 per month in addition to an initial Web site set-up fee of $500 or less. As a bonus, your ads can be easily and cheaply updated as well as customized to appeal to your prospects.

Your Web site can be accessed 24 hours a day and 7 days a week—even on holidays. This ease of access spells convenience. Convenience ranks as the most important buying consideration for home shoppers. Make it easy to order and they will buy.

Your Web page can be used as an online sales catalog. Browsers can peruse photos of your product line and get up-to-date prices. Video and audio clips or even animation can inform and entertain the prospective buyer. You enjoy the tremendous benefits of an enhanced catalog without the usual cost of printing and mailing the paper versions.

Ordering is easy and convenient. Numerous options exist for processing orders. Customers fill out your on-screen order form. Electronic payment may be made directly to you or through a third party. Naturally, online credit card information security is a big concern. Many vendors utilize data security systems to encrypt sensitive data, thus protecting the buyer's credit card information. Without the proper equipment, decryption of the scrambled data is impossible.

Since not all vendors are up to speed in utilizing data security systems, you should beware. Confirm that the vendor has a secure site. If you are setting up your own site for business, get on board with a data security system to ensure your customers' security.

Credit card companies are beginning to view business on the Internet as less risky than traditional retail business. It is far easier for a dedicated dumpster diver to steal your credit card information off a discarded carbon than to hack into and steal the information from encrypted computer files. If credit card companies are comfortable with credit card transactions on the Internet, then perhaps we should be too. Remember, if fraud occurs, it is the credit card company that carries most of the liability. The card holder assumes only a minuscule portion. A sensible precaution is for you to always scrutinize your monthly bill for any unauthorized charges.

Since some people still believe security of credit card numbers, expiry dates and PIN numbers is still questionable, many customers lean toward other ordering options. This is fine, particularly if you are dealing with a vendor without a secure site. The order form with the buyer's credit card number may be faxed. The buyer may choose to print the order form and mail it to the business with either the credit card information, check or money order. Another option: Use a toll-free number and credit card payment to complete the transaction.

Many Internet businesses can operate from out of a home. Your customers have no way of knowing how big your company is. Home-based Internet businesses can compete with large corporations and save money on operating costs. Your global reach enables you to project your presence without the added investment of many full-time salespeople.

A Web site can improve your public relations, provide customer services such as posting FAQs (frequently asked questions) and include a link to your email address for better communication between you and your customers.

Designing a successful Web site is not terribly difficult. Keep in mind the essential sales and marketing techniques which you use for your other marketing outlets. Applying these same rules to Web site development will help ensure the effectiveness of your ad. Heed the following guidelines to attain the success and profit you've planned and hoped for:

- Attract the interest of Internet users with an informative, well-designed site that is easy to use. Internet translation: Post a cool site. Browsers continually search for new, hot sites in their quest to be on the leading edge of the information age. Entertain them while getting your message across.

- Cultivate the user's trust by projecting an air of professionalism. Image is everything on the Internet. Customer concerns about information quality, product quality and vendor integrity are a major issue. These concerns must be addressed head on by taking steps to reassure your prospects. Polish your corporate image by disclosing your company biography. Welcome browsers to your Web site and entertain them with information about your products or services. Share news releases with them to show you are no stranger to the media and have established a reputation in your industry. Establish credibility.

- Effective ads continually emphasize the benefits to the consumer. Introduce the most important benefits early in the Web site. These key benefits are the basis for most buying decisions. To increase the likelihood of making the sale, reinforce these key benefits throughout your sales presentation. Be certain to give your prospects the information they need such as product or service features, warranties and options on your product line.

- Provide communication avenues as prospects will always have questions. If you make no provision to answer their questions, do you really expect them to buy? Of course not. Your customer must have adequate informa-

141

tion upon which to make a buying decision. You have to provide adequate information on your products and services on your electronic site. A list of FAQs can cover 90 percent of all questions likely to be asked. For other questions, provide a link to your email address to allow customers to contact you directly. The Web site can include a form for their questions or to request further information. This system of communication can also make customer feedback easy. You can conduct market research and enhance your public relations.

- Close the sale with an easy-to-understand system with several ordering and billing options. Because of credit transaction security concerns, direct online order payments are the exception rather than the rule. Encryption technology is making the system safer but mercantile protocols are still very experimental. Bear in mind, technology advances rapidly. Credit transaction security is rapidly improving and surpassing that of conventional merchant transactions with which we feel comfortable.

Whether you decide to design a Web site with in-house talent or go out-of-house with an Internet consultant, be certain you comprehend the Internet technology options and opportunities in order to make an intelligent investment in time, energy and money. We've presented some basic information on the Internet and Web site development and use. This is a starting point. If you see yourself on the Internet, check out the following resources for further research into an exciting new marketing challenge:

- *Marketing on the Internet: Multimedia Strategies for the World Wide Web*, by Jill H. Ellsworth and Matthew V. Ellsworth. New York: John Wiley and Sons, 1995.

- *On-Line Marketing Handbook: How to Sell, Advertise, Publicize and Promote Your Products and Services on the Internet and Commercial On-Line Systems*, by Daniel S. Janel. New York: Van Nostrand Reinhold, 1995.

Radio Advertising

Radio advertising presents a significant challenge for the direct marketer. You will encounter significant difficulty in targeting your audience. Don't despair, however, for it can be done. You must choose the right station. Careful research will identify the stations in your area that reach those listeners you've identified as your best prospects.

Radio is an inexpensive advertising medium. Best of all, advertising rates are quite negotiable and barter deals are often available. Great deals can be made for remnant space. Let's face it, the radio station has got to fill every second of air time. You get low cost exposure and the station has no time left unsold. Both parties win. Radio ads can be quickly produced, are easily revised and updated and if you put the ad together yourself, you get the 15 percent agency discount. Per-inquiry ads may be available but difficult to find. It's worth asking about though, for free air time is a great deal for a small business advertiser with a product that sells well on radio.

Radio presents the opportunity for low cost advertising to blanket a local area. In order to gain maximum effect for your ad dollar investment you must repeat your ads frequently. Don't make a deal for ads that are spread out over a long period of time. Concentrate your ads and repeat them. The listeners hear your ad again and again, giving them the impression your company is larger than it really is. Additionally, research shows it takes numerous exposures to an ad before it becomes memorable for listeners. You need to get your ad noticed if you want the orders.

Morning and afternoon drive times are the prime hours for radio advertising and also the most costly. If you seek less expensive rates look for late evening or overnight hours. If your demographics show your best prospects listen during these cheaper ad times, your direct marketing plans may flourish due to the low ad costs.

Hints for Successful Radio Ads

- Advertise when the greatest number of your prospects are listening.
- Concentrate your advertising at specific times in tight groups.
- Be creative and make your ad stand out with humor or simply entertain your audience.
- You have about three seconds to seize your audience's attention. Grab 'em!
- Insist upon professional ad production in a studio. Use professional announcers, background music and special effects to create a high quality ad.
- Employ plenty of repetition within your ad. Repeat your product name, company name, address and phone number.
- Make a call to action crystal clear. Tell your prospects what you want them to do. Come to your store? Phone in an order?

Direct marketers should utilize the radio talk-show circuit to promote and sell their products. If your company sells an interesting product or service that can be discussed on a talk show, you may be able to make significant sales for an incredibly small investment. Your product should be inexpensive enough to appeal to a mass audience.

The radio talk-show host will interview you over the phone so you never have to leave home. You get massive exposure for your product as you and the host promote it over the airwaves. You're getting free advertising, not just for 30 or 60 seconds, but significant portions of an hour. Your customers call in orders on your toll-free number and pay for the orders by credit card or check-by-phone.

To find out more about selling on radio talk-shows, contact *Radio-TV Interview Report (RTIR)* at (215) 259-1070.

Radio Advertising Resources

- Hillier, Newmark, Wechsler & Howard
  100 Park Avenue, 5th Floor
  New York, NY 10017-5516
  (212) 309-9000
  Radio advertising broker. Coordinates nationwide ad campaign with local radio stations.

- Katz Radio Group
  125 West 55th Street
  New York, NY 10019
  (212) 424-6490
  Radio advertising broker. Coordinates nationwide ad campaign with local radio stations.

- Radio Advertising Bureau
  1320 Greenway Drive, Suite 500
  Irving, TX 75038
  (800) 232-3131
  Trade association.

- *Radio Marketing Guide and Fact Book for Advertisers*
  1320 Greenway Drive, Suite 500
  Irving, TX 75038
  (800) 232-3131
  Published by Radio Advertising Bureau.

- *On the Air: How to Get on Radio and TV Talk Shows and What to Do When You Get There,* by Al Parinello. Career Press: 1991, Franklin Lakes, NJ.

- *How to Get on Radio Talk Shows All Across America Without Leaving Your Home or Office,* by Joe Sabah. Pacesetter Publications: 1997, Denver, CO.

TV Advertising

Should you buy time on television to advertise your products? At first glance you might think not with production costs ranging from $5,000 up to hundreds of thousands of dollars and prime time commercial air time so high you get a nosebleed. When a 30-second Super Bowl spot costs in excess of $1,000,000 you quickly realize only the big guys can afford the prime slots. But don't despair for there is good news. There are bargains.

Why would you choose television for advertising? Television is a visual medium. It blends the sense of sight with color and motion, and hearing with sound and music to seduce viewers. And seduce them it does for the average household watches in excess of seven hours of TV each day. Ninety-nine percent of the population believe they *cannot* live without it. Television is the most expensive ad medium because it is the most persuasive medium that reaches audiences of tremendous size. It's a wonderful medium in which to advertise because it's so easy to reach your target audience. Simply follow the programming. If you want to reach kids, advertise during cartoons. Selling cookware? Advertise during a cooking show. Interested viewers are there just waiting to be seduced by your ads.

When considering using television, consult with an advertising agency. Talk to them about your needs and get production and media-buying estimates. Production costs vary tremendously. It is possible to obtain a well-produced ad for several thousand dollars. If the ad is shoddily produced, you will be projecting a very poor image to your potential customers. You'll do more to harm than help.

Always negotiate for better TV and radio ad rates. Everyone will think you to be foolish if you fail to do so. TV rate cards are not carved in stone. To be successful, negotiate the lowest rates for the best ad times. If your expertise is not in negotiating then find an ad broker to do this for you.

Many television stations have production facilities for customizing canned or preproduced commercials to your company's needs. The station supplies the commercial for a very small fee. They insert a "tag line" to customize it for you, giving you inexpensive TV spots to promote your product or service.

You can produce your own TV commercial, reserving the final five seconds for a listing of local retailers who carry your product. Approach the local retailers you would like to carry your product. Most will be unwilling to stock your product unless you pay for shelf space. Make a deal with them. They will stock your product in their stores in exchange for listing their company and location on your commercial. Retailers love TV exposure and many will take you up on this deal.

Cable TV offers many more deals with commercial time running 10 to 20 percent of the cost of network time. Look for tie-ins with local cable features.

Inquire about cooperative advertising, fringe time, adjacencies, package plans and per inquiry deals. For promotional purposes, you might want to arrange to give away your product on game shows or get your product used on a TV show or movie. For game show giveaways contact Game Show Placements, 7011 Willoughby Avenue, Hollywood, CA 90038, or call (213) 874-7818. To get your product used on television or in the movies, contact large TV and movie prop houses in Hollywood. Check the *Yellow Pages* for their listings. Make sure you issue plenty of press releases publicizing your product's use on screen.

Cable TV Shopping Channels

QVC, the Home Shopping Network and other cable TV shopping channels continue to astound the world with their popularity and success. TV shopping is easy and addictive. Consumers enjoy being able to view products and order them from the comfort and security of their own home. Convenience is the name of the game. Make no mistake, it's not only the big guys who get their products on these shop-at-home networks. They actively seek budding entrepreneurs who offer innovative products with quality and appeal. National cable TV retailers routinely look to inventors to supply new product lines for their buying audience.

Competing with QVC and Home Shopping Network are smaller cable TV retailers such as Value-Vision International of Eden Prairie, Minnesota, Shop at Home of Knoxville, Tennessee, and a home-shopping show run by the Black Entertainment Television network in Washington, DC.

Small companies and recent start-ups with new products typically lack well-established distribution and their finances are tight. The cable TV home shopping networks can form a symbiotic relationship with these companies. The show provides a vital distribution channel for those experiencing difficulties with traditional distribution methods. It costs you nothing to place your product on the show. There are no shelf space or slotting fees. The smaller home shopping shows, in particular, do not have a large inventory requirement. This helps small companies that cannot afford major investments in inventory due to tight cash flows.

QVC has become one of the largest electronic retailers in the U.S. reaching an audience of 55 million homes. Savvy entrepreneurs take advantage of this popular marketing outlet. Request a vendor relations packet from QVC to have your product evaluated and considered for airing. Contact QVC at:

- QVC
  Studio Park
  Department 0846
  West Chester, PA 19380
  (610) 701-8282
  Fax (610) 701-1356

As a part of the vendor relations packet, you will find a product data sheet to fill out. The completed product data sheet and a picture of your product must be sent to QVC for a merchandise buyer to evaluate. A determination will be made and you will be contacted within three weeks. If you are fortunate enough for your product to be of interest to QVC, they will request a sample to be put to their rigorous quality assurance tests.

If selected, QVC requires the product be individually packaged, labeled and shipped directly to a QVC warehouse. Be sure to ask for their advice on product packaging. Your product must be priced so QVC can charge at least $15. The price range that seems to work best is between $20 and $100. You must plan ahead if you want your product to get on the air for a specific season. From issuance of a QVC purchase order, expect three months to pass before the product can be aired.

A special feature of QVC allows budding entrepreneurs the opportunity to showcase their own product for sale. QVC goes from state to state on their QVC 50 in 50 Tour, doing local shows featuring 50 local entrepreneur's products. It's a highly competitive contest to get your product on the air but if you're one of the lucky ones, it's a golden opportunity. Your product should be novel with a highly visual and appealing presentation. Remember, this is TV. If you don't entertain viewers, they will click that remote control. If you possess the type of personality that can charm the audience, all the better. The shopping networks love having the inventor make the product presentation.

For more information on how to get your small business' products aired on QVC's 50 in 50 Tour, call (610) 701-8282. If QVC has chosen your state for a broadcast, call your state's commerce department or Economic Development Commission to arrange for an invitation to participate in the screening trade show.

To request a vendor kit from the Home Shopping Network, call (813) 572-8585, extension 4750. HSN also allows a videotaped presentation of your product to be mailed to the company headquarters in St. Petersburg, Florida. If you find it convenient, you may call to request an interview with a buyer at their company headquarters.

How profitable is product placement on these TV shopping channels? Within the past few years we watched QVC sell fudge mix at Christmas. You might think to yourselves—why would anyone buy this? Every grocery store carries fudge mix. We learned it's not so much the product that counts but the presentation.

Two attractive spokespersons presented platters of fudge on a table decked out with Christmas decorations and holiday greenery. They made it festive and fun. The hosts talked it up, making the audience think about how tantalizing and tasty that melt-in-your-mouth fudge was. They sampled every kind, raving over each flavor. They sold the sizzle. It was magic. Their irresistible presentation made the sale. In just a few short minutes more than $40,000 worth of fudge mix sold. This example illustrates the incredible potential that lies in commerce in the electronic media.

Telephone Sales

Many direct marketers use telemarketing to reach their prospects. Judging from the calls we receive, few do it well. Telephone sales offer great potential as well as great peril. Telemarketing allows a company to approach the consumer with a very personal and persuasive sales pitch. It offers the benefit of directing your efforts toward a highly targeted group of prospects.

Their responses are immediate, giving you instant feedback to determine if your efforts are effective or not. With the use of inexpensive toll-free numbers, you can reach far and wide to your audience from the comfort of your own home or business.

The perils of telemarketing must be carefully considered if you plan to try it. Telemarketing costs are high. This means you must obtain high response rates for your campaign to work. You need to be well organized with a winning sales script and a personality ideal for this kind of work. Be advised . . . a significant number of consumers hate telemarketers. They despise the invasion of their privacy and interruption in their life. You must learn to take rejection well, and you must treat everyone with grace and tact.

If your prospects are already your own customers, they are more likely to be receptive to your call. Since you already have a personal relationship with them, they know you and your products, which gives you a foot in the door. A cold call to someone who never heard of you is almost doomed to failure if your aim is to make a sale.

The smart telemarketer uses the phone to generate an inquiry. Convince the consumer to meet with you for a one-on-one sales pitch or to accept your brochure in the mail. Used with conventional direct marketing, you can deliver an effective one-two punch to close the sale. You can also reverse this order and use the sales call as a follow-up to a previous mailing.

Some of the Best Uses of the Phone to Support Your Business

- Use the phone to answer inquiries instead of a sales letter. This personal touch can significantly increase your response rates and boost your profitability.

- Periodically go through your in-house list to generate sales of new products.

- Keep in touch with valued customers, especially if they are not local. Get feedback. Conduct market research. Service your customers' needs.

- Conduct immediate testing by phone for use in direct mail packages. Use these results to design your package to generate maximum responses. This technique gives you a fast roll-out time.

Telemarketing Hints

- Always emphasize the product's benefits.

- Follow a well-prepared script but be prepared to wing it without one if asked questions. Know the product.

- Be flexible in accepting payment. Make arrangements to accept several major charge cards such as Visa and MasterCard as well as COD, purchase orders and checks-by-phone.

- Don't confuse the customer. Make your pitch straightforward. Keep it honest.

- As always, use a highly targeted list of prospects.

- Use a referral if at all possible. You may also work with a partner organization with whom you share the profits. Examples: churches, charities.

- Check the *Business-to-Business Yellow Pages* under Telemarketing Research and Selling Services to investigate the resources available to business. A trade magazine worth reading is *Telemarketing Magazine*, One Technology Plaza, Norwalk, CT 06854; call (800) 243-6002 to order a subscription.

- Using AT&T's toll-free directory service can help you save a ton of money. Simply call (800) 555-1212 when you need the toll-free telephone number for a company you want to call. Give the AT&T representative the company's name and location. The representative gives you the toll-free number enabling you to call that company for free. This service is a tremendous boon not just for telemarketing but for all your business needs. Using toll-free numbers can shave a significant amount of money from your monthly telephone bill.

Manufacturers' Agents

Some entrepreneurs use manufacturers' agents to expand their sales force and penetrate previously untapped territories. If your sales efforts require face-to-face meetings and your business operates out of an east coast location, it becomes an onerous or even an impossible task to cover the nation's heartland or west coast. If you wish for your business to reach far and wide, help is out there—for a price, which is usually a straight commission on all sales in an exclusive territory.

Manufacturers' agents or sales agents can expand your sales territory without requiring any additional investment. The resulting wider distribution and faster sales boost your profits. Previously untapped markets open up because of the efforts of your supplemental sales force who bring their own vast network of contacts and expertise.

Wholesalers generally buy a product outright from you and service your order. They don't have sales agents. Recently, more and more wholesalers require you to give them your product on consignment instead of selling it to them.

Distributors operate on consignment. Expect to see your money 90 to 120 days after they make a sale. Their sales agents actively promote your product. They operate on incentive. To make money they must make a sale.

To track down manufacturers' agents who may wish to carry your product, contact the Manufacturers' Agents National Association (MANA) at P.O. Box 3467, Laguna Hills, CA 92654, (714) 859-4040. This 8,000-member trade association for sales agents and distributors will put you in touch with local and national agents who may be willing to promote and sell your products. Be sure to inquire about MANA's numerous and informative publications. MANA also offers business/sales agent contract assistance for setting up your business relationship.

Flea Markets

If you desire to start up a small business but your resources are limited, flea markets may be the opportunity you seek. Many people who experiment with flea markets have little capital and a full-time job. Their background in business is often nonexistent. This avenue for sales can be your training ground for building your own full-time business. Many people share this same dream yet too few dare to take a chance and turn their dream into reality.

Flea markets have become an amazing avenue for sales that continue to grow in popularity and dollars of business each year. For a rental fee of between $5 to $30, depending on geographic location, you can rent a space for your products. Nowhere can you find cheaper commercial space for opening your own "store." In one weekend the number of potential customers viewing your product line often outstrips what a conventional store sees in an entire week. Floor traffic at successful flea markets is often elbow-to-elbow because the vendors offer products customers want to buy. These flea markets offer an attractive, in-demand product mix. Customers don't frequent flea markets to buy yard sale items and assorted used items. Most don't want this junk. More often than not, the seller fails to present this merchandise in a professional, attractive manner. Sales are lost as a result. Garage and yard sale vendors devalue the overall flea market. Flea market industry managers look for a certain kind of vendor if they want their business to become successful and remain so.

Flea markets seek vendors who offer top-of-the-line new goods. Distributors can supply these goods at rock bottom prices allowing a healthy markup. You may be in a position to supply your own products if you manufacture or craft the items. Then again, your product may be a service you provide.

A professional presentation boosts sales. Plan to use sturdy tables covered with colorful tablecloth linen. Never display your product in a mishmash or piled in cardboard boxes. Don't display your products on a blanket on the ground. You are putting it too close to a child's level where it can be mishandled, especially if it is breakable. It can be accidentally kicked or tripped over.

Consider using an attention-getting centerpiece for display purposes only. Don't sell it (unless they offer you an obscene amount of money). Use it to attract interest to you and your products. Consider your appearance as a vendor. Strive to dress comfortably, yet clean, neat and professional in appearance. Most customers shy away from shady-looking vendors. Impress the public with not only your product line and presentation but your appearance as well. Remember to dazzle them with your smile.

Establish an identity for yourself in the marketplace. Don't try to remain anonymous. You should create a business name for yourself with the goal of separating yourself from your competition. Try to come up with a catchy, clever name that is easily remembered. It should describe your product line. Use this business name on your business cards and flyers to promote your business. In most towns you need only to go to your town clerk's office to file a doing business as (dba) form. This filing of a fictitious name statement allows you to legally use your new name. When you receive the application form for the dba you will receive instructions on the process. You may be required to pay some modest filing fee and advertise your intention to "do business as" for four consecutive weeks in a newspaper. This sort of sole proprietorship is the most common business entity in the U.S. with over two-thirds of all businesses organized in this fashion.

Don't think you're immune from state sales tax considerations if you market your products at flea markets. If your state levies a state sales tax then you as a vendor must obtain a tax permit and collect state sales tax on every sale you make. The penalties for tax evasion make ignoring the law a fool's game. The law directs vendors to display their state sales tax permit in full view at their place of business. You must collect sales tax money when due and make payments to the state.

If you've gone the route of patenting an invention and manufacturing it, sales of your product can begin. If you plan to test market your product to test proof of concept, a flea market may be the ideal place to do it. At the beginning of your venture you want to start out small and grow at a carefully controlled rate, if possible. You strive to keep expenses as low as possible. Your objective is to establish a modest but strong local market for your product. You must show that customers want to buy it. By investing a small amount of money and proving to yourself a market exists, you can decide whether you should expand your business or possibly even license or sell the patent rights and let someone else worry about the business of selling.

Flea markets offer many benefits. Be your own boss. Learn while you earn. Explore new business opportunities. Boost your income. You may find yourself having a lot of fun while you do all these things.

To further explore the opportunities flea markets offer, we heartily recommend the following resources:

The Merchandiser Group magazines bring you coast-to-coast coverage of the flea market and swap meet industry. Their pages are packed with sources of wholesale merchandise as well as articles bringing you the inside scoop on how to prosper in the fascinating world of flea markets and swap meets. The *East Coast Merchandiser, Midwest Merchandiser* and *Western Merchandiser* each cost $30 for a one-year subscription (12 issues).

The 1997 Guide to Active Flea Markets and Swap Meets is an authoritative compilation of active operating flea markets and swap meets throughout the United States. The listings include operating hours and descriptions of the markets. This directory will get you on the right road to active, operating, predominantly new merchandise markets across the United States. The cost is $10.

Cover magazine is a monthly wholesale purchasing guide. Throughout its pages you will find hundreds of offerings from America's leading importers and manufacturers. In addition, *Cover* is a top-quality editorial report, providing readers with the latest news, trends and strategies invaluable to the independent retailer. *Cover* costs $12 for a one-year subscription (12 issues).

The Merchandiser Group's Directory of Wholesalers, Importers and Liquidators is a listing of more than 2,000 product sources from around the nation in a huge variety of merchandise categories. Like a phone book, this handy reference source will keep the names, addresses and phone numbers of suppliers at your fingertips. The directory costs $20.

To obtain further information or place orders for any of these publications, contact: Sumner Communications, Inc., 24 Grassy Plain Street, Bethel, CT 06801-1725, (203) 748-2050 or fax (203) 748-5932. Email at sumcomm@aol.com. Visit their searchable directory of wholesale products and suppliers on the Internet at http://wholesalecentral.com. (Note: Publications' descriptions were reprinted by permission © Sumner Communications.)

Invention Stores

The greatest challenge for most entrepreneurial inventors is getting their patented product into the stores and onto the shelves. Patenting is a cinch compared to the marketing challenges you face. Since you're chomping at the bit to begin to make sales, it's understandable to become frustrated when attempting to penetrate the market with your new product. A new, unproven product from a company without a track record is a hard sell. Many companies simply are not interested. Don't despair, however, for there is hope for you. Believe it or not, numerous companies seek exactly the new and innovative products you offer.

The real trick is to find these companies. We've identified a list of retail stores or mail order houses that will be receptive to your novel or unusual products. Of these, Hammacher Schlemmer deserves special merit and mention. This New York–based specialty store and mail-order catalog house negotiates deals with a limited number of inventors to develop and arrange for manufacture of their product then sell it in the store and catalog. Hammacher Schlemmer continues to introduce numerous new products to the market and largely specializes in gadgets for the affluent. They have the distinction of offering the best in the world of various classes of products. Many of the products that started out with this company as gadgets for the rich have gone on to achieve widespread market penetration and success. Examples include microwave ovens, blenders and electric razors.

Stores and Catalogs Looking for Innovative Products

- B-N-Genius
- Brookstone Company
- Harriet Carter
- Walter Drake & Sons
- Gumps
- Hammacher Schlemmer
- Impact 2000
- JS & A
- Nature Co.
- Plow & Hearth
- Price of His Toys
- Sharper Image
- Lillian Vernon

The *Catalog of Catalogs* mail order directory lists these as well as other catalog stores likely to be receptive to your products. The directory lists each catalog's name, address, telephone number and a summary of their product line. This publication will prove itself to be your indispensable source of information for direct marketing catalog vendors.

Invention Shows

Invention shows allow inventors to showcase their new products for industry and the general public. Inventor's clubs and associations often sponsor these conventions to bring together inventors, manufacturers, investors, sales and marketing people, licensees, the media and the general public. The resulting exposure, which would be otherwise difficult to obtain, provides inventors with the opportunity to test market, sell, license or otherwise promote their invention.

With the media in attendance, you have the opportunity to gain valuable publicity with their news coverage and possibly even an interview. Be very cautious that their news coverage doesn't ambush you. Too frequently, the media enjoy portraying inventors as eccentric or even as crackpots. You don't need that kind of damaging publicity. Always present yourself as a professional and practical businessperson with your feet planted firmly on the ground.

There is a downside for exhibiting your invention at one of these shows. Many potential licensees abhor the idea of publicizing their future marketing plans for a product. They don't want their competition to know what they plan to introduce to the marketplace. If you publicize your invention at one of these shows you may doom any potential licensing deal you may have had if you approached the prospect quietly and directly. Additionally, if your product is Patent Pending, publicizing your invention may prevent you from obtaining foreign patents. A potential licensee may insist upon being able to obtain foreign rights as part of a licensing deal. This point alone may lose the deal for you. You have to evaluate the pros and cons of exhibiting at an invention show. It's helpful to attend one of these shows strictly as a visitor. Spend a little time with some of the exhibitors and ask if the show is working for them. To obtain a listing of major inventor shows throughout the United States, write to the Office of Inventions and Innovations, National Bureau of Standards, Washington, DC 20234.

There are two premier invention shows in the United States. The Invention Convention is produced by Invention Services International in Los Angeles. Call for information at (213) 460-4408. Information on the Patent and Trademark Office's Inventor's Conference and Exposition may be obtained by calling (703) 308-4357.

Trade Shows

Using trade shows as a promotional opportunity for your products can help you reach vast numbers of hot prospects. Your new and exciting products can be displayed and demonstrated with one main goal in mind—sales. Trade show statistics reveal more than 85 percent of attendees are the movers and shakers of industry—the decision makers who are empowered to buy. The value of these personal contacts goes beyond the possibility of an immediate sale. They become part of your business network who can help generate direct and indirect sales for years to come. Sounds good, doesn't it? However, if you do it wrong, you can waste a great deal of time and money and damage your business reputation. Read on for tips on how to do it right.

Trade shows exist for practically every industry. Because of the sheer number of relevant shows for each industry, you must be selective about which you plan to attend as an exhibitor and as a visitor. You need to query trade show management and examine the literature they provide.

The following are items of concern in evaluating any trade show:

1. What will my costs be? Ask about fees for exhibit space, tables and other furniture rentals, lights and power as well as other hidden costs.

2. How many people attend the show?

3. What is the demographic breakdown on the attendees? Look at past attendance and the reputation of the show. Make sure it is the right quality for your business. Examine job titles and functions and make certain they represent the industries to whom you wish to market.

4. Request an exhibit layout to calculate optimum placement of your own booth.

5. Request a listing of special events at the show.

Trade shows allow exhibitors the benefit of direct feedback from prospects as well as valuable market exposure for your products. You can generate instantaneous sales leads. We know of no better way to introduce a new product to the marketplace. A newly developed product can be quickly test marketed to gauge customer interest. The results of this test marketing may well determine market strategy for the product. Allowing your prospects to see product demonstrations and handle the product can result in much higher sales. These face-to-face encounters with targeted customers enable you, the exhibitor, to disseminate compelling information on your product or service. You reach prospects that ordinarily cannot be easily reached. Additionally, you have the opportunity to network with your colleagues and spy on your competition.

Trade Show Tips

- Design your display to attract the attention and interest of your prospects. Live demonstrations work best. A standard 10-foot by 10-foot booth will accommodate two salespeople. Keep it open and concentrate on showcasing your products and their benefits. Prospects expect giveaways; make it one of your products.

- Get publicity. Issue news releases to the local media in the city the event takes place. Highlight your unique product in the news release. Your customers should also receive a nice letter with your news release inviting them to the show. Send a news release to trade magazines in your field of industry to garner publicity.

- Everybody who stops at your booth expects a brochure. They may not read it but they do collect them. Do your best to make your copy stand out and be read. Print more brochures and business cards than you think you'll need.

- Plan your exhibit with a definite goal in mind. Introduce a new product. Expand into a new market. Generate sales. Concentrate on one goal and go for it!

- Mailing lists of show attendees are available from show management. These prospects should be invited to your booth. Give them directions on how to locate you at the show. Inform them of any publicity generating contests you plan to sponsor at the show. Give them your contest entry form to drop off at your booth.

- Put together a backup plan in case disaster strikes. Your booth may be lost, damaged or delayed in shipping. A key salesperson may get sick. Plan for these catastrophes.

- When you receive the business card of any prospective buyer, immediately record what that prospect desires. You can write it on the back of the business card, use a pocket tape recorder, log it in your business diary or enter the information into your computer. Don't wait. It's too easy to forget.

- Every lead generated by the trade show requires a follow-up. Using your stack of business cards, do a mailing of your sales information. Don't wait. Memories of the show will fade. Strike while the iron is hot.

- Issue a new news release. Send it to all on the registration list of trade show attendees. All of these people are now added to your company's mailing list.

Trade Show Resources

Consult *The Encyclopedia of Associations* for comprehensive listings of trade associations. Contact the appropriate trade association for your area of interest to inquire about trade shows. You can count on them to be generous and informative. Inquire with the Chambers of Commerce of the nearby cities with convention facilities for their listing of trade shows.

Other national resources include:

- *Directory of Fairs, Festivals and Expositions*
  Box 24970
  Nashville, TN 37202
  (615) 321-4251

- Meeting Planners International (MPI)
  1950 North Stemmons Freeway
  Dallas, TX 75207
  (214) 712-7700

- *Trade Show and Convention Guide*
  Box 24970
  Nashville, TN 37202
  (615) 321-4250

- *Trade Show and Professional Exhibits Directory*
  835 Penobscot Building
  Detroit, MI 48226
  (800) 877-4253

- *Trade Shows Worldwide*
  835 Penobscot Building
  Detroit, MI 48226
  (800) 877-4253

- *Trade Show Week Data Book*
  121 Chanlon Road
  New Providence, NJ 07974
  (800) 521-8110

- *Trade Shows USA!*
  24 Grassy Plain Street
  Bethel, CT 06801-1725
  (860) 748-2050

"Human subtlety . . . will never devise an invention more beautiful, more simple or more direct than does nature, because in her inventions nothing is lacking, and nothing is superfluous."
—Leonardo da Vinci

AFTERWORD

All of us are dedicated to the life-long search for our pot of gold at the end of the rainbow. Although many of us are content working nine-to-five for someone else, we are not likely to make our fortune doing so. Yes, it is possible to earn a good living and lead a comfortable life. Most people are quite content with this state of affairs. In their later years, as they look back on their life, they are content. A life well lived should contain no great regrets. Most peoples' goals, though modest, are well met. For them, their pot of gold at the end of the rainbow has been won and their life is a success.

We all measure success in different ways. How we define success defines the path we must take to acquire that success. The best definition of success we know is doing what you want in life. Freedom to choose our life work, who we associate with, who controls us and how we live our personal life is the essence of success. Independence is one of life's great treasures.

Many people confuse the trappings of success for the real thing. Wealth, influence, status and power are measures of success for many. Do they realize when they flaunt these trappings of success, what they are really saying is "look at me . . . I'm trying to compensate for my insecurity"? A person's character determines what is of importance to them.

How do you measure your pot of gold at the end of the rainbow? As an inventor, your goals probably include turning your ideas into reality, and then licensing or selling patent rights or starting a business to market and sell your invention. Sure, you want to make a bundle on the invention. That's every inventor's dream. But that is not the whole story. Every inventor is driven by the altruistic urge to better humankind's lot by advancing technology. Making all our lives better is a big part of what it means to be an inventor.

Inventing Made Easy showed you several useful tools to tap into your creativity to make you more productive in idea generation. We explored the ins and outs of the U.S. patent system. Learning the step-by-step process to protect your ideas with a patent is a key step towards attaining the rewards you deserve. Knowing the strengths and weaknesses of the system allows you to avoid the heartbreaking pitfalls which many others have stumbled into.

Difficult as it is, inventing a new product is relatively easy when compared to profiting from that invention. It is easy to be an inventor. What is so very hard is being a *successful* inventor. We don't just tell you how to invent something. We give you the information to market the heck out of your invention. The marketing outlets explored in this book are your key to commercial success. You have so many marketing options to explore.

You don't have to start your own company to manufacture and distribute your invention. However, if you decide to go that route, the information on business start-up will help you focus your efforts in the right direction. Running a successful business is quite a challenge. With the right advice early on, you are better able to meet that challenge and excel.

Licensing or outright sale of your patent has to be the holy grail of inventing. Patent your invention then let it go. Let someone else manufacture, market and sell it while you collect a nice, fat royalty check every month. Too good to be true? Not if you learn how to approach manufacturers with your proposal to license your invention (and do it right!).

As you have read this book you have no doubt noticed that we are at times critical of the U.S. patent system. Despite a few weaknesses, it is nevertheless the best system in the world to protect your intellectual property. Patenting your inventions is still the best way to protect them from unscrupulous competitors. To be successful, you need every advantage and every protection.

We believe *Inventing Made Easy* will guide you, the reader, whether you are an inventor or entrepreneur (hopefully both!), well on your way down the path to success. Although we cannot guarantee successful results in your endeavors, you are in a singularly unique position to benefit from our shared wisdom. With the powerful tools and insider secrets we have revealed, you certainly have a clear advantage. No one is going to put something over on you! It has been said that "in knowledge there is power." You now possess the power to make your dreams become a delicious reality. Your fantasies of success are now your goals. Go for it, my friends!

SECTION II

Invention Showcase

Most readers will agree that what you are about to read is unique in the realm of invention books. Section II presents a compendium of unpatented ideas and inventions the authors generated over several years of inventive effort. You won't see this in other books. All of the ideas in this disclosure section were dreamed up, evaluated and set aside in favor of other endeavors. The writing of *Inventing Made Easy* is one such project that took priority over the rest. This book is important to us (and hopefully you!) because of the benefits it can provide for the many struggling inventors who desperately need a guide.

As you read through the inventions you may notice that some are familiar. Some may already be on the market. We tip our hats to those individuals who got there first.

Part of the reason why we decided to disclose our inventions was in order to entertain and inform. However, the major reason for their disclosure is purely altruistic. *We are giving them all away!* That's right. Your eyes are not deceiving you. Any reader is free to use these ideas. No strings attached. No permission required.

Because disclosure in this book constitutes prior art, you are prevented from patenting them. Nevertheless, many have commercial possibilities. We hate to see promising ideas wasted and would enjoy seeing them become reality. If you wish to bring any of them to market, good for you and good luck.

Inventions

Twister Pen

The Twister Pen is designed as an inexpensive stick pen with a clip. This unique pen is constructed of only three molded plastic parts plus a standard ink cartridge. When the twist cap is screwed on tightly, the ink cartridge tip is exposed for writing. Conversely, when the twist cap is unscrewed to the stops, it covers the tip of the ink cartridge for protection of the tip when not in use. Since the twist cap cannot come off because of the stops, there is no worry about lost or misplaced caps.

The details:

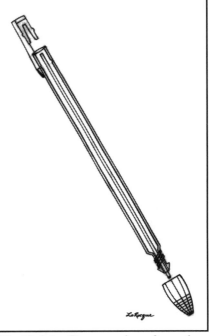

The Twister Pen; a unique four-piece retractable pen.

- One half turn screw for full in-out translation of the twist cap.

- Barrel stops prevent the twist cap from coming off.

- Ink cartridge never moves during operation.

- Standard ink cartridge is used. No spring. No crimps.

- Combination barrel cap and clip is made permanent by sonic welding and is not removable. No cam. No plunger.

- Barrel's internal cavity has tapered fit near tip to prevent hang-up of ink cartridge for fast autoassembly.

- Cap/clip's penetrating section is tapered to prevent hang-ups for fast autoassembly.

163

- Raised ridge on cap/clip slides into recessed slot in barrel for sonic welding.

- Pen assembly is simple and fast. Slide a bushing type ink cartridge down into barrel. Insert cap/clip. Press on screw cap. Assembly complete.

Fiber Optic Christmas Tree Lights

Oh Tanenbaum! Our fiber optic light guide system illuminates a Christmas tree in a dazzling display of color and special effects. Fiber optic strands are bundled together in a central vertical stack with an illumination source at the base. Individual fibers are drawn through the tree branches to place them in a pleasing distribution. The end of each fiber terminates in a splayed bundle of tiny fibers or a prism where the light effect is seen.

The light source, a high light output halogen lamp, is located in the base unit. Between the light source and the start of the fibers, a prism can be inserted to give prismatic color effects. The most important feature of this lighting system is the rheostat controlled rotating filter

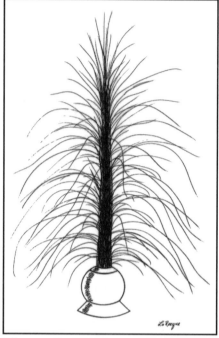

Fiber optic Christmas tree lights arranged in tree pattern. Fibers are drawn throughout the tree branches to attain a pleasing arrangement of lighting effects.

mask which provides an incredible variety of special effects. This unique filter mask is constructed of several layers of heat resistant filters arranged in patterns that generate these special effects.

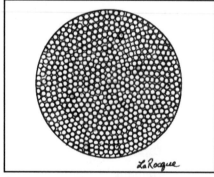

A cross-section of the fiber optic Christmas tree light guide bundle. Fibers bundled on the right side extend to the top-most branches of the tree. Moving to the left side of the light guide bundle, the fibers emanate lower in the tree, gradually reaching the bottom.

Integral to this system is the organized bundling of optic fibers in the base unit. The fibers that terminate at the top of the tree are clustered on the right side of the bundle at the base. The fibers are stacked sequentially, based on their height in the tree. The fibers that terminate on the lowest branches are bundled on the left side of the bundle at the base.

As the filter mask rotates above the light source, a kaleidoscope of colors and special effects are generated and displayed at the ends of the fibers. These interchangeable filter masks are capable of generating a myriad of wondrous effects such as:

- Flashing patterns with single or multiple colors.
- Twinkling starlight.
- Random prismatic effects yielding changing colors.
- Falling snowflake pattern.
- The full spectrum of waves of color washing over the tree.
- Geometric light effects.

Bear Hug Clothing

A lovable teddy bear can be your precious child's best friend. With Bear Wear, your child can take his or her best friend wherever they go. Best of all, they are huggable any time. This line of T-shirts, sweatshirts and sweaters is designed with a Velcro pad attached to the front of the garment where a delightfully plush teddy bear head may be attached and detached. A variety of teddy bear designs are available for interchangeable wear. Choose a different bear for every day of the week. Now your little one can hug a bear with Bear Wear from the Bear Hug Collection.

Heavy Duty Sickle Bar Brush Cutter

As anyone who does yard work knows, cutting weeds and brush is a major pain in the butt. The tools available just aren't up to the job. Let's look at what's available in power tools.

165

The weed-eater type tools usually utilize nylon line for weeds and a metal, circular saw blade for brush. The saw blade is a lousy design and incredibly dangerous. If you hit a rock or metal you will likely be faced with flying projectiles that can maim or kill.

A hedge trimmer is nearly perfect though underpowered and usually cannot cut larger sized brush. The stems or stalks are too wide to fit in the sickle bar's serrations. Besides, bending over to cut at ground level is murderous on your back and neck. Troy-Built sells a wonderful walk behind brush cutting sickle bar

Heavy duty sickle bar brush cutter.

mower, although it is rather expensive. Few people want to put out that kind of cash just to occasionally cut some brush. The Troy-Built mower's major drawback is simply that it is impractical for 90 percent of your brush cutting needs. Most of the brush you need to cut will be on uneven ground, side hills, rocky areas, near stonewalls and fences. Troy-Built's product is nearly useless in these places.

What you need is a hand-held tool utilizing the frame of a weed-eater trimmer, with a powerful engine to drive a heavy duty sickle bar mower blade. A small chainsaw motor provides the power to drive the sickle bar, which is capable of shearing the sizable brush that grows out here in the real world. This hybrid design is no backyard toy. It busts brush and can stand up to the rigors of commercial use.

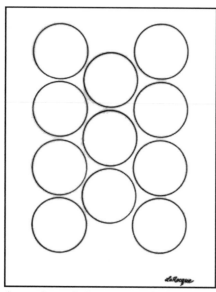

A section of the array of Chameloflage's pixel-like bubbles. A bi-layered, conductive plastic film contains the liquid crystal emulsion responsible for the light shutter effect.

Chameloflage

The chameleon-like abilities of the alien creature in the Arnold Schwarzenegger movie *Predator* stunned audiences. By exploiting adaptive camouflage the alien became next to impossible to locate or defend against in this science fiction movie. Now the high-tech soldier of the future can emulate this stealthy technology. A soldier wearing an outer garment capable of adaptive camouflage becomes capable of unparalleled stealthiness in a changing environment.

Utilizing liquid crystal light shutter window technology, an adaptive camouflage is possible. A liquid crystal emulsion contained in pixel-like bubbles, comprised of a bilayered, conductive plastic film, reacts to an electric field. Field-on and field-off conditions and electric field strength determine translucence and clarity of image. Microprocessor-controlled peripheral sensors sample the background environment then select an appropriate pattern to match the surroundings. Patterns are derived based on chemical formulas, spectral analysis and mathematical calculations to optimize stealthiness. Response time is in the millisecond range resulting in instantaneous adaptation to new backgrounds.

To an observer, an individual wearing this metamorphic camouflage will be rendered invisible. Under certain light conditions and from certain angles a faint trace of a shimmering effect may be noticed. This can easily be dismissed as heat waves or one's imagination playing tricks on the mind.

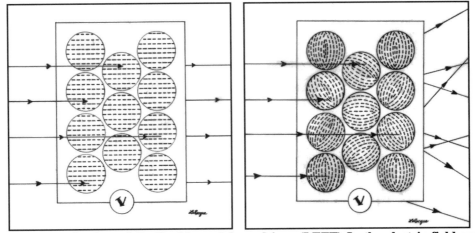

A microscopic view of the liquid crystal emulsion: (LEFT) In the electric field on condition. When the power is on, the electric field rotates crystals within each cell. The crystals align with the electric field and the light propagation axis. Light passes through without being scattered or attenuated. Each pixel-like bubble contains a multitude of these microscopic cells. (RIGHT) In the electric field off condition. When power is off, incoming light is scattered or diffracted by the liquid crystals in each cell. The liquid crystals are arranged in their naturally occurring curvilinear paths along the spherical walls of the cell. This results in light attenuation.

Campaign, Sports and Christmas Buttons With Music Chips

Pin-on buttons have been used for promotions and souvenirs for a long time. Newly developed and now inexpensive electronic technology makes it possible to add a new dimension: sound. Electronic music modules very similar to those used in Hallmark's musical greeting cards may be used on the buttons to play an appropriate song. Voice chips are becoming available as well and their prices continue to drop. The music module is affixed to the back of the button with the activating switch sticking out through a tiny hole in the pin-on button. A simple push with a finger activates the battery operated module and the song plays. These unique buttons are quite likely to become collector's items.

- Political theme. The campaign button is imprinted with the American flag, bald eagle, democratic donkey, republican elephant or candidate photo. It plays a rousing version of "Happy Days are Here Again."

- Sports theme: The baseball button is imprinted with a scene of the great American pastime, including a baseball, bat and ball; team name; player's picture or mascot. When you press the button, "Take Me Out to the Ballgame" plays.

- Holiday theme: The Christmas button is imprinted with a Christmoose, Christmas tree, reindeer, snowflake, Santa's sleigh or Jolly Old St. Nick. When you press the button, a Christmas Carol plays.

- Entertainment theme: The Disney button is imprinted with the Magic Kingdom's castle or Disney characters. The enchanting Disney theme "When You Wish Upon a Star" plays at the push of a button. Once children press the button and the music plays, they're hooked.

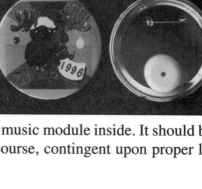

- For those of you with a sadistic sense of humor or just really do love him, Barney the purple dinosaur plays the show's unforgettable theme music.

The aforementioned designs can also be plastic molded with the electronic music module inside. It should be noted any of the above products are, of course, contingent upon proper licensing, where appropriate.

Magic Muck

There is a universal rule about little boys—they love nothing better than playing with a nice pile of mud. The muckier the mud is, the better. And the dirtier they get, the more fun it is. Surely there are millions of children in the cities and suburbs who will never know the pleasure of running their little fingers through a juicy pile of mud. These poor kids are truly deprived.

It's Magic Muck to the rescue. Packed in 1-gallon plastic jugs, this assortment of child-safe mud will thrill your little ones for hours. Free of lead and other toxins, these muds come in a rich and earthy assortment of colors:

- Barnyard Black
- Bog Brown
- Gray Glop

- River Bottom Red
- Creamy Crud
- Goober Green
- Toe Jam Tan

A plastic play sheet is included. Roll it out. Put on dirty old clothes . . . have fun! Let a kid be a kid. But why should only kids get to use this stuff? Mom can "borrow" a little for a mud mask. It's fun for the whole family!

Editing and Time-Compressing VCR

One reality the entertainment industry firmly embraces is that Americans have a short attention span. The MTV generation wants it now and you better be quick about delivering it to them. Additionally, we are constantly on the go, doing the best we can to juggle all the balls life has tossed our way. Time is a precious and ever more scarce resource as the complexity of our lives increases. Yet we love watching television. We were raised on TV and few of us would want to do without. Some consider watching TV to be an incredible waste of time, so our watching is really one of life's guilty pleasures. Think of the time you could save if you could make your viewing more efficient.

We really do need a new VCR capable of editing out the junk and time-compressing what is left. On this new model of VCR, the program is recorded then edited. All commercials are eliminated. Note to all you advertising agencies: Tough cookies! If you don't have the talent and creativity to make commercials that *entertain* us, don't expect us to sit still and watch your product. If you cannot entertain us and inform us at the same time, then you don't belong in the business. Boring commercials deserve to be excised. This cuts a 30-minute show down to 24 minutes. Time-compression will speed up the show but the effect will be imperceptible to viewers. Twenty percent compression will cut out 4.8 minutes from the show's running time. The end result is being able to watch a 30 minute TV show in about 19 minutes. Further advances in technology will allow the slow, boring parts of a show and pauses in dialogue to be excised to give viewers the short version of the show in 15 minutes or less. America is primed and ready for speed viewing.

Stackable Flower Vase

This plastic acrylic, stackable flower vase provides an attractive, stable support for a cut flower. The bell shaped vases nest tightly against one another for shipping and storage. A wide, sturdy base provides stability to pre-

Stackable flower vase.

169

vent tipping over. A water tube slides down into the vase from the top. It provides hydration for the cut bloom, extending its life and preserving its beauty.

A florist may apply a decal to the vase's base to send a message. It could be anything from "Thanks for a job well done" to "You are the love of my life." An electronic music or voice module may be adhered to the vase to send a special message in a tune or in words.

Hockey Power Puck

This is not your ordinary hockey puck. It is constructed not of the usual material but out of the same material superballs are made of. When a player slaps the puck with a hockey stick, the shot goes faster and farther. The puck rebounds off surfaces in a manic fashion. The game gets really fast, really intense and really, really wild.

Vehicle Security Camera

A vandal or a thoughtless clod slams his car door into the side of your brand new vehicle. A buffoon backs into your vehicle then takes off. No note. No apology. No responsibility. We've all suffered from these infuriating events. If only it could have been caught on film and the person responsible identified and made to pay. It can.

The base unit of the vehicle security camera is hidden in your vehicle. Two fiber optic light guides emanating from it can be snaked throughout your vehicle to allow a variety of placement choices for different views. The wide angle lenses at the end of the fiber optic light guides allow comprehensive coverage for your vehicle. An impact trips a sensor which activates the camera system. Several exposures are snapped at time intervals you can preset. Accidents and break-ins can be recorded to provide the authorities with the evidence they need to do their job.

Computerized Governor for Vehicles

American drivers love to speed in arrogant defiance of safety, common sense and reasonable laws. Aggressive driving and road rage take a heavy toll in the accidents this behavior causes. Too many drivers cannot mind their manners so something has to change. A technical solution is needed where a behavioral solution is not possible. A black box containing a tamperproof monitoring and controlling computer can be interlinked with a modern vehicle's computer. This new computer prevents the vehicle from exceeding a preset limit on speed. This computerized governor would make a reasonable top speed of 80 miles per hour the law of the land. Additionally, this device records your driving history, keeping track of the number of times and duration of incidents where the vehicle exceeds speed limits. The factory-installed black box can be checked for tampering yearly at emissions and safety checks.

Law enforcement personnel can stop a speeder and plug into the black box to download the vehicle's data. Fines can be calculated based upon number of speeding incidents and how fast the vehicle traveled. Insurance companies can be immediately notified of this history of excessive speed. Transmission and satellite uplink from the police cruisers or at the routine data dump at your yearly emissions and safety check will enable your insurance company to set your rates. It's only fair that those who drive faster pay higher auto insurance rates. Those who drive slower and are mindful of the law don't get their rates jacked up. Insurance companies will view this technology as revenue positive. They can make lots of money. Best of all, the system is fair with those drivers deserving high rates getting them.

Law enforcement will appreciate this device as it will allow them to concentrate assets more toward solving crime rather than catching speeders. Manning a speed trap is so boring. The only thing worse is monitoring a road construction site. Surely there are more important duties for these police officers to perform. Cost-benefit analysis should show the advantage of a $500 computer unit required in all new vehicles versus income from occasional traffic violations. Jobs will be created in the high-paying manufacture and servicing of this electronic unit. Massive amounts of tax money will be saved that we currently spend on law enforcement and the court system.

People shouldn't complain about the intrusiveness of this technology. Many truckers are already subjected to similar technology. Their driving history is recorded in their truck's computer and scrutinized by their employers. This is appropriate technology for our times to make the roads safer for all of us.

Soaring Suit

Skydiving appeals to many adventurous spirits. The exhilaration of freefall becomes an addictive high. Now you can savor it all the longer with

 a Soaring Suit. Wear this ultra-baggy jumpsuit to extend the precious moments of freefall. The design dirties your configuration and slows your fall as you plummet to earth. The baggy configuration with flaps between legs and flaps between arms and sides of the chest slow your fall like that of a flying squirrel. You glide earthward until you are ready to deploy your chute and complete your descent.

Soaring suit worn by skydiver in freefall.

Buzzard Drone for Reconnaissance

The ultimate in covert on-site intelligence gathering has arrived. Imagine you are responsible for guarding a "sensitive" site. You know when the reconnaissance satellites make their passes. You utilize cloud cover and darkness to the maximum. Your site relies upon the latest in camouflage technology. Your radar can detect any plane. But do you suspect a buzzard flying lazy circles 200 feet above you? Now you should because it may not be the real thing.

The technology exists today to create a life-size, realistic-looking, flight-capable model of a vulture or eagle. By riding the thermals, this semi-autonomously controlled model is capable of remaining aloft for hours. The Buzzard Drone can be preprogrammed to follow a specific course using GPS guidance. Upon reaching its target, it loiters overhead, while the desired intelligence is gathered. Film, video, audio or other data may be collected as it lurks above. Altitude maintenance and attitude control and stability are accomplished with the programmable onboard computer. After the mission objectives have been accomplished the drone returns to preset coordinates for recovery. This can be an inexpensive and versatile piece of reconnaissance and security apparatus for military, security and investigative missions.

Folding Apple Peeler

Many health conscious people won't eat an apple without peeling it to get rid of the pesticide residues which may be trapped on the skin. Others don't trust that the fruit was properly washed, or don't find eating wax appealing. Some don't want to eat the peel simply as a matter of personal preference. The Folding Apple Peeler is perfect for the apple-loving person on the go. This fruit peeler folds up just like a jackknife.

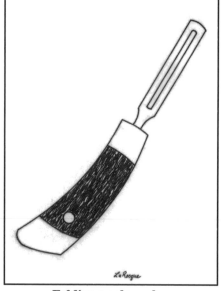

Folding apple peeler.

How to Conquer the Common Cold

The ubiquitous plague known as the common cold plunges humanity into an abyss of misery whenever it strikes. The hours of suffering lost to this virus stagger the mind. Americans suffer approximately 1 billion colds per year. Much of the misery could be avoided if only people would wash their hands more frequently to prevent the transmission of this nasty little bug.

It takes just a few viruses to precipitate a chain reaction in your body. Research shows the most vulnerable parts of our bodies to be the nose and eyes. The nose is the primary site where infection occurs because of the slightly cooler conditions there. Specifically, the virus must be in contact with the nasopharynx for infection to occur. Unless you have an immunity to the specific cold virus, infection will occur after a three to five day incubation period. Woman seem to suffer from more colds than men, perhaps since many women spend more time with children. Close indoor contact seems most conducive to spreading colds.

Medical researchers have discovered more than 200 different viruses that cause the common cold. To fight these viruses, a body requires a good diet rich in vitamins as well as a positive mental attitude to keep the immune system at peak performance. Regular consumption of yogurt helps boost your immunity and decreases cold symptoms by one-third.

When a person contracts a bacterial infection doctors can prescribe an antibiotic to combat it. Since antibiotics don't work with viral infections, doctors can only prescribe plenty of rest and fluids for a cold. A ton of cold remedies jam the drug stores' shelves, none of which fight the viral infection. They only provide some measure of relief from the symptoms of the infection. Some are actually useless, relying upon a placebo effect or the giant pharmaceutical company's marketing power to push the product on the public.

Anti-viral agents do exist, however. Central plains and eastern U.S. Native peoples have long known of and used a perennial herb called Echinacea to fight colds. Modern medical science now recognizes its utility as a powerful anti-viral agent. This agent's mode of action is said to be in the stimulation of the immune system, increasing lymphatic filtration and stimulating increased production of infection fighting white blood cells (specifically T-cells). Researchers report tumor inhibiting properties as well.

The herb can be found in drugstores and health food stores in a tea or capsule form. Many herbalists sell the dried root, which contains the highest concentration of anti-viral agents. It can be made into a tea or a tincture. We've used Echinacea and heartily recommend it as an effective cold fighter.

This season's hottest new cold remedy is zinc gluconate. When taken in lozenge form, it reduces the duration of cold symptoms by about three days. Since there is no vaccine or effective therapy for the common cold, all cold sufferers can hope for is a reduction in the duration of the symptoms. Zinc gluconate seems to be powerful and effective in cutting the duration of cold symptoms in half. The combination of Echinacea and Cold-Eeze brand zinc gluconate lozenges used by cold sufferers may portend dire consequences for the $3 billion per year cold remedy market. If duration of cold symptoms is cut in half, significantly less sales will occur of the traditional cold remedies foisted upon us by the giant pharmaceutical companies.

With what we know today about fighting the common cold, we see a market opportunity for a new product:

Cold Kicker Chicken Soup
Ingredients:
free-range chicken
Echinacea herb
zinc gluconate
vitamin C
low salt
capsaicin
garlic

Chicken growers raise free-range chicken to be healthier, more natural and tastier than the conventional growers' product. Getting fresh air and exercise in conjunction with a healthier diet produces better chickens in a more humane environment. Conventional processors eviscerate the birds then soak them in a vat of cold water to chill them. While soaking in this bacteria-contaminated "fecal soup" the bird soaks up to 10 to 15 percent of its weight of this water. In contrast, properly processed free-range chicken is sprayed with chilled, clean water to quickly cool the dressed bird. The chicken remains cleaner and thus less likely to harbor dangerous bacteria. The taste has to be better without the fecal soup flavor in the meat.

Studies show that chicken soup does fight colds. Chicken protein contains the amino acid cysteine which is released when the soup simmers. Cysteine is chemically similar to acetylcysteine, a prescription drug for respiratory infections. Both have the pharmacological action of thinning mucus in the lungs. The aromatic nature of chicken soup helps clear the airways.

Adding Echinacea to the chicken broth seasons the soup with the added benefit of its anti-viral properties. Zinc gluconate assists in boosting the body's immune functions. The aromatic nature of hot, steamy soup delivers the zinc gluconate precisely where the body needs it. Vitamin C contributes its disease fighting anti-oxidant capability and protects delicate lung tissue.

Low salt content should be a prerequisite. The major soup manufacturers continue to dump too much salt in their product. They know the hazards of excessive dietary sodium but don't seem to care. They need to add a ton of salt to make their soups taste palatable. High salt in your diet exacerbates respiratory illness. Excessive sodium throws the sodium-potassium ratio out of balance. This leads to inflammation.

Cold sufferers benefit from hot and spicy foods. The pharmacologically active part of hot peppers is capsaicin. It acts as a mucus moving agent by thinning lung secretions. The drug guaifenesin is chemically similar. Guaifenesin is an expectorant that is the active ingredient in most over-the-counter cough syrups, expectorants and cold tablets. Capsaicin acts to flush out the sinuses and wash away irritants as well as break up congestion in the lungs. Because viruses thrive in dried-out environments, capsaicin is beneficial because of its moistening action in your airways.

Garlic benefits cold sufferers due to allicin, from which garlic derives its unique flavor. When metabolized by the body, allicin becomes similar to the pharmacologically active ingredient in Mucodyne, which regulates mucus flow.

Cold Kicker Chicken Soup could be marketed like Ensure brand liquid dietary supplement. Ensure is available off-the-shelf in drugstores in convenient, easy-to-open single serving cans. Available in a six-pack, Ensure sells for about $10. Cold Kicker Chicken Soup could be similarly marketed at a very premium price, ensuring a high profit margin for both manufacturer and pharmacy or retailer.

SECTION III

Invention Notebook

For your convenience, we have included an Invention Notebook in this section to allow you to create the all-important record of conception, building and testing of your next invention. Creating this official record will help you secure your patent rights. Should your patented invention be challenged, this record will be the cornerstone of your legal defense.

Chapter 1 discussed the importance of the comprehensive use of this record-keeping tool. You now know that logging each and every step in the invention process is wise and necessary. Keep referring to the instructions in Chapter 1 as you make entries. By following these guidelines, you organize and streamline the patent process and strengthen your patent rights.

PROJECT TITLE:

WORK CONTINUED FROM PAGE

WORK CONTINUED TO PAGE

Inventor: _____   Date: _____

Inventor: _____   Date: _____

Disclosed to & Understood by: _____   Date: _____

Disclosed to & Understood by: _____   Date: _____

PROJECT TITLE:

WORK CONTINUED FROM PAGE

WORK CONTINUED TO PAGE

Inventor: _____ **Date:** _____

Inventor: _____ **Date:** _____

Disclosed to & Understood by: _____ **Date:** _____

Disclosed to & Understood by: _____ **Date:** _____

PROJECT TITLE:

WORK CONTINUED FROM PAGE

WORK CONTINUED TO PAGE

Inventor: _____ Date: _____

Inventor: _____ Date: _____

Disclosed to & Understood by: _____ Date: _____

Disclosed to & Understood by: _____ Date: _____

PROJECT TITLE: _____

WORK CONTINUED FROM PAGE

WORK CONTINUED TO PAGE

Inventor: _____ **Date:** _____

Inventor: _____ **Date:** _____

Disclosed to & Understood by: _____ **Date:** _____

Disclosed to & Understood by: _____ **Date:** _____

PROJECT TITLE:

WORK CONTINUED FROM PAGE

WORK CONTINUED TO PAGE

Inventor: _____ Date: _____

Inventor: _____ Date: _____

Disclosed to & Understood by: _____ Date: _____

Disclosed to & Understood by: _____ Date: _____

PROJECT TITLE:

WORK CONTINUED FROM PAGE

WORK CONTINUED TO PAGE

Inventor: _____ Date: _____

Inventor: _____ Date: _____

Disclosed to & Understood by: _____ Date: _____

Disclosed to & Understood by: _____ Date: _____

PROJECT TITLE:

WORK CONTINUED FROM PAGE

WORK CONTINUED TO PAGE

Inventor: _____   Date: _____

Inventor: _____   Date: _____

Disclosed to & Understood by: _____   Date: _____

Disclosed to & Understood by: _____   Date: _____

APPENDIX 1

Communications with the Patent and Trademark Office

Mail Address

General written correspondence should be directed to the following address:

Commissioner of Patents and Trademarks
Washington, DC 20231

PTO Telephone and Fax Numbers

The following list of Patent and Trademark Office telephone and fax numbers is current as of January 2, 1998. You should be aware the numbers change often so you may wish to check the *Official Gazette* for the updated telephone list. Unless otherwise specified, use area code 703.

General information:

308-HELP (308-4357)
(800) PTO-9199
Fax 305-7786
TDD 305-7785

Attorneys/Agents Registered to Practice Before PTO List:

PTO 308-5316, extension 17
Government Printing Office (202) 512-1800
Diskette, Tape or CD-ROM 306-2600

Bulletin Board System (BBS) information:
306-2600

Disclosure Document Program:
308-0900

Fee rates:
308-HELP; (800) PTO-9199

Forms:
308-HELP; (800) PTO-9199

Maintenance fees:
308-5068; 308-5069;
Fax 308-5077

Official Gazette subscriptions:
Government Printing Office (202) 512-1800

Patent and Trademark Copy sales—uncertified copies:
Weekdays, 7:30 A.M. to 8:00 P.M., EST/EDT
305-8716; Fax 305-8759

Patent & Trademark Depository Library Program:
308-5558

Search Facilities—Patent Search Room (Crystal Plaza 3, 1A03):
Weekdays, 8:00 A.M. to 8:00 P.M., EST/EDT
308-0595

PTO Internet Addresses

PTO Home Page:
http://www.uspto.gov

Patent & Trademark Copy Sales:
http://www.uspto.gov/web/offices/ac/ido/opr/ptcs/

APPENDIX 2
Inventors Associations

Inventors Associations work to advance the interests of their members by providing a common forum for the discussion of development, patenting and marketing of their inventions. Individuals can draw upon the collective expertise and experience of the group in solving their particular invention related problems. The membership usually consists of a broad cross-section of inventors with a vast pool of knowledge. We recommend joining such an organization.

Agencies exist to provide an aspiring inventor or entrepreneur with valuable services and guidance in conducting their business. Call your state headquarters of the SBA's Small Business Development Centers (SBDCs) to inquire about programs to assist inventors. The SBDCs provide management assistance as well as counseling, training and technical assistance.

Affiliated Inventors Foundation (AIF)
902 North Circle Drive, No. 208
Colorado Springs, CO 80909-5200
(719) 635-1234
Toll free (800) 525-5885
Fax (719) 635-1578
Membership 400 independent inventors.
Affiliated with Technology Transfer Society.

American Society of Inventors (ASI)
P.O. Box 58426
Philadelphia, PA 19102-8426
(215) 546-6601
Membership 150 engineers, scientists and businessmen.
Affiliated with National Congress of Inventors Organizations.

Intellectual Property Owners
1255 23rd Street NW, Suite 850
Washington, DC 20037
 (202) 466-2396
Fax (202) 466-2893
Web site http://www.ipo.org
Nonprofit association whose members own patents, trademarks, copyrights and trade secrets. Membership open to individuals, organizations and companies.

Inventors Assistance League, International
345 West Cypress Street
Glendale, CA 91204
 (818) 246-6540
Membership 6,942 inventors and manufacturers.
Affiliated with National Inventors Foundation.

Inventors Clubs of America (ICA)
P.O. Box 450261
Atlanta, GA 31145-0261
 (404) 355-8889
Toll free (800) 336-0169
Fax (404) 355-8889
Membership 6,000 inventors, scientists and manufacturers.

Inventor's Guild
Box 132
Plainview, TX 79073
For-profit group promoting invention.

Inventors Workshop International Education Foundation (IWIEF)
1029 Castillo Street
Santa Barbara, CA 93101-3736
 (805) 962-5722
Fax (805) 899-4927
Membership 27,000 amateur and professional inventors providing education and assistance on patent matters.

National Congress of Inventors Organizations (NCIO)
c/o Intervention Services International Corporation
P.O. Box 93669
Los Angeles, CA 90093-6690
 (213) 878-6959
Fax (213) 962-8588
Membership 63 inventors involved in inventor education including idea development, protection and marketing. Call toll-free 888-695-4455 for information on the perils and pitfalls of dealing with Invention Promotion Firms.

National Inventors Foundation (NIF)
345 West Cypress Street
Glendale, CA 91204
 (818) 246-6540
Membership 10,071 independent inventors united to educate and assist others on patent matters.

Non profit Organizations Offering Assistance to Inventors and Entrepreneurs

This comprehensive listing of organizations offering assistance to inventors and entrepreneurs is graciously provided by Robin Conger of the Pacific Northwest National Laboratory. The information in this section was compiled by the U.S. Department of Energy's Pacific Northwest National Laboratory for the Department's Office of Industrial Technology. This information was excerpted with permission from the fourth edition of the *Inventor Assistance Source Directory*. The directory contents were compiled for the Inventions and Innovations Program, U.S. Department of Energy, by Segren Goodey and Margaret Axelson, Program Assistants. The information is available free of charge from the Office of Industrial Technology's Innovative Concepts Program. Call (509) 372-4270 or fax your request to (509) 372-4369.

ALASKA

Jamie Kenworthy
Exec. Director
AK Science/Technology Foundtn.
4500 Diplomacy Drive #515
Anchorage, AK 99508-5918
(907) 272-4333 Fax (907) 274-6228

Charles Christy
Database Admin.
AK Tech. Transfer Assistance Ctr.
430 W. 7th Ave., Ste. 110
Anchorage, AK 99501
(907) 274-7232 Fax (907) 274-9524

Pamela Middaugh
Executive Director
Alaska Inventors & Entrepreneurs
Association, Inc.
P.O. Box 241801
Anchorage, AK 99524-1801
(907) 276-4337 Fax (907) 276-4337
inventor@arctic.net

Clyde Johnson
Director
Kenai Peninsula SBDC
P.O. Box 3029
Kenai, AK 99611-3029
(907) 283-3335 Fax (907) 283-3913

E Wall
Lead Subcenter Dir.
University of Alaska SBDC
430 W. 7th Ave., Ste. 110
Anchorage, AK 99501
(907) 274-7232 Fax (907) 274-9524

ALABAMA

Director
Near SBDC
P.O. Box 168
Huntsville, AL 35804-0168
(205) 535-2061 Fax (205) 535-2050
small bus@hsvchamber.org

Gary Hannem
Director
SBDC, Auburn University
108 COB Lowder Bldg.
Auburn, AL 36849-5243
(334) 844-4220 Fax (334) 844-4268
ghannem@business.auburn.edu

Wilson L. Harrison
Director
UAB Office for the Advancement
of Developing Industries
1075 13th St. South
Birmingham, AL 35294-4440
(205) 934-2190 Fax (205) 934-1037

Carolyn Long
Account Executive
Univ. of North Alabama, SBDC
Box 5250
Florence, AL 35632-0001
(205) 760-4629 Fax (205) 760-4813

ARKANSAS

James T. Benham
AR Science & Technology Authority
100 Main St., Suite 450
Little Rock, AR 72201
(501) 324-9006 Fax (501) 324-9012

Janet Nye
State Director
Univ. of Arkansas at Little Rock, SBDC
100 S. Main St., Suite 401
Little Rock, AR 72212
(501) 324-9043 Fax (501) 324-9049

ARIZONA

Deborah Elver
Program Coordinator
Cochise College SBDC
901 N. Colombo
Sierra Vista, AZ 85635
(520) 515-5478 Fax (520) 515-5437
elverdeb@tron.cochise.cc.az.us

Susan Moore
President
Inventors Association of AZ
2201 N. Camino Principal, Suite 4
Tucson, AZ 85715
(520) 296-4464 Fax (520) 290-8164

Jennee Miles
Director
Mohave Comm. College SBDC
1971 Jagerson Ave.
Kingman, AZ 86401
(520) 757-0895 Fax (520) 757-0836
jenmil@pops.mohave.cc.az.us

Linda Andrews
Regional Director
Pima Community College SBDTC
4905A E. Broadway Blvd., #110
Tucson, AZ 85709-1260
(602) 748-4906 Fax (602) 748-4585

Christina Gonzalez
Manager,
SBDC
1414 W. Broadway #165
Tempe, AZ 85281-6941
(602) 966-7786 Fax (602) 966-8541

Rich Senopole
Director,
SBDC
117 E. Gurley St. #206
Prescott, AZ 86301
(520) 776-2373 Fax (520) 778-3109
sba_rich@sizzle.yavapai.cc.az.us

Dr. Rita C. Manak
Director,
University of Arizona
Office of Technology Transfer
P.O. Box 210158, Room 515
Tucson, AZ 85721-0158
(520) 621-5000 Fax (520) 626-4600

CALIFORNIA

Tiffany Haugen
Director, Accelerate Technology
SBDC
4199 Campus Drive #240
Irvine, CA 92715
(714) 509-2990 Fax (714) 509-2997

Kenneth Romano
CACT Director
CACT-Sierra College
5000 Rocklin Road
Rocklin, CA 95677
(916) 781-0433 Fax (916) 781-0410
romano_ke@email.sierra.cc.ca.us

Bradford L. Friedman
Law & Tech. Advisor
California Invention Center
California State University
675 Sharon Park Drive #237
Menlo Park, CA 94025
(510) 885-3805 Fax (510) 885-8039
cic@csuhayward.edu

Lawrence J. Udell
Executive Director
California Invention Center
School of Business & Economics
Cal State Hayward
Hayward, CA 94542-3066
(510) 885-3805 Fax (510) 885-2039

Denise Arend
State Dir. of SBDC
California Office of Small Business
801 K Street, Suite 1700
Sacramento, CA 95814
(916) 322-5790 Fax (916) 322-5084

Carole Enmark
Director
Cascade SBDC
737 Auditorium Drive HA
Redding, CA 96001
(916) 247-8100 Fax (916) 241-1712

Randy Mason
Program Manager
Central California SBDC
430 W. Calowell #D
Visalia, CA 93277
(209) 625-3051 Fax (209) 625-3053

John Christensen
President
Central Valley Inventor's
Association, Inc.
P.O. Box 1551
Manteca, CA 95336-1551
(209) 239-5414

Brad Mix
Business Consultant
Coachella Valley SBDC
501 S. Indian Cyn #222
Palm Springs, CA 92264
(619) 864-1311 Fax (619) 864-1319

Sherm Fishman
Contra Costa Inventors Club
295 Stevenson Dr.
Pleasant Hill, CA 94523-4149
(510) 934-1331 Fax (510) 934-1132

Bob Smith
CEO
Experimental Cities, Inc.
"A Flash of Genius"
P.O. Box 731
Pacific Palisades, CA 90272-0731
(310) 276-0686 Fax (310) 274-7401
gmarcus@igc.apc.org

Steve Schneider
Program Coordinator
Idea to Market Network
P.O. Box 12248
Santa Rosa, CA 95406
800-ITM-3210 Fax (707) 584-4161

Debbie Trujillo
Manager
Imperial Valley SBDC
301 N. Imperial, Suite B
El Centro, CA 92243
(619) 312-9800 Fax (619) 312-9838

Teri Corrazzini Ooms
Executive Director
Inland Empire SBDC
2002 Iowa Avenue, Ste. 110
Riverside, CA 92507
(909) 781-2345 Fax (909) 781-2353

Michael Roessler
Assistant Director
Inland Empire SBDC
2002 Iowa Avenue, Ste 110
Riverside, CA 92507
(909) 781-2345 Fax (909) 781-2353

Martha Regan
Co-President
Inventors Alliance
5666 Arboretum Drive
Los Altos, CA 94024
(415) 967-0220 Fax (415) 967-0720

Jim Mitsouka
President
Inventors Forum
P.O. Box 8008
Huntington Beach, CA 92615-8008
(714) 253-0952 Fax (714) 836-5609

Greg W. Lauren
Coordinator
Inventors Forum of San Diego
11190 Poblado Road
San Diego, CA 92127-1306
(619) 673-4733 Fax (619) 451-6154

Alan A. Tratner
President
Inventors Workshop International
1029 Castillo Street
Santa Barbara, CA 93101-3736
(805) 962-5722 Fax (805) 899-4927

Maggie Weisberg
Partner
M & M Associates
P.O. Box 1020
Fort Jones, CA 96032-9712
(916) 468-2282 Fax (916) 468-2238

Melvin L. Fuller
Partner
M & M Associates
VVC Productions
P.O.Box 1020
Fort Jones, CA 96032-1020
(916) 468-2282 Fax (916) 468-2238

Stephen Paul Gnass
President
National Congress of Inventor
Organizations
P.O. Box 93669
Los Angeles, CA 90093-6690
(213) 878-6952 Fax (213) 962-8588

Gillian Murphy
Director
San Joaquin Delta College
SBDC
814 N. Hunter Street
Stockton, CA 95202
(209) 474-5089 Fax (209) 474-5605

Charles Robbins
Director
Sawyer Center
520 Mendocino Ave., Ste. 210
Santa Rosa, CA 95401
(707) 524-1770 Fax (707) 524-1772

Director
SBDC
4275 Executive Square
La Jolla, CA 92037
(619) 453-9388 Fax (619) 450-1997
sbdc@smallbiz.org

Director
SBDC
560 Wall Street, Ste. J
Auburn, CA 95603
(916) 885-5488 Fax (916) 823-2831

Paul Hischar
Manager
SBDC
375 S. Main Street, Ste. 101
Pomona, CA 91766
(909) 629-2247 Fax (909) 629-8310

Kenneth Symington
Business Coordinator
SBDC
3233-C Donald Douglas Loop South
Santa Monica, CA 90405
(310) 398-8883 Fax (310) 398-3024

Kenneth Symington
Business Coordinator
SBDC
21221 S. Western Ave.
Torrance, CA 90501
(310) 787-6466 Fax (310) 782-8607

Teresa Thomae
Director
SBDC
6500 Soquel Drive
Aptos, CA 95003
(408) 479-6136 Fax (408) 479-6166

Sherm Fishman
Executive Director
Small Entity Patent Owners Assn.
295 Stevenson Drive
Pleasant Hill, CA 94523-4149
(510) 934-1331 Fax (510) 934-1132

192

A. Wayne Snodgrass
President
Small Manufacturers' Institute
6000 J Street, Ste. 83053
Sacramento, CA 95819-6122
(916) 278-4877 Fax (916) 367-3270
wsnodgrass@aol.com

Jeffrey Johnson
Director
Weill Institute
SBDC
1706 Chester Ave. #200
Bakersfield, CA 96330
(805) 322-5881 Fax (805) 322-5663

COLORADO

Lewis Kontnik
President
CO BioMedical Venture Center
1610 Pierce Street
Lakewood, CO 80214
(303) 237-3998 Fax (303) 237-4010

Jim Reser
Director
Fort Lewis College SBDC
1000 Rim Drive
Durango, CO 81301-3999
(970) 247-7009 Fax (970) 247-7623
reser_j@fortlewis.edu

Steve Madone
Executive Director
Fremont County D C
402 Valley Road
Canon City, CO 81212
(719) 275-8601 Fax (719) 275-4400

Director
Greeley SBDC
1407 8th Avenue
Greeley, CO 80631
(970) 352-3661 Fax (970) 352-3572

Director
SBDC
School of Business 105
Alamosa, CO 81102
(719) 587-7372 Fax (719) 587-7522

Joseph Bell
Director
SBDC
2440 Pearl Street
Boulder, CO 80302
(303) 344-2145

Sonny Lastrella
Deputy State Dir.
SBDC
State of Colorado-OBD
Denver, CO 80202
(303) 892-3840 Fax (303) 892-3848

Dennis O'Connor
Director
SBDC
136 West Main Street
Trinidad, CO 81082
(719) 846-5644 Fax (719) 846-4550

Frank Pryor
Director
SBDC
2627 Redwing Rd., Ste. 105
Fort Collins, CO 80526
(970) 226-0881 Fax (970) 204-0385

Selma Kristel
Dir., Business Growth
South Metro Denver Chamber
7901 South Park Plaza
Littleton, CO 80120
(303) 795-0142 Fax (303) 795-7520

Julie Morey
SBDC Director
Western CO Bus. Dev. Corp.
304 W. Main Street
Grand Junction, CO 81505
(970) 243-5242 Fax (970) 241-0771
mesastate@attmail.com

CONNECTICUT

Julie Rader
Director
Connecticut Innovations, Inc.
Technology Assistance Center
40 Cold Spring Road
Rocky Hill, CT 06419
(860) 563-5851 Fax (860) 563-4877

Dennis Gruell
Regional Director
CT SBDC
1800 Asylum Ave., Univ. of CT
West Hartford, CT 06117
(860) 241-4986 Fax (860) 241-4907
dennis@ct.sbdc.uconn.edu

Ilene G. Oppenheim
Director
CT Small Business
Development/Outreach Center
101 South Main Street
Waterbury, CT 06706
(203) 757-8937 Fax (203) 756-9077

Harold Meyer III
President
Innovators Network of Greater
Danbury
52 Bank Street, Suite A
New Milford, CT 06776-2706
(860) 350-2709 Fax (860) 355-8752

John A. Ruckes
Lead Planning Analyst
State of Connecticut/OPM
P.O. Box 341441 MS# 52ENR
Hartford, CT 06134-1441
(860) 418-6384 Fax (860) 418-6495

DISTRICT OF COLUMBIA
John Curtin Esq.
Assoc. of Trial Lawyers of America
1050 31st Street
Washington, DC 20007
(202) 965-3500 Fax (202) 625-7312

Woodrow McCutchen
Executive Director
Howard University SBDC
2600 6th Street NW
Washington, DC 20059
(202) 806-1550 Fax (202) 806-1777
husbdc@cldc.howard.edu

Terry Levinson
Director
U.S. Department of Energy
Inventions & Innovations
1000 Independence Ave.
EE 521, 5E052
Washington, DC 20585
(202) 586-1478 Fax (202) 586-1605

DELAWARE
David J. Freschman
President
Delaware Innovation Fund
3828 Kennett Pike #100
Wilmington, DE 19807
(302) 777-1616 Fax (302) 777-1620

Clinton Tymes
Director
Delaware SBDC Network
005 Purnell Hall
Newark, DE 19716
(302) 831-1555 Fax (302) 831-1423

FLORIDA
Doug L. Davis
Director
Bay County Incubator
2500 Minnesota Ave.
Lynn Haven, FL 32444
(904) 271-1108 Fax (904) 271-1109

Victoria H. Peake
Coordinator
Brevard Community College SBDC
3865 N. Wickham Road
Melbourne, FL 32935-2399
(407) 242-9416 Fax (407) 634-3721
peake.v@al.brevard.cc.fl.us

Marcela E. Stanislaus
VP Sm. & Mi. Bus.
Central FL Development
600 N. Broadway Avenue
Bartow, FL 33830
(941) 534-4370 Fax (941) 533-1247

Edward A. Cobham Jr.
Comm. Asst. Consult.
Department of Community Affairs
Florida Energy Office
2740 Centerview Drive
Tallahassee, FL 32399-2100
(904) 488-2475 Fax (904) 488-7688

Dr. Gary Nelson
President
Edison Inventors Association, Inc.
P.O. Box 07398
Ft. Myers, FL 33919
(941) 275-4332 Fax (941) 267-9746

Earnie DeVille
President
Emerald Coast Inventors Society
c/o UWF SBDC
11000 University
Pensacola, FL 32514-5752
(904) 474-2908 Fax (904) 474-2126
urnmani@aol.com

Scott Faris
President
Enterprise Corporation
1111 N.W. Shore Blvd., Ste 200-B
Tampa, FL 33607
(813) 288-0445 Fax (813) 554-2356

William Healy
Regional Director
FIU SBDC
46 SW 1st Avenue
Dania, FL 33004
(954) 987-0100 Fax (954) 987-0106

Director
Florida Atlantic Univ. SBDC
777 Glades Road
Boca Raton, FL 33431
(561) 362-5620 Fax (561) 362-5623

Royland Jarrett
Regional Manager
Florida Intl. Univ. SBDC
HM112A N. Miami Campus
N. Miami, FL 33181
(305) 940-5790 Fax (305) 940-5792

Doug L. Davis
Director
GCCC SBDC
2500 Minnesota Ave.
Lynn Haven, FL 32444
(904) 271-1108 Fax (904) 271-1109

Richard J. Carreno
Master Instructor
Indian River Comm. College
3209 Virginia Ave.
Fort Pierce, FL 34981
(407) 462-4756 Fax (407) 462-4830

Pamela H. Riddle
CEO
Innovative Product Technologies
4131 NW 13th Street, Ste. 220
Gainesville, FL 32609
(352) 373-1007 Fax (352) 337-0750

Frederic Bonneau
Director
Miami-Dade Comm. College
Entrepreneurial Education Center,
SBDC
6300 NW 7th Avenue
Miami, FL 33150-4322
(305) 237-1900 Fax (305) 237-1908

Radcliffe S. Weaver
President
Naples Entrepreneurial Enterprise
Development
40 9th Avenue South
Naples, FL 33940-6844
(941) 649-4094 Fax (941) 435-1718

Jerome Zajic
Tech. Spec. & PE
PSPI, Inc.
15 Dahoon Court South
Homosassa, FL 34446-8922
(352) 382-1535

Philip R. Geist
Program Manager
SBDC
110 E. Silver Springs
Ocala, FL 34470-6613
(352) 622-8763 Fax (352) 351-1031
sbdcoca@mercury.net

Patricia N. McGowan
Executive Director
SBDC
1157 E. Tennessee St.
Tallahassee, FL 32308
(904) 599-3407 Fax (904) 561-2409

Daniel V. Regelski
Cert. Bus. Analyst
SBDC
8099 College Parkway SW
Fort Meyers, FL 33919
(941) 489-9201 Fax (941) 489-9051

Raymond V. Purdy
Director
Tampa Bay Inventors Council
13543 Periwinkle Avenue
Seminole, FL 34646
(813) 391-0315

Walter B. Craft
Manager
The Univ. of West Florida SBDC
1170 MLK Jr. Blvd. 2/250
Ft. Walton Beach, FL 32547
(904) 863-6543 Fax (904) 863-6564

Martha J. Cobb
Area Manager
UWF SBDC
11000 University Bld. 8
Pensacola, FL 32514-5752
(904) 474-2908 Fax (904) 474-2126

GEORGIA

Mary-Frances Panettiere
Head, Tech. Resources
Georgia Institute of Technology
Library and Information Center
Atlanta, GA 30244-0900
(404) 894-4508 Fax (404) 894-8190

Elizabeth S. Robertson
Program Manager
Governor's Ofc. Energy Resources
100 P Street NW, Ste 2090
Atlanta, GA 30303-1911
(404) 656-3887 Fax (404) 656-7970

Alexander T. Marinaccio
Chairman
Inventors Clubs of America, Inc.
P.O. Box 450261
Atlanta, GA 31145-0261
(404) 355-1692 Fax (404) 355-8889

Ronald L. Henderson
Teamleader
U.S. Department of Energy
Atlanta Support Office
730 Peachtree St. NE, Ste 876
Atlanta, GA 30308
(404) 347-7139 Fax (404) 347-3098

Jeffrey R. Sanford
Area Director
Univ. of Georgia SBDC
1061 Katherine Street
Augusta, GA 30904-6105
(706) 737-1790 Fax (706) 731-7937
sbdcaug@uga.cc.uga.edu

Ron E. Simmons
Area Director
University of Georgia BOS
500 Jesse Jewell Pkwy., Ste 304
Gainesville, GA 30501-3773
(770) 531-5681 Fax (770) 531-5684

Lynn H. Vos
Savannah Area Director
University of Georgia
Business Outreach Services
450 Mall Blvd., Suite H
Savannah, GA 31406-4824
(912) 356-2755 Fax (912) 353-3033

Thomas Snyder
University of Georgia BOS
928 45th Street, Room 523
Columbus, GA 31904-6572
(706) 649-7433 Fax (706) 562-9645

John R. Miquelon
Business Consultant
University of Georgia BOS
P.O. Box 13212
Macon, GA 31208
(912) 751-6592 Fax (912) 751-6607
sbdcmac@uga.cc.uga.edu

HAWAII

Janice Kato
Business Devel. Mgr.
High Tech. Devel. Corp.
2800 Woodlawn Dr. #100
Honolulu, HI 96822
(808) 539-3814 Fax (808) 539-3611

Randy Gingras
Center Director
UHH SBDCN
3-1901 Kaumualii Hwy.
Lihue, HI 96766-9591
(808) 246-1748 Fax (808) 245-5102
randy@aloha.net

Darryl Mleynek
State Director
University of Hawaii at Hilo SBDC
200 W. Kawili Street
Hilo. HI 96720-4091
(808) 933-3515 Fax (808) 933-3683
darrylm@interpac.net

IOWA

Lori Harmening
Executive Director
Circle West/SBDC
P.O. Box 204
Audubon, IA 50025
(712) 563-2623 Fax (712) 563-2301

William R. Berkland
Indust. Spec. Comm.
Cntr. for Indust. Research Serv.
500 ISU Research Park
2501 N. Loop Drive
Ames, IA 50010-8286
(515) 294-3420

Ben C. Swartz
Director
Drake University SBDC
INVENTURE Program
2507 University Ave.
Des Moines, IA 50311
(515) 271-2655 Fax (515) 271-1899

Sharon Tahtinen
Executive Officer
Iowa Dept. of Natural Res.
Wallace State Office Bldg.
Des Moines, IA 50319-0001
(515) 281-7066 Fax (515) 821-6794

Steven T. Carter
Director
ISU BDC
2501 No. Loop Dr., Bldg. #1, Ste 615
Ames, IA 50010-8283
(515) 296-7828 Fax (515) 296-6714
stc@iastate.edu

Charles Tonn
Director
NE Iowa SBDC
770 Town Clock Plaza
Dubuque, IA 52001-6837
(319) 588-3350 Fax (319) 557-1591

Paul D. Heath
Director
SBDC
5160 PBAB
Iowa City, IA 52242
(319) 335-3742 Fax (319) 353-2445
paul-heath@uiowa.edu

Richard Petersen
Director
SBDC
500 College Drive
Mason City, IA 50401
(515) 422-4341 Fax (515) 422-4129

Mark Laurenzo
Bureau Chief
SBRO
Dept. of Economic Development
200 E. Grand Avenue
Des Moines, IA 50309
(515) 242-4740 Fax (515) 242-4809

Robin Travis
Director
Southwestern SBDC
1501 West Townline Road
Creston, IA 50801
(515) 782-4161 Fax (515) 782-3312

IDAHO

John Wordin
President
E. Idaho Inventors Forum
P.O. Box 452
Shelley, ID 83274-0452
(208) 346-6763 Fax (208) 346-6763

Bob Shepard
Regional Director
ID SBDC
1910 University Dr.
Boise, ID 83725
(208) 385-3875 Fax (208) 385-3877
bshepard@bsu.idbsu.edu

Gerald Fleischman
Bioenergy Specialist
Idaho Dept. of Water Resources
P.O. Box 83720
Boise, ID 83702-0098
(208) 327-7959 Fax (208) 327-7866

Rick R. Ritter
Bus. Develop. Spec.
Idaho Innovation Center
2300 N. Yellowstone
Idaho Falls, ID 83401
(208) 523-1026 Fax (208) 523-1049

James R. Steinfort
Executive Director
Idaho Manufacturing Alliance
1021 Manitou Ave.
Boise, ID 83706
(208) 385-3689 Fax (208) 385-3877

Laurence C. Bonar
Director Tech. Lic.
Idaho Research Foundation, Inc.
121 Sweet Avenue
Moscow, ID 83843-2309
(208) 885-3548 Fax (208) 882-0105

James E. Hogge
State Director
Idaho SBDC
State Office - Boise State Univ.
1910 University Drive
Boise, ID 83725
(208) 385-1640 Fax (208) 385-3877

Burt Knudson
Tech Srvcs. Consult.
Idaho SBDC
1910 University Drive
Boise, ID 83725-1655
(208) 385-3870 Fax (208) 385-3877
bknudson@bsu.idbsu.edu

Helen M. Leboef-Binninger
Regional Director
Idaho SBDC
Lewis-Clark State College
500 8th Avenue
Lewiston, ID 83501
(208) 799-2465 Fax (208) 799-2878

Mary Capps
Regional Director
Idaho State University SBDC
2300 N. Yellowstone, Ste 121
Idaho Falls, ID 83401
(208) 523-1087 Fax (208) 523-1049
cappmary@fs.isu.edu

Paul Cox
Regional Director
SBDC
1651 Alvin Ricken Dr.
Pocatello, ID 83201
(208) 232-4921 Fax (208) 233-0268

John Lynn
Regional Director
SBDC
505 W. Clearwater Loop
Post Falls, ID 83854
(208) 769-3444 Fax (208) 769-3223
jlynn@nidc.edu

ILLINOIS

Andrew Fox
Portfolio Manager
ARCH Development Corp.
1101 East 58th Street
Chicago, IL 60637
(312) 702-1692 Fax (312) 702-0741

David K. Gay
Manager
College of DuPage SBDC
22nd Street and Lambert
Glen Ellyn, IL 60137-6599
(630) 942-2771 Fax (630) 942-3789

Camilla McKinney
Manager
Decatur Industry & Technology
Center
2121 S. Imboden Court
Decatur, IL 62521
(217) 423-2832 Fax (217) 423-7214

Kriss Knowles
Small Business Spec.
Elgin Comm. College SBDC
1700 Spartan Dr.
Elgin, IL 60123-7193
(847) 888-7675 Fax (847) 931-3911

Thomas E. Parkinson
Evanston Business Inv. Co.
1840 Oak Avenue
Evanston, IL 60202
(847) 866-1817 Fax (847) 866-1808

Paul Peterson
Deputy Director
Greater North - Pulaski Dev.
4054 W. North Avenue
Chicago, IL 60639-5220
(312) 384-2262 Fax (312) 384-3850

Mindy B. Solomon
Executive Director
Illinois Recycling Association
9400 Bormet Drive, Ste 5
Mokena, IL 60448
(708) 479-3800 Fax (708) 479-4592

Jeffrey J. Mitchell Sr.
Director
Illinois SBDC
620 E. Adams Street
Springfield, IL 62701
(217) 524-5700 Fax (217) 524-0171
jeff.mitchell@accessil.com

Jim Charney
Director
Illinois SBIR Center
7500 S. Pulaski Road 200
Chicago, IL 60652
(312) 838-0319 Fax (312) 838-0303

Bruce R. Baumeister
CEO
Innovation Development Corporation
P.O. Box 1185
Calumet, IL 60409
(708) 891-0316 Fax (708) 891-0316

Don Moyer
Patent Agent
Inventors' Council
431 S. Dearborne #705
Chicago, IL 60605
(312) 939-3329 Fax (312) 922-7706

Boyd Palmer
Director
IVCC SBDC
815 N. Orlando Smith Rd.
Oglesby, IL 61348
(815) 223-1740 Fax (815) 224-3033
bpalmer@rs6000.ivcc.edu

Denise F. Mikulski
Manager
Joliet Junior College SBDC
214 N. Ottowa
Joliet, IL 60432
(815) 727-6544 Fax (815) 722-1895
dmikulsk@jjc.cc.il.us

Bob Duane
Manager
Lewis & Clark Community College
SBDC
5800 Godfrey Road
Godfrey, IL 62035
(618) 467-2370 Fax (618) 466-0810

Carson A. Gallagher
Director
Loop SBDC
100 W. Randolph St. S3-400
Chicago, IL 60601-3218
(312) 814-6111 Fax (312) 814-5247
carson.gallagher@accessil.com

Joseph R. McLennan
President
Management Association of Illinois
2809 S. 25th Avenue
Broadview, IL 60153
(708) 344-6400 Fax (708) 344-6989

Susan R. Whitfield
Director
McHenry County College SBDC
8900 US Hwy. 14
Crystal Lake, IL 60012-2761
(815) 455-6098 Fax (815) 455-9319
sue.whitfield@accessil.com

Lisa N. Payne
Director
Rend Lake College SBDC
Route 1
Ina, IL 62895
(618) 437-5321 Fax (618) 437-5353
payne@rendlake.ric.cc.il.us

Richard C. Holbrook
Director
SBDC
1840 Oak Avenue
Evanston, IL 60201
(708) 866-1817 Fax (708) 866-1808

Alan Hauff
Director
SIU - E SBDC
Campus Box 1107
Edwardsville, IL 62026-1107
(618) 692-2929 Fax (618) 692-2647

Becky Williams
Director
Southeastern IL College SBDC
303 S. Commercial
Harrisburg, IL 62946-2125
(618) 252-5001 Fax (618) 252-0210

Lynn Lindberg
Coordinator
Southern IL Mfg. Ext. Svc.
150 E. Pleasant Hill
Carbondale, IL 62901-6891
(618) 536-4451 Fax (618) 453-5040
lindberg@siu.edu

Raymond C. Lenzi
Executive Director
Southern Illinois University
Office of Econ. & Reg. Div.
Carbondale, IL 62901-6891
(618) 536-4451 Fax (618) 453-5040
lenzi@siu.edu

Sheree Kirby
Manager
Technology Commercial Lab
2004 S. Wright Street
Urbana, IL 61801
(217) 244-7742 Fax (217) 244-7757
kirby@uxl.cso.uiuc.edu

Thomas V. Thornton
President
The Illinois Coalition
100 West Randolph Street, 11-600
Chicago, IL 60601
(312) 814-3482 Fax (312) 814-4942

Melvin J. Degeeter
Director
University of Illinois
Res. & Technology Mgnt.
417 Swanlund 601 E. John
Champaign, IL 61820
(217) 333-7862 Fax (217) 244-3716

INDIANA

Adele Purlee
Executive Director
Bedford Chamber of Commerce
1116 16th Street
Bedford, IN 47421
(812) 275-4493 Fax (812) 279-5998
bedford@tima.com

Davida E. Parks
Assistant Director
BIDC - Purdue University
1220 Potter Drive
West Lafayette, IN 47906-1383
(800) 787-2432 Fax (317) 474-1352

Randall N. Redelman '
Treasurer
IN Inventors Association
P.O. Box 2388
Indianapolis, IN 46206-2388
(317) 745-5597

Robert Humbert
President
Indiana Inventors Association
5514 South Adams
Marion, IN 46953-6141
(317) 674-2845

W. Sidney Johnson
Director
Industrial Research Liaison Program
One City Center, Suite 200
Bloomington, IN 47404-3929
(800) 624-8315 Fax (812) 855-8570

Robert P. Quadrozzi
Executive Director
Jay County Development Corp.
121 West Main Street, Suite A
Portland, IN 47371
(219) 726-9311 Fax (219) 726-4477

Vivian G. Sallie
Executive Director
Minority Business Develop.
401 E. Colfax Ave., Suite 30
South Bend, IN 46634
(219) 234-0051 Fax (219) 289-0358

James W. Byrd
Executive Director
Randolph County Comm. & Econ. Dev.
P.O. Box 529
Winchester, IN 47394
(317) 584-3266 Fax (317) 584-3622

John D. Weber
Director
Regional Mfg. Ext. Center
33 South 7th Street
Richmond, IN 47374
(317) 966-3909 Fax (317) 966-0882

Julie A. Hogsett
Executive Director
Rush Co. Industrial Development Corp.
P.O. Box 156
Rushville, IN 46173-0156
(317) 932-5610 Fax (317) 932-4191

Carolyn J. Anderson
Regional Director
SBDC
300 Michigan Street
South Bend, IN 46601
(219) 282-4350 Fax (219) 236-1056

Cliff Fry
Director
SBDC
33 S. 7th Street, Suite 3
Richmond, IN 47374
(317) 962-2887 Fax (317) 966-0882

David Miller
Director
SBDC
P.O. Box 248
Bloomington, IN 47402-0248
(812) 339-8937 Fax (812) 335-7352

Patricia A. Stroud
Director
Southern Indiana SBDC
1613 E. Eight St., P.O. Box 1567
Jeffersonville, IN 47131
(812) 288-6451x160 Fax (812) 284-8327

Beth A. Clark
Coordinator
Sullivan Co. Chamber of Commerce
P.O. Box 325
Sullivan, IN 47882
(812) 268-4836 Fax (812) 268-4836

Ray E. Dickerson
Executive Director
Union Co. Development Corp.
27 West Union
Liberty, IN 47353-1349
(317) 458-5976 Fax (317) 458-5976

Bruce A. Storm
President
Wabash Area Chamber of Commerce
111 South Wabash St., P.O. Box 371
Wabash, IN 46992-0371
(219) 563-1168 Fax (219) 563-6920

William E. Bradley Jr.
Executive Director
Wabash Econ. Development Corp.
111 S. Wabash, P.O. Box 795
Wabash, IN 46992-0795
(219) 563-5258 Fax (219) 563-6920

KANSAS

Bill Sander
Regional Director
Garden City Comm. College SBDC
801 Campus Drive
Garden City, KS 67846
(316) 276-9632 Fax (316) 276-9630
sbdc@gcnet.com

Brenda I. Gallo
Senior Secretary
Johnson County Comm. College
SBDC
12345 College Blvd.
Overland Park, KS 66210-1299
(913) 469-3878 Fax (913) 469-4415

Michael F. Renk
Director
Kansas State University
2409 Scanlan
Salina, KS 67401
(913) 826-2616 Fax (913) 826-2630
mfr@mail.sal.ksu.edu

Clayton Williamson
President
Kansas Association of Inventors
1300 Kansas Avenue
Great Bend, KS 67530
(316) 793-1950 Fax (316) 793-1952

State Director
Kansas SBDC
700 SW Harrison St., Suite 1300
Topeka, KS 66603-3712
(913) 296-5298 Fax (913) 296-3490

Clyde C. Engert
Vice President Reser
KS Technology Enterprise
214 SW 6th First Floor
Topeka, KS 66603
(913) 296-3686 Fax (913) 296-1160

Fredrick H. Rice
Director
KSU SBDC
2323 Anderson, Suite 100
Manhattan, KS 66502-2912
(913) 532-5529 Fax (913) 532-5827

Kathryn S. Richard
Regional Director
SBDC, Pittsburg State University
Pittsburg, KS 66762-7560
(316) 235-4920 Fax (316) 232-6440
krichard@pittstate.edu

Tom Cornelius
Director
Seward County Comm. College
Business & Industry/Community Services
1801 N. Kansas, Box 1137
Liberal, KS 67905-1137
(316) 629-2650 Fax (316) 629-2725

Wayne Glass
Director
Washburn University SBDC
1700 College
Topeka, KS 66621
(913) 231-1010x130 Fax (913) 231-1063
zzsbdc@acc.wuacc.edu

Joann Ard
Acting Regional Director
Wichita State University SBDC
1845 Fairmount
Wichita, KS 67260-0148
(316) 689-3193 Fax (316) 689-3647

KENTUCKY
William R. Keelen
Program Manager
Center for Manufacturing
University of Kentucky
Lexington, KY 40506-0108
(606) 257-6262 Fax (606) 257-1071

Mohamed H. Nasser
Coordinator
Central KY Inventors &
Entrepreneurs Council
117 Carolyn Dr.
Nicholasville, KY 40356
(606) 885-9593 Fax (606) 887-9856

Kimberly A. Jenkins
Gen. Mgt. Consult.
Morehead/Ashland SBDC
1401 Winchester Ave., Suite 305
Ashland, KY 41101
(606) 329-8011 Fax (606) 324-4570
k.jenkins@morehead-st.edu

LouAnn Allen
Director
SBDC
238 West Dixie
Elizabethtown, KY 42701
(502) 765-6737 Fax (502) 769-5095

Richard Horn
Director
SBDC
2355 Nashville Road
Bowling Green, KY 42101-4144
(502) 745-1905 Fax (502) 745-1931
rshorn@wku.edu

Ken Blandford
Mgmt. Consultant
University of Louisville SBDC
Shelby Campus
Louisville, KY 40292
(502) 852-7854 Fax (502) 852-8573
klblan01@ulkyvm.louisville.edu

LOUISIANA

Charles D'Agostino
Executive Director
Louisiana Business Technology
Center
South Stadium Drive LSU
Baton Rouge, LA 70803
(504) 334-5555 Fax (504) 388-3975

Ronald H. Schroeder
Director
Loyola University New Orleans SBDC
College of Business Administration
6363 St. Charles Ave., Campus Box 134
New Orleans, LA 70118-6195
(504) 865-3187 Fax (504) 865-3496

Peggy Connor
Director
LSUS SBDC
One University Place
Shreveport, LA 71115-2399
(318) 797-5144 Fax (318) 797-5208
ameachum@pilot.lsus.edu

Windell Millicks
Business Resource Spec.
Macon Ridge Economic Dev.
P.O. Drawer 746
Ferriday, LA71373
(318) 757-3033 Fax (318) 757-4212

Paul Dunn
Director
NLU SBDC
700 University Avenue
Monroe, LA 71209
(318) 342-1224 Fax (318) 342-1209

Laverne Jasek
Informational
State Dept. of Economic
P.O. Box 94185
Baton Rouge, LA 70804-9185
(504) 342-5368 Fax (504) 342-5349

Thomas C. Arata
Assistant to Director
UNO SBDC
1600 Canal St., Suite 620
New Orleans, LA 70112
(504) 539-9292 Fax (504) 539-9295
unosbdc@www.gnofn.org

MASSACHUSETTS

Steven Cressy
President
Cape Cod Inventors Association
1600 Falmouth Road, Suite 123
Centerville, MA 02632
(508) 428-8792

Donald Job
President
Innovative Products Research &
Services
393 Beacon Street
Lowell, MA 01850
(978) 934-0035 Fax (978) 459-8126

Donald L. Gammon
President Emeritus
Inventors Assoc. of New England
P.O. Box 335
Lexington, MA 02173
(978) 474-0488 Fax (978) 474-0488

Robert Allen
Program Officer
U.S. Department of Energy
One Congress Street, Suite 1101
Boston, MA 02114
(617) 565-9715 Fax (617) 565-9723

MARYLAND

Lanny Herron
Lab to Mrkt. Prin.
Merrick School of Business
1420 N. Charles Street
Baltimore, MD 21201
(410) 837-5069 Fax (410) 837-5675
lherron@ubmail.ubalt.edu

Jacob Rabinow
National Institute of Standards &
Technology
Gaithersburg, MD 20899
(301) 975-5502 Fax (301) 975-3839

Jack E. Pevenstein
Engr./Outreach Coord.
Office of Technology Innovation
Natl. Inst. of Stds. & Technology
Gaithersburg, MD 20899-0001
(301) 975-5500 Fax (301) 975-3839

Robin B. Douglas
Executive Director
SBDC
3 Commerce Drive
Cumberland, MD 21502
(301) 724-6716 Fax (301) 777-7504
robindougl@metbiz.net

Mary Ann Garst
Director
SBDC
7932 Opossumtown Pike
Frederick, MD 21702
(301) 846-2683 Fax (310) 846-2689

Pam Schaller
Consultant
SBDC
Chesapeake College
Wye Mills, MD 21617
(410) 827-5286 Fax (410) 827-5286

Michael E. McCabe
Senior Evaluator
U.S. Department of Commerce
NIST
Building 820, Room 251
Gaithersburg, MD 20899
(301) 975-5517 Fax (301) 975-3839

MAINE

Cheri Cooledge
MSBDC
AVCOG
125 Manley Road
Auburn, ME 04210
(207) 783-9186 Fax (207) 783-5211

James A. Burbank
Director Bus. Assist.
Costal Enterprises
Box 268
Wiscasset, ME 04578
(207) 882-4340 Fax (207) 882-4456

Richard Angotti Jr.
President
Katahdin Regional Development
Center
P.O. Box 449
East Millinocket, ME 04430
(207) 746-5338 Fax (207) 746-9535
krdc@agate.net

James A. Burbank
Director
SBDC
P.O. Box 268, Water St.
Wiscasset, ME 04578-0268
(207) 882-4340 Fax (207) 882-4456
jab@cei.maine.com

Brian Burwell
Business Counselor
SBDC
96 Falmouth Street, P.O. Box 9300
Portland, ME 04104-9300
(207) 780-4420 Fax (207) 780-4810

James S. Ward
Dir. Indus. Coord.
University of Maine
5717 Corbett Hall
Orono, ME 04469-5717
(207) 581-1488 Fax (207) 581-1479

MICHIGAN

Dennis K. Whitney
Counselor
Business Development Center
131 South Hyne
Brighton, MI 48116
(810) 227-3556 Fax (810) 227-3080

Janet E. Masi
Vice President
Chamber of Commerce
30500 Van Dyke, Suite 118
Warren, MI 48093
(810) 751-3939 Fax (810) 751-3995
janet-masi@chambercom.com

Ram Kesavan
Director
College of Business Administration
University of Detroit Mercy
4001 W. McNichols, P.O. Box 19900
Detroit, MI 48219-0950
(313) 993-1115 Fax (313) 993-1052
kesavar@udmercy.edu

Todd J. Brian
Executive Director
Industrial Development Corp.
800 Military Street
Port Huron, MI 48060
(810) 982-9511 Fax (810) 982-9531

Carl R. Shook
Director
Kalamazoo College SBDC
1327 Academy Street
Kalamazoo MI 49001
(616) 337-7350 Fax (616) 337-7415
sbdc@kzoo.edu

Dennis K. Whitney
Director
Livingston County SBDC
131 Hyne Street
Brighton, MI 48116
(810) 227-3556 Fax (810) 227-3080

Donald L. Morandini
Director
Macomb County Business Assistance
Center
115 S. Groesbeck
Macomb, MI 48043
(810) 469-5118 Fax (810) 469-6787
bacmac@bizserve.com

Thomas Kubanek
Executive Director
Manistee County Economic
Development Office
375 River Street, Suite 205
Manistee, MI 49660
(616) 723-4325

Dani Topolski
Manager
MCIDC Genesis Center for Ent.
Devel.
111 Conant Avenue
Monroe, MI 48161
(313) 243-5947 Fax (313) 242-0009

Christine M. Greve
Regional Director
MI SBDC at SVSU
7400 Bay Road
University Center, MI 48710
(517) 790-4388 Fax (517) 790-4983
cmgreve@tarois.svsu.edu

Carol R. Lopucki
Director
Michigan SBDC
301 W. Fulton 718 S
Grand Rapids, MI 49504-6495
(616) 771-6693 Fax (616) 458-3872
lopuckic@gvsu.edu

Sarah McCue
Dir. of Publications
Michigan SBDC
2727 Second Avenue
Detroit, MI 48201
(313) 964-1798 Fax (313) 964-3648

Chuck Persenaire
Executive Director
Oceana County E.D.C.
P.O. Box 168
Hart, MI 49420-0168
(616) 873-7141 Fax (616) 873-5914

Ken Rizzio
Executive Director
Ottawa County Economic Development
Office
6676 Lake Michigan Drive
Allendale, MI 49401
(616) 892-4120 Fax (616) 895-6670

Charles S. Fitzpatrick
Director
SBDC
256 AB CMU
Mt. Pleasant, MI 48859
(517) 774-3220 Fax (517) 774-7992
34ntjen@cmuvm.csu.cmich.edu

Ed Zimmer
President
The Entrepreneur Network
1683 Plymouth Road
Ann Arbor, MI 48105-1891
(800) 468-8871 Fax (313) 663-9657

Richard J. Beldin
Executive Director
Traverse Bay Enterprise Forum
P.O. Box 506
Traverse City, MI 49685-0506
(616) 929-5017 Fax (616) 929-5012

Matthew T. Meadors
Vice President
Traverse City Chamber
P.O. Box 387
Traverse City, MI 49685-0387
(616) 947-5075 Fax (616) 946-2565

MINNESOTA

Tom Trutna
Director
Dakota Co. Technical College SBDC
1300 145th Street E.
Rosemount, MN 55068-2999
(612) 423-8262 Fax (612) 322-1501

Jim Jordan
SBDC Bus. Counselor
Hennepin Technical College
1820 Xenium Lane
Plymouth, MN 55441
(612) 550-7156 Fax (612) 550-7272

Danelle J. Wolf
Director
Hennepin Technical College SBDC
1820 N. Xenium Lane
Plymouth, MN 55441
(612) 550-7218 Fax (612) 550-7272
dwolf@henn.tec.mn.us

Frank W. Allen
Director
Icasca Development Corp.
19 NE Theid Street
Grand Rapids, MN 55744
(218) 326-9411 Fax (218) 327-2242
idcsbdc.uslink.net

Randall D. Olson
Executive Director
Minnesota Project Innovation, Inc.
111 Third Avenue South, Suite 100
Minneapolis, MN 55401-2551
(612) 338-3280 Fax (612) 338-3483

David Hepenstal
Tech. Info. Spec.
Minnesota Technology, Inc.
111 Third Avenue South, Suite 400
Minneapolis, MN 55401
(612) 338-7722 Fax (612) 339-5214

Lisa V. McGinnes
Executive Director
Owatonna Incubator
P.O. Box 505
560 Dunnell Drive, Suite 203
Owatonna, MN 55060-0505
(507) 451-0517 Fax (507) 455-2788

James L. Antilla
Director
SBDC
1515 E. 25th Street
Hibbing, MN 55746
(218) 262-6703 Fax (218) 262-6717
j.antilla.hi.cc.mn.us

Paul G. Paris
President
Society of MN Inventors
20231 Basalt Street
Anoka, MN 55303
(612) 753-2766 Fax (612) 753-2766

Andrew J. Amoroso
Econ. Develop. Spec.
U.S. Small Business Administration
610-C Butler Square
100 N. Sixth Street
Minneapolis, MN 55403-1563
(612) 370-2324 Fax (612) 370-2303

Lee Jensen
Director
UMD Center for Econ. Development
150 SBE 10 University Drive
Duluth, MN 55812-2496
(218) 726-6192 Fax (218) 726-6338
ced@d.umn.edu

Fred Amram
Professor
University of Minnesota
General College
240 Appleby Hall
Minneapolis, MN 55455
(612) 625-2531 Fax (612) 626-7848

MISSOURI

Mark Manley
Patent Agent
Center for Technology
Central MO State University
Warrensburg, MO 64093
(816) 543-4402 Fax (816) 543-8159

Ed Stout
Consultant to Board
Mid-America Inventors Association
2018 Baltimore
Kansas City, MO 64108
(816) 221-2442 Fax (816) 221-3995

Darrell R. Drammer
Technology Coord.
Missouri SBDC
CMSY Grinstead #8
Warrensburg, MO 64093-5037
(816) 543-4402 Fax (816) 543-8159

Morris R. Hudson
Program Manager
MO Procurement Assistance Center
300 University Place
Columbia, MO 65203
(573) 882-3597 Fax (573) 884-4297
mopcol@ext.missouri.edu

Glen E. Giboney
Director
SBDC
100 E. Normal
Kirksville, MO 63501
(816) 785-4307 Fax (816) 785-4357

Fred Goss
Director
Technology Search SBDC
104 Nagogami Terr UMR
Rolla, MO 65409
(573) 341-4559 Fax (573) 341-6495

Nick Arends
Business Counselor
Univ. of Missouri-Columbia SBDC
Mid-Missouri Inventor Association
1800 University Place
Columbia, MO 65211
(573) 882-7096 Fax (573) 882-9931

Paul F. Cretin
Business Specialist
University Extension
200 North Main
Rolla, MO 65401
(573) 364-3147 Fax (573) 364-0436

V. E. Lorton
Business Specialist
University Extension
1012A Thompson Blvd.
Sedalia, MO 65301
(816) 827-0591 Fax (816) 827-4888

Ray Marshall
Business Ind. Spec.
University Extension
417 E. Urbandale
Moberly, MO 65270
(816) 626-3534 Fax (816) 263-1874
marshallr@ext.missouri.edu

Rebecca L. How
University of Missouri
Business/Industry
P.O. Box 71
Union, MO 63084

Gerald G. Udell
Director
Wal-Mart Innovation Network
901 S. National
Springfield, MO 65804
(417) 836-5671 Fax (417) 836-7666

MISSISSIPPI

Robert D. Russ
Director
Copiah Lincoln Community College SBDC
11 Coin Circle
Natchez, MS 39120
(601) 445-5254 Fax (601) 446-1221

Marguerite H. Wall
Director
Hinds Community College SBDC
P.O. Box 1170
Raymond, MS 39154
(601) 857-3536 Fax (601) 857-3535

Henry C. Thomas
Director
JSU SBDC
931 Highway 80 West Box 43
Lackson, MS 39204
(601) 968-2795 Fax (601) 968-2796

Bobby Lantrip
Mgr. Tech. Services
Mississippi SBDC
216 Old Chemistry Blg.
University, MS 38677
(601) 232-5001 Fax (601) 232-5650

Robert L. Palmer
Director
Mississippi State University
Technology Transfer
P.O. Box 6156
Mississippi State, MS 39762
(601) 325-3521 Fax (601) 325-3803

Chuck Herring
Director
MS Delta Community College SBDC
P.O. Box 5607
Greenville, MS 38704-5607
(601) 378-8183 Fax (601) 378-5349

Lucy R. Betcher
Director
SBDC
136 Beach Park Place
Long Beach, MS 39560
(601) 865-4578 Fax (601) 865-4581

Dean P. Brown
Director
SBDC
P.O. Box 100
Gautier, MS 39553
(601) 497-7723 Fax (601) 497-7696

Heidi C. McDuffie
Director
SBDC
5448 US Highway 49 South
Hattiesburg, MS 39401
(601) 544-0030 Fax (601) 544-0032

Dr. William Blair
President
Society of MS Inventors
P.O. Box 13004
Jackson, MS 39236-3004
(601) 982-6229 Fax (601) 982-6610

MONTANA

Randy O. Hanson
Director
Bear Paw Development Corp.
SBDC
306 3rd Avenue, Box 170
Havre, MT 59501-0170
(406) 265-9226 Fax (406) 265-5602

Gene Marcille
Director
Commerce SBDC
1424 9th Avenue
Helena, MT 59620-0501
(406) 444-4780 Fax (406) 444-1872

Fred E. Davison
President
Creativity Innovation, Productivity, Inc.
RR#1, Box 37
Highwood, MT 59450
(406) 733-5031 Fax (406) 733-2039

Ann P. Keenan
Sr. Reg. Director
Montana Business Connections
Montana State University
Reid Hall
Bozeman, MT 59717
(406) 994-2024 Fax (406) 994-4152

John Balsam
Regional Director
Montana Business Connections:
The Entrepreneurship Center
School of Business, Univ. of Montana
Missoula, MT 59812
(406) 243-4009 Fax (406) 243-4030

Howard E. Haines
Montana Dept. of Environmental Quality
P.O. Box 200901
Helena, MT 59620-0901
(406) 444-6773 Fax (406) 444-1804

David P. Desch
Sr. Investments Mgr.
Montana Science & Tech. Alliance
1424 9th Avenue
Helena, MT 59620
(406) 444-2778 Fax (406) 444-1585

Bruce A. Hofmann
Bus. Development
Montana Tradeport Authority
2720 3rd Avenue North
Billings, MT 59101-1931
(406) 256-6871 Fax (406) 256-6877

Thomas C. McKerlick
Bus. Devel. Manager
Montana Tradeport Authority
2722 3rd Avenue North, Suite 300
Billings, MT 59101
(406) 256-6873 Fax (406) 256-6877

Roxanne L. Bunker
Director
SBDC
123 West Main
Sidney, MT 59270
(406) 482-5024 Fax (406) 482-5306

Bret George
SBDC Coordinator
WEDGO
127 N. Higgins
Missoula, MT 59802
(406) 543-3550 Fax (406) 721-4584

Warren T. George
Yellowstone Inventors
3 Carrie Lynn
Billings, MT 59102
(406) 259-9110

NORTH CAROLINA

John Hogan
Facilities Manager
First Flight Venture Center
P.O. Box 13169
Research Technical Park, NC 27709-3169
(919) 990-8558 Fax (919) 588-8802

Michael R. Twiddy
Business Counselor
NC SBTDC
Wesleyan College
3400 N. Wesleyan Blvd.
Rocky Mount, NC 27804
(919) 985-5130 Fax (919) 977-3701

Wauna L. Dooms
Director
SBTDC
Elizabeth City State University
Campus Box 874
Elizabeth City, NC 27909
(919) 335-3247 Fax (919) 335-3648

Counselor
SBTDC at UNCC
BCC at 8701 Mallard Creek Road
Charlotte, NC 28262
(704) 548-1090 Fax (704) 548-9050

NORTH DAKOTA

Bruce Gjovig
Director
Center for Innovation
Box 8372, UND Station
Grand Forks, ND 58202
(701) 777-3132 Fax (701) 777-2339

Chuck Pineo
Consultant
Center for Innovation
Box 8372
Grand Forks, ND 58202-8372
(701) 777-3132 Fax (701) 777-2339

Jan M. Peterson
Regional Director
ND SBDC
400 East Broadway Ave., Suite 416
Bismark, ND 58501-4071
(701) 223-8583 Fax (701) 255-7228
janpeter@prarie.nodak.edu

Wally Kearns
State Director
North Dakota SBDC
P.O. Box 7308
Grand Forks, ND 58202-7308
(701) 777-3700 Fax (701) 777-3225

Brian Argabright
Regional Director
SBDC
P.O. Box 940
Minot, ND 58702
(701) 852-8861 Fax (701) 838-2488
brian@minot.ndak.net

Beverly Fischer
Admin. Officer
Technology Transfer, Inc.
1833 East Bismark Expressway
Bismark, ND 58504
(701) 328-5329 Fax (701) 328-5320

NEBRASKA

Roger Reyda
President
Lincoln Inventors' Association
92 Ideal Way
Brainard, NE 68626
(402) 545-2179 Fax (402) 545-2179

Kay Payne
Director
NBDC
19th and University Drive
Kearney, NE 68849
(308) 865-8344 Fax (308) 865-8153
paynek@platte.unk.edu

Mary Woita
Asst. State Director
Nebraska Business Development
Center
1313 Farnam, Suite 132
Omaha, NE 68182-0248
(402) 595-2381 Fax (402) 595-2385

Melinda K. Cruz
Consultant
Nebraska Business Development
Center
1313 Farnam, Suite 132
Omaha, NE 68182
(402) 595-2381 Fax (402) 595-2385

Jeanne P. Eibes
Director
Nebraska Business Development
Center
Omaha Center
1313 Farnam, Suite 132
Omaha, NE 68182
(402) 595-2381 Fax (402) 595-2385
jeibes@unomaha.edu

Cliff N. Hanson
Director
Nebraska Business Development
Center
1000 Main Street
Chadron, NE 69337
(308) 432-6286 Fax (308) 432-6430
chanson@csc1.csc.edu

Herbert Hoover
Info. Specialist
University of NE-Lincoln
UN Engineering Extension
W191 Nebraska Hall
Lincoln, NE 68588-0535
(402) 472-5611 Fax (402) 472-0015

NEW HAMPSHIRE

Jon Cavicchi
IP Librarian/Lecture
Franklin Pierce Law Center
Intellectual Property Library
2 White Street
Concord, NH 03301
(603) 228-1541 Fax (603) 228-0388
jcavicchi@fplc.edu

James O'Donnell
Business Counselor
MicroEnterprise Assistance Program
P.O. Box 628, Room 325
Portsmouth, NH 03802-0628
(603) 431-2000 Fax (603) 427-1526

Gary Cloutier
Regional Manager
New Hampshire SBDC
Blake House - Keene Street
Keene, NH 03435-2101
(603) 358-2602 Fax (603) 358-2612
gc@christa.unh.edu

Janice B. Kitchen
Regional Manager
New Hampshire SBDC
MSC 24A Plymouth State College
Plymouth, NH 03264
(603) 535-2523 Fax (603) 535-2850
j.kitchen@plymouth.edu

Elizabeth Lamoreux
State Director
New Hampshire SBDC
University of New Hampshire
108 McConnell Hall
Durham, NH 03824
(603) 862-2200 Fax (603) 863-4876

Anka Verweij-Jacobs
NH SBDC ITRC
International Training
601 Spaulding Turnpike #29
Portsmouth, NH 03801
(603) 334-6074 Fax (603) 334-6110

Robert C. Wilburn
Regional Manager
SBDC
One Indian Head Plaza
Nashua, NH 03060
(603) 886-1233 Fax (603) 595-0188
sbdc-bw@mv.mv.com

NEW JERSEY

Mira Kostak
Director
Kean College SBDC
215 North Avenue
Union, NJ 07083
(908) 527-2946 Fax (908) 527-2960

Harry Roman
Vice President Prog.
NJ Inventors Congress Hall of Fame
25 Laurel Avenue
East Orange, NJ 07017-2113
(210) 430-6646 Fax (210) 504-8414

LeRoy A. Johnson
Director
SBDC
180 University Avenue - 3rd Floor
Newark, NJ 07102-1895
(201) 648-5950 Fax (201) 648-1175

NEW MEXICO

Terry R. Sullivan
Director
Dona Ana Community College SBDC
Box 30001, Dept. 3DA
Las Cruces, NM 88003
(505) 527-7601 Fax (505) 527-7515

Erich Strebe
Program Manager
Industry Network Corporation
1155 University SE
Albuquerque, NM 87106
(505) 843-4250 Fax (505) 843-4255

James M. Greenwood
Exec. Dir.
Los Alamos Economic Development Corp.
P.O. Box 715
Los Alamos, NM 87544
(505) 662-0001 Fax (505) 662-0099

Allan Gutjahr
Vice President
New Mexico Tech
Brown 200C New Mexico Tech
Socorro, NM 87801
(505) 835-5646 Fax (505) 835-5649

Lily F. Tercero
State Director
NM SBDC
P.O. Box 4187
Santa Fe, NM 87502-4187
(505) 483-1362 Fax (505) 438-1237
ltercero@santa-fe.cc.nm.us

Michael McDiarmid
Engineer
NM State Energy & Minerals
2040 South Pacheco Street
Santa Fe, NM 87505
(505) 827-5948 Fax (505) 827-5912

Susan Glenn-James
Director
SBDC
911 S. 10th Avenue
Tucumcari, NM 88401
(505) 461-4413 Fax (505) 461-1901

Clemente Sanchez
Director
SBDC
709 E. Roosevelt Avenue
Grants, NM 87020
(505) 287-8221 Fax (505) 287-2125

Cal Tingey
Director
SBDC
4601 College Blvd.
Farmington, NM 87402
(505) 599-0346 Fax (505) 599-0385

Dwight Harp
Director
SBDC at NMSUA
1000 Madison, Suite C
Alamagordo, NM 88310
(505) 434-5272 Fax (505) 434-5272
dharp@nmsua.nmsu.edu

Richard Reisinger
Dir. Product Develop.
Technology Ventures Corporation
1155 University SE
Albuquerque, NM 87106
(505) 843-4286 Fax (505) 246-2891

Ray A. Garcia
Director, SBDC
UNM Valencia Campus SBDC
280 La Entrada
Los Lunas, NM 87031
(505) 925-8980 Fax (505) 925-8981
rayg@unm.edu

NEVADA

Donald G. Costar
Editor/Spokesman
Nevada Inventors Association
P.O. Box 9905
Reno, NV 89507-0905
(702) 322-9636 Fax (702) 322-0147

Robert Holland
Bus. Develop. Spec.
Nevada SBDC
University of Nevada Las Vegas
4504 Maryland Parkway, Box 456011
Las Vegas, NV 89154-6011
(702) 895-0852 Fax (702) 895-4095
nsbdc@ccmail.nevada.edu

Sharolyn Craft
Director
Nevada SBDC
University of Nevada Las Vegas
4505 Maryland Parkway, Box 456011
Las Vegas, NV 89154-6011
(702) 895-0852 Fax (702) 895-4095

Bryan Leipper
Staff Liaison
Nevada Technology Council
4001 S. Virginia Street
Reno, NV 89502
(702) 829-9000 Fax (702) 829-9000

Nicole H. Maher
Management Consult.
SBDC
P.O. Box 820
Winnemucca, NV 89446-0820
(702) 623-1064 Fax (702) 623-5999

Thomas Gutherie
President/CEO
Southern Nevada CDC
2770 S. Maryland Parkway, Suite 212
Las Vegas, NV 89109
(702) 732-3998 Fax (702) 732-2705

Teri Williams
Executive Director
Tri-County Development
P.O. Box 820
Winnemucca, NV 89446
(702) 623-5777 Fax (702) 623-5999

NEW YORK

Jeffrey A. Kohler
Dir. of Commercial.
Aztech, Inc.
1576 Sweet Home Road
Amherst, NY 14228
(716) 636-3626 Fax (716) 636-3630

Eugene Williams
Director
Bronx - SBDC
Bronx Community College
McCracken Hall
W. 181st University Avenue
Bronx, NY 10453
(718) 563-3570 Fax (718) 563-3572

H. Walter Haeussler
President
Cornell Research Foundation, Inc.
Cornell Bus. & Tech.
20 Thornwood Drive, Suite 105
Ithaca, NY 14850
(607) 257-1081 Fax (607) 257-1015

Philip Knapp
NY Society of Professional Inventors
116 Stuart Avenue
Amityville, NY 11701
(516) 598-3228 Fax (516) 598-3241

Daniel Weiss
President
NY Society of Professional Inventors
Box 216
Farmingdale, NY 11735-9998
(516) 798-1490

Maria A. Circosta
Coordinator
NYS SBDC
555 Broadway
Dobbs Ferry, NY 10566
(914) 674-7485 Fax (914) 693-4996

Merry Gwynn
Coordinator
NYS SBDC
Clinton Community College
Platsburgh, NY 12901
(518) 562-4260 Fax (518) 563-9759

Joanne Bauman
Regional Director
SBDC
Binghampton University
Binghampton, NY 13902-6000
(607) 777-4024 Fax (607) 777-4029
sbdcbu@spectra.net

Peter J. George
SBDC
135 Western Avenue
Albany, NY 12222
(518) 442-5577 Fax (518) 442-5581

Judith M. McEvoy
Director
SBDC
State University of New York
Stony Brook, NY 11794-3775
(516) 632-9070 Fax (516) 632-7176

Joseph Schwartz
Director
SBDC
State University of Technology
Campus Commons
Farmingdale, NY 11735
(516) 420-7930 Fax (516) 293-5243
schwarjf@snyfarva.farmingdale.edu

Charles L. Van Arsdale
Executive Director
SBDC SUNY Geneseo
111 South
Geneseo, NY 14451-1485
(716) 245-5429 Fax (716) 245-5430

Thomas Reynolds
Director
SBDC Manufacturing Field Office
385 Jordan Road
Troy, NY 12180-7602
(518) 286-1014 Fax (518) 286-1006
mfo@wizvax.net

Sandra J. Bordeau
Director of Admin.
SUNY Brockport SBDC
74 N. Main Street
Brockport, NY 14428
(716) 637-6660 Fax (716) 637-2102

John Petersen
Deputy Director
The Research Foundation of SUNY
Technology Transfer
SUNY at Stony Brook
Stony Brook, NY 11794-3368
(516) 632-6955 Fax (516) 632-9839

Carol Oldenburg
Administrative Coord.
United Inventors Assoc. of the USA
P.O. Box 23447
Rochester, NY 14692-3447
(716) 359-9310 Fax (716) 359-1132

OHIO
Michael Lehere
Director
Akron Industrial Incubator
526 S. Main Street
Akron, OH 44811
(330) 375-2173 Fax (330) 762-3657

David E. Guza
Princ. Research Engineer
Battelle Memorial Institute
11-2-065
505 King Avenue
Columbus, OH 43201-2693
(614) 424-5516 Fax (614) 424-3228

Karen A. Patton
Executive Director
Enterprise Development
900 E. State Street, #101
Athens, OH 45701-2116
(614) 592-1188 Fax (614) 593-8283

Nicholas J. Cashier
Business Development
Great Lakes Industrial Technology
Business Strategy Development
25000 Great Northern Corporate
Center, Suite 260
Cleveland, OH 44070-5310
(216) 734-7553 Fax (216) 734-0686

Nicola Harmon
President
Innovation Alliance
2000 Henderson Road 140
Columbus, OH 43220
(614) 326-3822 Fax (614) 326-3824

Murray H. Henderson
President
Inventors Connection CLEY
P.O. Box 360804
Cleveland, OH 44136
(216) 226-9681

Henry B. Ferguson
Secretary/Treasurer
Inventors Council Lorian
Inventors Council of Greater Lorin
County
1101 Park Avenue
Elyria, OH 44035
(216) 322-1540

Richard A. Hagle
President
Inventors Network, Inc.
1275 Kinnear Road
Columbus, OH 43212
(614) 470-0144

Tom Farbizo
Director
Kent Tuscarawas SBDC
330 University Drive NE
New Philadelphia, OH 44663
(330) 339-9070 Fax (330) 339-2637

Nancy J. Morcher
Executive Director
London Area Chamber of Commerce
66 West High Street
London, OH 43140
(614) 852-2250 Fax (614) 852-5133

Barbara A. Harmony
Director
Mid Ohio SBDC
P.O. Box 1208
Mansfield, OH 44901
(919) 525-1614 Fax (919) 522-6811
mosbdc@rich.net

Dinah Adkins
Executive Director
National Business Incubation Association
20 E. Circle Drive, #190
Athens, OH 45701
(614) 593-4331 Fax (614) 593-1996

Joseph F. Wilson
Director
North Central SBDC
Terra Community College
2830 Napoleon Road
Fremont, OH 43420
(419) 334-8400 Fax (419) 334-9414
wilson_j@kwik.terra.cc.oh.us

Mary Ann Reis
Research Associate
Ohio Applied Tech. Transfer
1080 Carmack, Room 216
Columbus, OH 43210-1002
(614) 892-5485 Fax (614) 292-1893

Ronald L. Docie
Vice-President
Ohio Inventors Association
73 Maplewood Drive
Athens, OH 45701-1910
(614) 594-5200 Fax (614) 594-4004
docie@docie.com

Anne Blum-Hach
Director
SBDC
200 Tower City Center
Cleveland, OH 44113
(216) 621-3300 Fax (216) 621-4617

Thomas M. Farbizo
Director
SBDC
124 Chestnut Street
Coshocton, OH 43812
(614) 622-6535 Fax (614) 622-9902

Linda S. Steward
Vice President
SBDC
37 High Street
Columbus, OH 43215
(614) 225-6910 Fax (614) 469-8250

Warren Holden
Acting Executive Director
SBDC, Inc.
300 E. Auburn Avenue
Springfield, OH 45505
(513) 322-7821 Fax (513) 322-7874

Amber Wilson
Consultant
Southeast SBDC
P.O. Box 488
US Route 52 & Solida Road
South Point, OH 45680
(614) 894-3838

Bill Floretti
Director
UC SBDC
1111 Edison Drive
Cincinatti, OH 45216-2265
(513) 948-2081 Fax (513) 948-2007

Thomas A. Knapke
Director
Wright State University SBDC
Lake Campus
7600 State Route 703
Celina, OH 45822
(419) 586-3055 Fax (419) 586-0358
sbdc@lady.lake.wright.edu

OKLAHOMA

Bill Gregory
Coordinator
Inventors Resource Center
100 S. University Avenue
Enid, OK 73701
(405) 242-7989 Fax (405) 242-7989

Kenneth F. Addison Jr.
President
Oklahoma Inventors Congress
P.O. Box 27850
Tulsa, OK 74149-0850
(918) 245-6465 Fax (918) 245-2947

Danielle Coursey
Bus. Devel. Spec.
Oklahoma SBDC
309 N. Muskogee Avenue
Tahlequah, OK 74464-2399
(918) 458-0802 Fax (918) 458-2105

Bill W. Gregory
Coordinator
Oklahoma SBDC
100 S. University Bldgs.
Enid, OK 73701
(405) 242-7989 Fax (405) 242-7989

Alan H. Simon
Bus. Devel. Spec.
Oklahoma SBDC
215 I Street NE
Miami, OK 74354
(918) 540-0575 Fax (918) 540-0575

Susan Urbach
Regional Director
SBDC
115 Park Avenue
Oklahoma City, OK 73102-9005
(405) 232-1968 Fax (405) 232-1967
sbdc@aix1.ucok.edu

Dale A. Davis
President
Week-End Entrepreneurs
12516 E. 37th Street
Tulsa, OK 74146-3719
(918) 664-5831 Fax (918) 664-5831

OREGON

Robert L. Newhart II
Director
Central Oregon Community College BDC
2600 NW College Way
Bend, OR 97701-5998
(503) 383-7290 Fax (503) 383-7503
newhart@metolius.cocc.edu

Phil Goodenough
Counselor
Chmeketa SBDC
365 Ferry Street SE
Salem, OR 97301-3622
(503) 399-5088 Fax (503) 581-6017
philg@chemek.cc.or.us

John Prosnik
Director
Eastern Oregon State College SBDC
1410 L Avenue
La Grande, OR 97850-2899
(541) 962-3895 Fax (541) 962-3668
prosnij@eosc.osshe.edu

Bill Nasset
Public Info. Provider
Little Inventor Association
3923 Lancaster Drive NE
Salem, OR 97305
(503) 391-4464 Fax (503) 391-4887
patwiz@inventorworld.com
Web Page: inventorworld.com

Robert L. Newhart II
Acting CEO
Oregon Innovation Center
P.O. Box 1510
Redmond, OR 97756
(541) 383-7299 Fax (541) 317-0265
oic@cocc.edu

John A. Beaulieu
President
Oregon Resource and Technology
Development Fund
4370 NE Halsey Street
Portland, OR 97213-1566
(503) 282-4462 Fax (503) 282-2976

Nancy Hudson
Counselor
SBDC
332 W. 6th Street
Medford, OR 97501
(541) 772-3478 Fax (541) 734-4813

Jan S. Stennick
Director
SBDC
7616 SE Harmony
Milwaukie, OR 97222
(503) 656-4447 Fax (503) 652-0389

Gerald E. Wood
Director
SBDC
37 SE Dorion
Pendleton, OR 97801
(541) 276-6233 Fax (541) 276-6819

Nancy L. Hudson
SBDC Counselor
Southern OR Inventors Council
332 W. 6th
Medford, OR 97501
(541) 772-3478 Fax (541) 734-4813

Jon Richards
Director
Southwestern Oregon Community
College SBDC
340 Central
Coos Bay, OR 97420
(541) 269-0123 Fax (541) 269-0323
jrichards@oretel.org

Kathleen A. Simko
Director
TVCC SBDC
88 SW 3rd Avenue
Ontario, OR 97914
(541) 889-2617 Fax (541) 889-8331

PENNSYLVANIA

Jay W. Cohen
President
American Society of Inventors
P.O. Box 58426
Philadelphia, PA 19102
(215) 546-6601

Mary T. McKinney, PhD
Director
Duquesne University SBDC
Rockwell Hall
600 Forbes
Pittsburgh, PA 15282
(412) 396-6233 Fax (412) 396-5884
duqsbdc@duq.edu

Bruce M. Smackey
Lehigh University
Technology Commercialization
621 Taylor Street
Bethlehem, PA 18015-3117
(610) 758-3446 Fax (610) 758-5865

Charles W. Duryea, Sr.
Director
Pennsylvania Inventors Association
10819 Wales Road
Erie, PA 16510
(814) 739-2928 Fax (814) 489-3572

Gregory L. Higgins, Jr.
State Director
Pennsylvania SBDC
Vance Hall, 4th Floor, 3733 Spruce St.
Philadelphia, PA 19104-6374
(215) 898-1219 Fax (215) 573-2135
pasbdc@wharton.upcnn.edu

Elaine M. Tweedy
Director
SBDC
800 Linden Street
Scranton, PA 18510-4639
(717) 941-7588 Fax (717) 941-4053
tweedye1@uofs.edu

Geraldine A. Perkins
Director
Temple SBDC
Room 6 Speakman Hall
Philadelphia, PA 19122
(215) 204-7282 Fax (215) 204-4554
perkins@sbm.temple.edu

Robert S. Krutsick
Exec. Vice President
University City Science Center
3624 Market Street
Philadelphia, PA 19104-2614
(215) 387-2255 Fax (215) 382-0056

Ann Dugan
Director
University of Pittsburgh SBDC
208 Bellefield Hall
Pittsburgh, PA 15213
(412) 648-1544 Fax (412) 648-1636

Ruth Hughes
Business Consultant
Wilkes University SBDC
192 South Franklin Street
Wilkesbarr, PA 18766
(717) 831-4340 Fax (717) 824-2245
sbdc@wilkes.edu

RHODE ISLAND

Claudia Terra
Executive Director
Rhode Island Partnership for
Science & Technology
One West Exchange Street
Providence, RI 02903
(401) 277-2601 Fax (401) 277-2102

Domenic Bucci
President
Rhode Island Solar Energy Assoc.
42 Tremont Street
Cranston, RI 02920-2543
(401) 942-6691

Samuel F. Carr
Manager, E. Bay Ofc.
RI SBDC
45 Valley Road
Middletown, RI 02842
(401) 849-6900 Fax (401) 849-5848

Janice McClanaghan
Energy Program Manager
RI State Energy Office
275 Westminster Street
Providence, RI 02907
(401) 277-3370 Fax (401) 277-1260

SOUTH CAROLINA

Johnny Sheppard
President
Carolina Inventors Council
2960 Dacusville Highway
Easley, SC 29640
(803) 859-0066

George L. Long
Area Manager
Clemson University SBDC
P.O. Box 1366
Greenwood, SC 29648-1366
(864) 941-8071 Fax (864) 941-8090
glong@sisn.com

Jackie W. Moore
Area Manager
SBDC
171 University Parkway
Aiken, SC 29801-6309
(803) 641-3646 Fax (803) 641-3647
jackiem@aiken.sc.edu

Matt L. Scarborough
Area Manager
SBDC
School of Business
Coastal Carolina University
Conway, SC 29526
(803) 349-2169 Fax (803) 349-2455
matthew@coastal.edu

John W. Gadson, Sr.
Director
South Carolina State University SBDC
P.O. Box Campus - 7176
Orangeburg, SC 29117
(803) 536-8445 Fax (803) 536-8066

Judy Clements
Manager
University of South Carolina/Aiken
Private Investor Network
171 University Parkway
Aiken, SC 29801
(803) 641-3518 Fax (803) 641-3362

Merry S. Boone
Area Manager
USC SBDC
5900 Core Drive, #104
W. Charleston, SC 29406
(803) 740-6160 Fax (803) 740-1607
sbdc1@infoave.net

SOUTH DAKOTA

Bryce K. Anderson
Regional Director
S. Dakota SBDC
620 15th Avenue SE
Aberdeen, SD 57401-7610
(605) 626-2565 Fax (605) 626-2667
andersob@wolf.northern.edu

Valerie S. Simpson
Regional Director
SBDC
444 N. Mt. Rushmore Road, #208
Rapid City, SD 57701
(605) 394-5311 Fax (605) 394-6140

Robert J. Knecht
Chairman
SCORE
P.O. Box 747
Rapid City, SD 57709-0747
(605) 341-9007

Steven M. Wegman
SD Public Utilities Comm.
State Capitol Bldg.
Pierce, SD 57501
(605) 773-3201 Fax (605) 773-3809

Kent W. Rufer
Program Manager
South Dakota State University
Box 2220, Harding Hall
Brookings, SD 57007-0199
(605) 688-4184 Fax (605) 688-5880

TENNESSEE

David G. Beall
President
Innovative Ventures Corporation
1055 Commerce Park Drive
Oak Ridge, TN 37830
(615) 483-5060 Fax (615) 483-3938

Robert B. Braid
Senior Scientist
Oak Ridge National Lab
Energy Related Inventions Program
P.O. Box 2008, 4500 N Mail Stop 6205
Oak Ridge, TN 37830-6205
(423) 576-7071 Fax (423) 574-8884

Joseph R. Schultz
Executive Director
Rivervalley Partners, Inc.
835 Georgia Avenue, Suite 800
Chattanooga, TN 37402
(423) 265-3700 Fax (423) 265-7924

Teri T. Brahams
Director
SBDC
301 East Church Avenue
Knoxville, TN 37915
(423) 525-0277 Fax (423) 971-4439
tbrahams@pstcc.cc.tn.us

Robert Lytle
Business Counselor
SBDC
1501 University Blvd.
Kingsport, TN 37660
(423) 392-8017 Fax (423) 392-8017

Donna G. Marsh
Small Business Specialist
SBDC
100 Cherokee Blvd., Suite 202
Chattanooga, TN 37405
(423) 753-1774 Fax (423) 752-1925

John X. Volker
Director
SBDC
P.O. Box 4775 APSU
Clarksville, TN 37044
(615) 648-7764 Fax (615) 648-5985
volkerj@apsu0s.apsu.edu

Robert A. Justice
Director
TN SBDC
East TN State University
P.O. Box 70698
Johnson City, TN 37614-0698
(423) 929-5630 Fax (423) 461-7080
justiceb@etsu-tn.edu

Sharon Taylor McKinney
Small Business Specialist
TN SBDC
320 South Dudley Street
Memphis, TN 38104
(901) 527-1041 Fax (901) 527-1047

Dorothy A. Vaden
Business Specialist
TN SBDC
P.O. Box 63
Hartsville, TN 37074
(615) 374-9521 Fax (615) 374-4608

Janis Elsner
Associate Director
Vanderbilt University
Office of Technology Transfer
405 Kirkland Hall
Nashville, TN 37240
(615) 343-2430 Fax (615) 343-0488

TEXAS
Worth Hefley
President
Amarillo Inventors Association
P.O. Box 15023
Amarillo, TX 79105
(806) 376-8726 Fax (806) 376-7753

Thomas J. Stephenson
Director of Edu.
Austin Technology Incubator
3925 West Braker Lane, Suite 400
Austin, TX 78759-5321
(512) 305-0000 Fax (512) 305-0009

Samuel A. Harwell
Director
Brazos Valley SBDC
4001 East 29th
Bryan, TX 77802
(409) 260-5222 Fax (409) 260-5229
sam@bvsbdc

Charles Mullen
Chairman
Houston Inventors Association
204 Yacht Club Lane
Seabrook, TX 77586
(713) 326-1795 Fax (713) 326-1795

Tim Bigham
Principle Researcher
Information Insights
906 Stillhouse Spring
Round Rock, TX 78681
(512) 246-7040 Fax (512) 451-1885

Beth S. Huddleston
Director
International SBDC
Box 580299
Dallas, TX 75258
(214) 747-1300 Fax (214) 748-5774

Timothy L. Thomas
Director
MSU SBDC
3410 Taft
Wichita Falls, TX 76308
(817) 689-4373 Fax (817) 689-4374

Wessie Cramer
Executive Director
Network of American Inventors &
Entrepreneurs
11371 Walters Road
Houston, TX 77007-2615
(713) 537-8277 Fax (713) 537-1548

Ray Bell
Technology Counselor
SBDC
1500 Houston Street
Fort Worth, TX 76102
(817) 871-6028 Fax (817) 336-5086

Pat Bell
Director
SBDC
2400 Clarksville Street
Paris, TX 75460
(903) 784-1802 Fax (903) 784-1801
pssbdc@stargate.istarnet.com

Donna Dulfer
Acting Director
SBDC
3110 Mustang Road
Alvin, TX 77511
(713) 388-4686 Fax (713) 388-4903

Chris Jones
Director
SBDC
4800 Preston Park Blvd., Box 15
Plano, TX 75243
(214) 985-3770 Fax (214) 985-3775

Catherine J. Keeler
Director
SBDC
1525 W. California
Gainesville, TX 76240
(817) 668-4220

Karl V. Painter
Director
SBDC
4901 E. University
Odessa, TX 79762
(915) 552-2455 Fax (915) 552-2433
evans_c@utpb.edu

Howard N. Sheward
Director
SBDC
250 N. Sam Houston Parkway
Houston, TX 77060
(713) 591-9373 Fax (713) 591-9324

Elizabeth Soliz
Director
SBDC
635 East King
Kingsville, TX 78863
(512) 595-5088 Fax (512) 592-0866

Frank X. Viso
Director
SBDC
1530 SSW Loop 323, Suite 100
Tyler, TX 75701
(903) 510-2975 Fax (903) 510-2978
fviso@tyler.net

Mrs. Eloyd Murphy
President
Texas Inventors Association
4000 Rock Creek Drive, #100
Dallas, TX 75204-1626
(817) 265-1540 Fax (214) 526-6725

Daniel Altman
Field Engineer
Texas Manufacturing Assistance Center
Gulf Coast
1100 Louisiana Street
Houston, TX 77002
(713) 752-8434 Fax (713) 756-1515

Al E. Sammann
Director
Texas Tech. University SBDC
2579 S. Loop 289
Lubbock, TX 79423
(806) 745-3973 Fax (806) 745-6207

David Gerhardt
Executive Director
The Capital Network
3925 W. Braker Lane, #406
Austin, TX 78759
(512) 305-0826 Fax (512) 305-0836

Jill Fabricant, PhD
Director
The Enterprise Center
2200 Space Park Drive
Houston, TX 77058
(713) 335-1250 Fax (713) 333-9285

Roy Serpa
Region Director
TMAC Gulf Coast
1100 Louisiana, #500
Houston, TX 77002
(713) 752-8440 Fax (713) 756-1515
royserpa@uh.edu

Mike Young
Director Lead Center
UH SBDC
1100 Louisiana, Suite 500
Houston, TX 77502-5211
(713) 752-8400 Fax (713) 756-1515

David I. Armstrong
Director
UT Pan American SBDC
1201 W. University
Edinburgh, TX 78540
(210) 381-3361 Fax (210) 381-2322
armstrong@panam.edu

Morrison Woods
Director
UTSA SBDC
1222 N. Main, Suite 450
San Antonio, TX 78212
(210) 558-2460 Fax (210) 558-2464

Judith Ingalls
Director
UTSA SBDC Technology Center
1222 N. Main, Suite 450
San Antonio, TX 78212
(210) 558-2458 Fax (210) 558-2464

UTAH

Karen Gudmundson
Marketing Director
CEDO
777 S. State Street
Orem, UT 84058
(801) 226-1521 Fax (801) 226-2678

David Morrison
Patent & Trademark Librar.
Documents Division, Marriott Library
University of Utah
Salt Lake City, UT 84112
(801) 581-8394 Fax (801) 585-3464

John Winder
President
Intermountain Society of Inventors
& Designers
9888 Darin Drive
Sandy, UT 84070
(801) 571-2617

Rod J. Linton
Director
Office of Technology Development
324 S. State Street, Suite 500
Salt Lake City, UT 84111
(801) 538-8770 Fax (801) 538-8773

Barry L. Bartlett
Director
SBDC
Salt Lake City Community College
8811 South 700 East
Sandy, UT 84070
(801) 255-5878 Fax (801) 255-6393
bartleba@slcc.edu

Derek Snow
Director
SBDC
351 West Center
Cedar City, UT 84720
(801) 586-5400 Fax (801) 586-5493

Denise E. Beaudoin
Info. Specialist
State of Utah
Office of Energy Services
324 South State, Suite 230
Salt Lake City, UT 84111
(801) 538-8690 Fax (801) 538-8660

Josie Valdez
Asst. District Dir.
US Small Business Administration
125 South State Street
Salt Lake City, UT 84101
(801) 524-3210 Fax (801) 524-5604

Peter R. Genereaux
Utah Info. Technologies Assoc.
6995 Union Park Center, Suite 490
Midvale, UT 84047
(801) 568-3500 Fax (801) 568-1072

Bruce Davis
Director
Weber State University SBDC
3815 University Circle
Ogden, UT 84408-3815
(801) 626-6070 Fax (801) 626-7423
brdavis@weber.edu

VIRGINIA

Martha Morales
Associate Executive Director
AIPLA
2001 Jefferson Davis Highway, Suite 203
Arlington, VA 22202
(703) 415-0780 Fax (703) 415-0786

Deirdre Le
Secretary
Association of SBDC's
1300 Chain Bridge Road, Suite 201
McLean, VA 22101-3967
(703) 448-6124 Fax (703) 448-6125

Taylor K. Cousins
Executive Director
Capitol Area SBDC
One N. Fifth Street
Richmond, VA 23219
(804) 648-7838 Fax (804) 648-7849

Phillip Shaw
President
Capitol Inventors Society
3212 Old Dominion Blvd.
Alexandria, VA 22305
(703) 739-0868

Cathy Renault
Managing Director
Center for Innovative Technology
2214 Rock Hill Road
Herndon, VA 22070
(703) 689-3000 Fax (703) 689-3041

William J. Martin
Financial Specialist
EREC Energy Efficiency
Renewable Energy Clearinghouse
P.O. Box 3048
Merrifield, VA 22116
(800) 363-3732 Fax (703) 893-0400

Paul G. Hall
Director
Geo Mason University SBDC
3401 N. Fairfax Drive
Arlington, VA 22201
(703) 993-8129 Fax (703) 993-8130
phall@osfi.gmu.edu

Julie Janoski
Director
George Mason University SBDC
4031 University Drive
Fairfax, VA 22030-3409
(703) 277-7700 Fax (703) 277-7722

Roger Crosen
Coordinator
Lord Fairfax SBDC
P.O. Box 47
Middletown, VA 22645
(540) 869-6649 Fax (540) 868-7002

Tim B. Blankenbecler
Director
Mountain Empire Community College
SBDC
P.O. Drawer 700, Rt. 23 S.
Big Stone, VA 24219
(540) 523-6529 Fax (540) 523-8139

Joy L. Bryant
President
NAPP
435-2 Oriana, Box 215
Newport News, VA 23608
(800) 216-9588 Fax (804) 874-6278

Sally Rood
Associate Director
National Technology Transfer Center
Wheeling Jesuit College
2121 Eisenhower Ave., Suite 400
Alexandria, VA 22314
(703) 518-8800 Fax (703) 518-8986

David O. Shanks
Director
NRV SBDC
600 H. Norwood Street
Radford, VA 24141
(540) 831-6056 Fax (540) 831-6057
dshanks@runet.edu

Donald Kelly
Director
Patent & Trademark Office
U.S. Department of Commerce
P.O. Box 2863
Arlington, VA 22202
(703) 308-0975 Fax (703) 305-3463

James B. Boyd
Director
SVCC SBDC
Richlands, VA 24641
(540) 964-7345 Fax (540) 964-5788
jim_boyd@sw.cc.us

Robert A. Hamilton
Director
SBDC
918 Emmet Street North, Suite 200
Charlottesville, VA 22903-4878
(804) 295-8198 Fax (804) 295-7066
hamilton@sbdc.acs.virginia.edu

William J. Holloran, Jr.
Sr. Vice President
SBDC
525 Butler Farm Road
Hampton, VA 29670
(804) 825-2957 Fax (804) 825-2960

Wanda Hylton
Conference Coordinator
Virginia Tech. Graduate Center
2990 Telestar Court
Falls Church, VA 22042
(703) 698-6016 Fax (703) 698-6062

Rob Edwards
Director
Wytheville Community College SBDC
1000 East Rain Street
Wytheville, VA 24382
(540) 223-4798 Fax (540) 223-4716

VERMONT
James B. Stewart
Executive Director
Addison Co. Econ. Develop. Corp.
RR 4, Box 1309A
Middlebury, VT 05753-8626
(802) 388-7953 Fax (802) 388-0119

Samiko A. Cartin
SBDC
P.O. Box 455
Morrisville, VT 05661
(802) 888-5640 Fax (802) 888-7612

Area Specialist
Vermont SBDC
256 North Main Street
Rutland, VT 05701-2413
(802) 773-9147 Fax (802) 773-2772

Don Kelpinski
State Director
Vermont SBDC
P.O. Box 422
Randolph, VT 05060-0422
(802) 728-9101 Fax (802) 728-3026

WASHINGTON
Edmund F. Baroch
Business Specialist
Big Bend Community College
Business Development Center
7662 Chanute Street
Moses Lake, WA 98837
(509) 762-6289 Fax (509) 762-6329

Glynn Lamberson
Director
Columbia Basin College SBDC
901 N. Colorado
Kennewick, WA 99336
(509) 735-6222 Fax (509) 735-6609

Jack A. Wicks
Director
Edmonds Community College SBDC
20000 68th Avenue West
Lynnwood, WA 98036
(206) 640-1435 Fax (206) 640-1532
jwicks@edcc.ctc.edu

Jeevan Rego
Innov./Tech. Specialist
Innovation Assessment Center
WSU SBDC
501 Johnson Tower
Pullman, WA 99164-4851
(509) 335-7869 Fax (509) 935-0949

Barbara Campbell
Director NW Office
NASA - Far West RTTC
12318 NE 100th Place
Kirkland, WA 98033
(206) 827-5136 Fax (206) 827-5430

Ann Tamura
Export Devel. Spec.
North Seattle Community College
SBDC
2001 6th Ave., Ste 650, Westin Bldg.
Seattle, WA 98121
(206) 553-0052 Fax (206) 553-7253
atamura@doe.gov

Marvin Clement
Manager
Pacific Northwest National Laboratory
Entrepreneurial Pgms. Econ. Dvl. Ofc.
ORTA
P.O. Box 999 MSIN K9-87
Richland, WA 99352
(509) 375-2789 Fax (509) 375-6731

Janet A. Harte
Business Development Specialist
SBDC
Washington State University - Vancouver
217 SE 136 Ave., Suite 105
Vancouver, WA 98684-6929
(360) 693-2555
harte@vancouver.wsu.edu

Richard Monacelli
Business Development Specialist
SBDC
500 Tausick Way
Walla Walla, WA 99362
(509) 527-4681 Fax (509) 525-3101

Lynn Trzynka
Director
SBDC
Western Washington University
College of Business and Economics
Bellingham, WA 98225-9073
(360) 650-3899 Fax (360) 650-4844
trzynka@cbe.wwu.edu

Terry Chambers
Group Coordinator
SIRTI
665 N. Riverpoint Blvd.
Spokane, WA 99202-1665
(509) 358-2042 Fax (509) 358-2019
terryc@sirti.org

John J. Ryan
Group Coordinator
Spokane Intercollegiate Research &
Technology Institute (SIRTI)
665 N. Riverpoint Blvd.
Spokane, WA 99202-1665
(509) 358-2023 Fax (509) 358-2019

Dr. Norman Brown
President
Technology Targeting, Inc.
4579 144th Avenue SE
Bellevue, WA 98006
(206) 603-1940 Fax (206) 603-1972

Laura L. Dorsey
Marketing Manager
The Washington Technology Center
Box 352140
Seattle, WA 98195-2140
(206) 685-1920 Fax (206) 543-3059

Ray K. Robinson
Chairman
Tri-Cities Commercialization Partnership
200 Hillview Drive, Suite 100
Richland, WA 99352
(509) 627-6135 Fax (509) 627-6141

Johan Curtiss
Tech. Assit. Mngr.
Tri-Cities Enterprise Association
2000 Logston Blvd.
Richland, WA 99352
(509) 375-3268 Fax (509) 375-4838
jcurtiss@owt.com

Susan Sande
Resource Center Manager
Tri-Cities Enterprise Association
2000 Logston Blvd.
Richland, WA 99352
(509) 375-3268 Fax (509) 375-4838
erc@owt.com

Stuart R. Leidner
Coord. Innov. & Rsrc.
Washington SBDC
Washington State University
501 Johnson Tower
Pullman, WA 99164-4851
(509) 335-1576 Fax (509) 335-0949

Neil Delisanti
Business Development Specialist
Washington State University SBDC
950 Pacific Avenue, Suite 300
Tacoma, WA 98402
(206) 272-7232 Fax (206) 597-7305

LoAnn Ayers
Mgr. Admin. & Plng.
Washington State University - Tri-Cities
100 Sprout
Richland, WA 99352
(509) 372-7252 Fax (509) 372-7100
ayers@beta.tricity.wsu.edu

Steven Loyd
Chairman
Western Investment Network
411 University St. #1200
Seattle, WA 98101
(206) 441-3123 Fax (206) 463-6386

Corey Hansen
Business Development Specialist
Yakima Valley Community College SBDC
P.O. Box 1647
Yakima, WA 98907-1647
(509) 575-2284 Fax (509) 454-4155
yvccsbdc@televar.com

WISCONSIN
Louie M. Rech
Tech. Devel. Coord.
Technology Deployment Fund
Wisconsin Dept. of Development
P.O. Box 7970
Madison, WI 53707-7970
(608) 267-9382 Fax (608) 267-0436

Carla Lenk
Director
UW - Whitewater SBDC
Room 2000 Carlson Hall
Whitewater, WI 53190-1790
(414) 472-3217 Fax (414) 472-5692
lenk@uwwvax.uww.edu

Debra Malewicki
Director
Wisconsin Innovation Service Center
UW - Whitewater
402 McCutchan Hall
Whitewater, WI 53190
(414) 472-1365 Fax (414) 472-1600

Milissa E. Guenterberg
Research Manager
Wisconsin Innovation Service Center
402 McCutchan Hall
Whitewater, WI 53190
(414) 472-1365 Fax (414) 472-1600

WEST VIRGINIA
Daniel Tryon
Manager
Discovery Lab
W.V.U.
P.O. Box 6107
Morgantown, WV 26506-6101
(304) 293-3612 Fax (304) 293-3472

Dale Bradley
Program Director
Fairmont State College SBDC
1201 Locust Avenue
Fairmont, WV 26554
(304) 367-4125 Fax (304) 366-4870

Kenneth S. Peters
Program Manager
SBDC
P.O. Box AG
Beckley, WV 25802-2830
(304) 255-4022 Fax (304) 252-9584
sbdc@cwv.edu

James R. Martin
Business Analyst
SBDC / Elkins
10 Eleventh Street, Suite 1
Elkins, WV 26241
(304) 637-7205 Fax (304) 637-4902
jrjm@access.mountain.net

James E. Epling
Program Director
W. Virginia Institute of Technology SBDC
Engineering Building Room 102
Montgomery, WV 25136
(304) 442-5501 Fax (304) 442-3307
jepling@olie.wvitcoe.wvnet.edu

Edward R. Huttenhower
Director
W. Virginia Northern Community College
SBDC
1704 Market Street
Wheeling WV 26003
(304) 233-5900 Fax (304) 232-0965
ehuttenhower@nccvax.wvnet.edu

Hazel K. Palmer
Director
West Virginia SBDC
950 Kanawha Avenue SE
Charleston, WV 25301
(304) 558-2960 Fax (304) 558-0127
palmerh@mail.wvnet.edu

Gregory A. Hill
Director
WVU-P SBDC
Route 5, Box 167A
Parkersburg, WV 26101
(304) 424-8277 Fax (304) 424-8315

WYOMING

Larry Stewart
Regional Director
Mid-America Mfg. Tech. Center
P.O. Box 3362 Univ. Station
Laramie, WY 82071-3362
(307) 766-4811 Fax (307) 766-4818
lstewart@uwyo.edu

Kay Stucker
U.S. Small Business Administration
P.O. Box 2839
Casper, WY 82602-2839
(307) 261-6500 Fax (307) 261-6535

Leonard Holler
Director
WSBDC
111 West 2nd, Suite 502
Casper, WY 82601
(307) 234-6683 Fax (307) 577-7014

Bill Ellis
Region 1 Director
Wyoming SBDC
P.O. Box 1168
Rock Spring, WY 82902-1168
(307) 352-6894 Fax (307) 352-6876

Dwayne Heintz
Regional Director
Wyoming SBDC
Box 852
Powell, WY 82435
(307) 754-2139 Fax (307) 754-0368
nwwsbdc@wave.park.wy.us

Arlene M. Soto
Region 4 Director
Wyoming SBDC
1400 E. College Drive
Cheyenne, WY 82007-3298
(307) 632-6141 Fax (307) 632-6061
sewsbdc@wyoming.com

Diane Wolverton
State Director
Wyoming SBDC
Box 3922
Laramie, WY 82071-3922
(307) 766-3505 Fax (307) 766-3406
ddw@uwyo.edu

FOREIGN COUNTRIES

JoAnn M. Robertson
President
B.C. Inventors Society
P.O. Box 5086
Vancouver, BC, Canada V6B 4A9
(604) 877-1871

Bob Huehn
Senior Analyst
Canadian Industrial Innovation Centre
156 Columbia Street West
Waterloo, Ontario, Canada N2L3L3
(519) 988-5870 Fax (519) 885-5729

Chris Webb
Chairperson
Canadian Young Inventors' Fair Society
c/o Box 12151
1220 - 808 Nelson Street
Vancouver, BC, Canada V6Z 2H2
(604) 689-3626 Fax (604) 684-4589

Vince Kehoe
Executive Vice President
CIPAC
1518 333 7 Avenue SW
Calgary, Alberta, Canada T2P 2Z1
(403) 265-3011 Fax (403) 266-4091

Alex Zodiacal
Business Development Specialist
Economic Development Planning Office
American Samoa Government
Pago Pago, American Samoa 96799
(684) 633-5155 Fax (684) 633-4195

Victor Davila Sola
Patents Coordinator
Economic Development Administration
P.O. Box 362350
San Juan, Puerto Rico 00936-2350
(787) 765-7171 Fax (787) 765-0285

Chris Webb
Publisher
IDEAS Digest Newsmagazine
Box 12151 1220 - 808 Nelson Street
Vancouver, BC, Canada V6Z 2H2
(604) 689-3626 Fax (604) 684-4589

Pedro G. Cruz Sanchez
Executive Director
INDUNIV
P.O. Box 364984
San Juan, Puerto Rico 00936-4984
(809) 250-0000 Fax (809) 735-7355

Farag Moussa
President
International Federation of Inventors
Association (IFIA)
IFIA 3 Bellot
Geneva, CH, Switzerland 1206
41227893074 Fax 41227893076

Mark Ellwood
President
Inventors' Alliance of Canada
47 Kenneth Avenue
Toronto, Ontario, Canada M6P 1J1
(416) 762-3453 Fax (416) 762-3301

Boris Plahteanu
Prof PhD
National Inventics Institute of Jassy
Bld. Copou 3-5, P.O. Box 727
lasi-3, Romania RO-6600
(403) 221-4764 Fax (403) 221-4763
bplaht@ini.tuiasi.ro

Stephen Guerin
Industrial Tech. Adv.
NRC - IRAP
c/o Design Exchange
234 Bay Street
Toronto, Ontario, Canada M5K 1B2
(416) 216-2104 Fax (416) 368-0684

Rene Batiz-Ortiz
Director
Puerto Rico SBDC
UPR Ponce Box 7186
Ponce, Puerto Rico 00732
(787) 841-2641 Fax (787) 844-0883

Marian Diaz
Director
Puerto Rico SBDC
P.O. Box 5253 College Station
Mayaguez, Puerto Rico 00681-5253
(787) 834-3590 Fax (787) 834-3790

Jorge Hernandez
State Director
Puerto Rico SBDC
P.O. Box 364984
San Juan, Puerto Rico 00936-4983
(787) 250-0000 Fax (787) 282-6882

Chester Williams
State Director
SBDC, Univ. of the VI
Nisky Center, Suite 202
St. Thomas, Virgin Islands 00802-5804
(809) 776-3206 Fax (809) 775-3756

John Fraser
Director
University/Industry Liaison
Simon Fraser University
Burnby, BC, Canada V5A 1S6
(604) 291-4292 Fax (604) 291-3477

Susan Best
Co-Director
Women Inventors Project
1 Greensboro Dr., Suite 302
Etobicoke, Ontario, Canada M9W1C8
(416) 243-0668 Fax (416) 243-0688

APPENDIX 3

Patent and Trademark Depository Library List

The following list of libraries scattered throughout the United States have been designated as Patent and Trademark Depository Libraries (PTDL). The general public may use these library resources to perform preliminary patent searches, examine patents or conduct other patent- and trademark-related research. As well as maintaining patent collections, each facility offers the publications of the U.S. Patent Classification System. These include *The Manual of Classification, Index to the U.S. Patent Classification, Classification Definitions* and others.

A technical staff is available to assist the public in their patent research. The *Classification and Search Support Information System (CASSIS)* is a computerized database allowing the user unprecedented ease of access and effectiveness in their patent research.

Always phone the PTDL before your visit to inquire about the scope of their patent collection, hours of service to the general public as well as costs to obtain paper copies from either microfilm or bound volumes. The following is a complete PTDL list, current as of October 1997.

Alabama
Auburn University: Ralph Brown Draughon Library, Auburn University, (334) 844-1747
Birmingham: Birmingham Public Library, (205) 226-3620

Alaska
Anchorage: Z. J. Loussac Public Library, Anchorage Municipal Libraries, (907) 562-7323

Arizona
Tempe: Daniel E. Noble Science and Engineering Library/Science/Reference, Arizona State University, (602) 965-7010

Arkansas
Little Rock: Arkansas State Library, (501) 682-2053

California
Los Angeles: Los Angeles Public Library, (213) 228-7220
Sacramento: California State Library, Library-Courts Building, (916) 654-0069
San Diego: San Diego Public Library, (619) 236-5813
San Francisco: San Francisco Public Library, (415) 557-4500
Sunnyvale: Sunnyvale Center for Innovation, Invention and Ideas, (408) 730-7290

Colorado
Denver: Denver Public Library, (303) 640-6220

Connecticut
No PTDL in state

Delaware
Newark: University of Delaware Library, (302) 831-2965

District of Columbia
Washington: Founders Library, Howard University, (202) 806-7252

Florida
Fort Lauderdale: Broward County Main Library, (954) 357-7444
Miami: Miami-Dade Public Library, (305) 375-2665
Orlando: University of Central Florida Libraries, (407) 823-2562

Tampa: Tampa Campus Library, University of South Florida, (813) 974-2726

Georgia
Atlanta: Library and Information Center, Georgia Institute of Technology, (404) 894-4508

Hawaii
Honolulu: Hawaii State Library, (808) 586-3477

Idaho
Moscow: University of Idaho Library, (208) 885-6235

Illinois
Chicago: Chicago Public Library, (312) 747-4450
Springfield: Illinois State Library, (217) 782-5659

Indiana
Indianapolis: Indianapolis-Marion County Public Library, (317) 269-1741
West Lafayette: Siegesmund Engineering Library, Purdue University, (317) 494-2872

Iowa
Des Moines: State Library of Iowa, (515) 281-4118

Kansas
Wichita: Ablah Library, Wichita State University, (316) 978-3155

Kentucky
Louisville: Louisville Free Public Library, (502) 574-1611

Louisiana
Baton Rouge: Troy H. Middleton Library, Louisiana State University, (504) 388-8875

Maine
Orono: Raymond H. Fogler Library, University of Maine, (207) 581-1678

Maryland
College Park: Engineering and Physical Sciences Library, University of Maryland, (301) 405-9157

Massachusetts
Amherst: Physical Sciences and Engineering Library, University of Massachusetts, (413) 545-1370
Boston: Boston Public Library, (617) 536-5400, extension 265

Michigan
Ann Arbor: Media Union Library, The University of Michigan, (313) 647-5735
Big Rapids: Abigail S. Timme Library, Ferris State University, (616) 592-3602
Detroit: Great Lakes Patent and Trademark Center,
Detroit Public Library, (313) 833-3379

Minnesota
Minneapolis: Minneapolis Public Library & Information Center, (612) 372-6570

Mississippi
Jackson: Mississippi Library Commission, (601) 359-1036

Missouri
Kansas City: Linda Hall Library, (816) 363-4600
St. Louis: St. Louis Public Library, (314) 241-2288, extension 390

Montana
Butte: Montana Tech of the University of Montana Library, (406) 496-4281

Nebraska
Lincoln: Engineering Library, Nebraska Hall, 2nd Floor West, (402) 472-3411

Nevada
Reno: University Library, University of Nevada-Reno, (702) 784-6500, extension 257

New Hampshire
Concord: New Hampshire State Library, (603) 271-2239

New Jersey
Newark: Newark Public Library, (201) 733-7782
Piscataway: Library of Science and Medicine, Rutgers University, (908) 445-2895

New Mexico
Albuquerque: Centennial Science and Engineering Library, The University of New Mexico, (505) 277-4412

New York
Albany: New York State Library, Science, Industry and Business Library, (518) 474-5355
Buffalo: Buffalo and Erie County Public Library, (716) 858-7101
New York: Science, Industry and Business Library, (212) 592-7000

North Carolina
Raleigh: D. H. Hill Library, North Carolina State University, (919) 515-3280

North Dakota
Grand Forks: Chester Fritz Library, University of North Dakota, (701) 777-4888

Ohio
Akron: Akron-Summit County Public Library, (330) 643-9075
Cincinnati: The Public Library of Cincinnati and Hamilton County, (513) 369-6936
Cleveland: Cleveland Public Library, (216) 623-2870
Columbus: Ohio State University Libraries, (614) 292-6175
Toledo: Toledo/Lucas County Public Library, (419) 259-5212

Oklahoma
Stillwater: Oklahoma State University, (405) 744-7086
Oregon
Portland: Paul L. Boley Law Library, Lewis and Clark College, (503) 768-6786

Pennsylvania
Philadelphia: The Free Library of Philadelphia, (215) 686-5331
Pittsburgh: The Carnegie Library of Pittsburgh, (412) 622-3138
University Park: Pattee Library—C207, Pennsylvania State University, (814) 865-4861

Puerto Rico
Mayagüez: General Library, University of Puerto Rico, (787) 832-4040, extension 3459

Rhode Island
Providence: Providence Public Library, (401) 455-8027

South Carolina
Clemson: R.M. Cooper Library, Clemson University, (864) 656-3024

South Dakota
Rapid City: Devereux Library, South Dakota School of Mines and Technology, (605) 394-6822

Tennessee
Memphis: Memphis & Shelby County Public Library, and Information Center, (901) 725-8877
Nashville: Stevenson Science and Engineering Library, Vanderbilt University, (615) 322-2717

Texas
Austin: McKinney Engineering Library, The University of Texas at Austin, (512) 495-4500
College Station: Sterling C. Evans Library, Texas A&M University, (409) 845-3826
Dallas: Dallas Public Library, (214) 670-1468
Houston: The Fondren Library—MS 44, Rice University, (713) 527-8101, extension 2587
Lubbock: Texas Tech University, (806) 742-2282

Utah
Salt Lake City: Marriott Library, University of Utah, (801) 581-8394

Vermont
Burlington: Bailey/Howe Library, University of Vermont, (802) 656-2542

Virginia
Richmond: James Branch Cabell Library, Virginia Commonwealth University, (804) 828-1104

Washington
Seattle: Engineering Library, University of Washington, (206) 543-0740

West Virginia
Morgantown: Evansdale Library, West Virginia University, (304) 293-2510, extension 113

Wisconsin
Madison: Kurt F. Wendt Library, University of Wisconsin-Madison, (608) 262-6845
Milwaukee: Milwaukee Public Library, (414) 286-3051

Wyoming
Casper: Natrona County Public Library, (307) 237-4935

For more information, contact:
Patent and Trademark Depository Library Program
United States Patent and Trademark Office
Crystal Park 3, Suite 461
Washington, DC 20231
(703) 308-5558
Fax (703) 306-2654

APPENDIX 4

Patent and Trademark Office Fees

Inquiries regarding fee amounts and requests for a copy of the PTO fee schedule may be directed to the General Information Services Division. Contact them by phone at (800) 786-9199 [PTO-9199] or (703) 308-4357 [308-HELP] or by fax at (703) 305-7786. The Patent and Trademark Office updates its fee structure yearly. The following is a list of current PTO fees, effective October 1, 1997:

Basic Filing Fee	$790
Basic Filing Fee (Small Entity)	$395
Independent Claims	$82
Independent Claims (Small Entity)	$41
Claims in Excess of 20	$22
Claims in Excess of 20 (Small Entity)	$11
Multiple Dependent Claims	$270
Multiple Dependent Claims (Small Entity)	$135
Surcharge —Late Filing Fee	$130
Surcharge—Late Filing Fee (Small Entity)	$65
Design Filing Fee	$330
Design Filing Fee (Small Entity)	$165
Plant Filing Fee	$540
Plant Filing Fee (Small Entity)	$270
Reissue Filing Fee	$790
Reissue Filing Fee (Small Entity)	$395

Reissue Independent Claims $82
Reissue Independent Claims (Small Entity) $41
Reissue Claims in Excess of 20 .... $22
Reissue Claims in Excess of 20 (Small Entity) $11
Provisional Application Filing Fee $150
Provisional Application Filing Fee (Small Entity) $75
Surcharge—Incomplete Provisional
      Application Filed $50
Surcharge—Incomplete Provisional
      Application Filed (Small Entity) $25
Extension—First Month $110
Extension—First Month (Small Entity) $55
Extension—Second Month..................... $400
Extension—Second Month (Small Entity) $200
Extension—Third Month $950
Extension—Third Month (Small Entity) $475
Extension—Fourth Month $1,510
Extension—Fourth Month (Small Entity) $755
Extension—Fifth Month...................... $2,060
Extension—Fifth Month (Small Entity).......... $1,030
Notice of Appeal $310
Notice of Appeal (Small Entity) $155
Filing a Brief............................... $310
Filing a Brief (Small Entity).................... $155
Request for Oral Hearing $270
Request for Oral Hearing (Small Entity) $135
Petition—Not All Inventors $130
Petition—Correction of Inventorship $130
Petition—Decision on Questions $130
Petition—Suspend Rules $130
Petition—Expedited License $130
Petition—Scope of License $130
Petition—Retroactive License $130
Petition—Refusing Maintenance Fee............. $130
Petition—Refusing Maintenance Fee—Expired Patent $130
Petition—Interference $130
Petition—Reconsider Interference $130
Petition—Late Filing of Interference $130
Petition—Correction of Inventorship $130
Petition—Refusal to Publish SIR $130
Petition—For Assignment $130
Petition—For Application..................... $130

Petition—Late Priority Papers $130

Petition—Suspend Action $130

Petition—Divisional Reissues to Issue Separately . . . $130

Petition—For Interference Agreement $130

Petition—Amendment After Issue $130

Petition—Withdrawal After Issue $130

Petition—Defer Issue $130

Petition—Issue to Assignee $130

Petition—Accord a Filing Date Under 1.53 . . . . $130

Petition—Accord a Filing Date Under 1.62 . . . . $130

Petition—Make Application Special $130

Petition—Public Use Proceeding $1,510

Non-English Specification $130

Petition—Revive Unavoidably

    Abandoned Application $110

Petition—Revive Abandoned

    Application (Small Entity) $55

Petition—Revive Unintentionally

    Abandoned Application $1,320

Petition—Revive Unintentionally

    Abandoned Application (Small Entity) $660

SIR—Prior to Examiner's Action $920

SIR—After Examiner's Action $1,840

Submission of an Information Disclosure

    Statement (1.97) $240

Petition—Correction of Inventorship (Prov. App.) $50

Petition—Accord a filing date (Prov. App.) $50

Petition—Entry of submission after

    final rejection (Prov. App.) $50

Filing a submission after final rejection (1.129(a)) . . $790

Filing a submission after final rejection

    (1.129(a)) (Small Entity) $395

Per additional invention to be examined (1.129(b)) . . $790

Per additional invention to be examined

    (1.129(b)) (Small Entity) $395

Utility Issue Fee $1,320

Utility Issue Fee (Small Entity) $660

Design Issue Fee $450

Design Issue Fee (Small Entity) $225

Plant Issue Fee $670

Plant Issue Fee (Small Entity) $335

Copy of Patent $3

Patent Copy—Overnight delivery to PTO box or
  overnight fax $6
Patent Copy Ordered by Expedited Mail or Fax—
  express service $25
Plant Patent Copy $12
Copy of Utility Patent or SIR in Color $25
Certified Copy of Patent Application as Filed $15
Certified Copy of Patent Application as
  Filed, Expedited $30
Certified or Uncertified Copy of Patent—Related
  File Wrapper/Contents $150
Certified or Uncertified Copies of Office Records,
  per Document $25
For Assignment Records, Abstract of Title and
  Certification $25
Library Service $50
List of Patents in Subclass $3
Uncertified Statement—Status of Maintenance
  Fee Payment $10
Copy of Non–U.S. Patent Document $25
Comparing and Certifying Copies, Per Document,
  Per Copy $25
Duplicate or Corrected Filing Receipt $25
Certificate of Correction $100
Re-examination $2,520
Statutory Disclaimer $110
Statutory Disclaimer (Small Entity) $55
Maintenance Fee—3.5 Years $1,050
Maintenance Fee—3.5 Years (Small Entity) $525
Maintenance Fee—7.5 Years $2,100
Maintenance Fee—7.5 Years (Small Entity) $1,050
Maintenance Fee—11.5 Years $3,160
Maintenance Fee—11.5 Years (Small Entity) $1,580
Surcharge—Maintenance Fee—6 Months $130
Surcharge—Maintenance Fee—6 Months
  (Small Entity) $65
Surcharge—Maintenance After Expiration—
  Unavoidable $700
Surcharge—Maintenance After Expiration—
  Unintentional $1,640
Extension of Term of Patent Under 1.740 . . . . $1,120
Initial Application for Interim Extension Under 1.790 $420

Subsequent Application for Interim Extension
   Under 1.790 .... $220
Application Fee (nonrefundable) $40
Registration Examination Fee $310
Registration to Practice....................... $100
Reinstatement to Practice $40
Certificate of Good Standing $10
Certificate of Good Standing, Suitable Framing $20
Review of Decision of Director, OED $130
Regrading of A.M. section
   (PTO Practice and Procedure) $230
Regrading of P.M. section (Claim Drafting)........ $540
Establish Deposit Account $10
Service Charge Below Minimum Balance $25
Filing a Disclosure Document $10
Box Rental $50
International Type Search Report $40
Self-Service Copy Charge (per page) $0.25
Recording Patent Property $40
Publication in the *Official Gazette* $25
Labor Charges for Services (per hour) $40
Unspecified Other Services .... At Cost
Terminal Use APS-CSIR (per hour) $50
Retaining abandoned application $130
Processing Returned Checks $50
Handling Fee—Incomplete Application $130
Terminal Use APS—TEXT $40
Coupons for Patent and Trademark Copies $3
Handling Fee—Withdrawal SIR................. $130

APPENDIX 5

Better Business Bureaus

Better Business Bureaus (BBBs) are the place to turn if you have a consumer question or complaint. BBBs seek to monitor ethics in business as a public service to you, the consumer. The nonprofit organization's major goal is to encourage honest advertising and selling practices and, if necessary, to provide alternative dispute resolution.

Consumer services provided include: making available consumer education publications, providing answers to consumer questions, providing a history of complaints or other problems for a particular company, making information about charities available and sponsoring alternative dispute resolution such as mediation and arbitration services.

The Council of Better Business Bureaus located in Arlington, Virginia, is the national umbrella organization for the BBBs. Concerns regarding business or charities dealing on a national level should be directed here.

To contact your local BBB, refer to the list below. You may call your local BBB to inquire about their services but you must submit any complaints in writing so the BBB can maintain an accurate record of the dispute. You can go online through the Internet to access the BBB's Web site at http://www.bbb.org/bbb/ to obtain information about their programs, services and locations. You may also file a complaint online as well as obtain a BBB report on any of the 1.3 million businesses the BBB maintains in its database.

COUNCIL
Council of Better Business
Bureaus, Inc.
4200 Wilson Boulevard
Arlington, VA 22203
(703) 276-0100

BUREAUS
Alabama
1210 South 20th Street
P.O. Box 55268
Birmingham, AL 35205
(205) 558-2222

102 Court Street, Suite 512
Florence, AL 35630
(800) 239-1642 (toll free)

501 Church Street, N.W.
P.O. Box 383
Huntsville, AL 35801-5549
(205) 533-1640 (24 hours)

100 North Royal Street
Mobile, AL 36602-3295
(334) 433-5494
(800) 544-4714
(toll free south Alabama)

60 Commerce Street
Suite 806
Montgomery, AL 36104-3559
(334) 262-5606

Alaska
2805 Bering Street, Suite 2
Anchorage, AK 99503-3819
(907) 562-0704

P.O. Box 74675
Fairbanks, AK 99707
(907) 451-0222

P.O. Box 1229
Kenai, AK 99611
(907) 283-4880

Palmer-Wasilla Highway
Suite 107
Mat-Su Valley, AK 99654
(907) 376-4324

Arizona
4428 North 12th Street
Phoenix, AZ 85014-4585
(900) 225-5222 ($.95/min.)

3620 North 1st Avenue
Suite 136
Tucson, AZ 85719
(520) 888-5353 (inquiries)
(520) 888-5454 (complaints)
(800) 696-2827 (toll free
south Arizona only)

Arkansas
1415 South University
Little Rock, AR 72204-2605
(501) 664-7274
(800) 482-8448 (toll free
in Arkansas)

California
705 18th Street
Bakersfield, CA 93301-4882
(805) 322-2074

290 N. 10th Street, Suite 206
P.O. Box 970
Colton, CA 92324-0814
(900) 225-5222 ($.95/min.)

6101 Ball Road, Suite 309
Cypress, CA 90630-3966
(900) 225-5222 ($.95/min.)

2519 West Shaw, #106
Fresno, CA 93711
(209) 222-8111

3727 West 65th Street
Suite 607
Los Angeles, CA 90020-2538
(900) 225-5222 ($.95/min.)

494 Alverado Street, Suite C
Monterey, CA 93940-2717
(408) 372-3149

510 16th Street, Suite 550
Oakland, CA 94612-1584
(510) 238-1000 (24 hours)

400 S Street
Sacramento, CA 95814-6997
(916) 443-6843

5050 Murphy Canyon
Suite 110
San Diego, CA 92123
(619) 496-2131

114 Sansome Street
Suite 1108
San Francisco, CA 94104
(415) 243-9999

1530 Meridian Avenue
Suite 100
San Jose, CA 95125
(408) 445-3000

400 South El Camino Real
Suite 350
P.O. Box 294
San Mateo, CA 94402-1706
(415) 696-1240

213 Santa Barbara Street
P.O. Box 129
Santa Barbara, CA 93102
(805) 963-8657

509 W. Weber, Suite 202
Stockton, CA 95203
(209) 948-4880

Colorado
3622 North El Paso
P.O. Box 7970
Colorado Springs, CO
80907-5454
(719) 636-1155

1780 South Bellaire, Suite 700
Denver, CO 80222-4350
(303) 758-2100
(inquiries, 24 hours)
(303) 758-2212 (complaints)
(303) 758-4786 (TDD, 24 hours)

1730 South College Avenue
Suite 303
Fort Collins, CO 80525-1073
(303) 484-1348
(307) 778-2809 (Cheyenne)

119 West 6th Street, Suite 203
Pueblo, CO 81003-3119
(719) 542-6464

Connecticut
2345 Black Rock Turnpike
P.O. Box 1410
Fairfield, CT 06432-1410
(203) 374-6161
(203) 798-7300 (Danbury)
(203) 853-0659 (Norwalk)
(203) 359-9892 (Stamford)
(203) 597-1177 (Waterbury)

621 North Main Street Ext.
Wallingford, CT 06492-2420
(203) 269-2700

Delaware
2055 Limestone Road
Suite 200
Wilmington, DE 19808-5532
(302) 996-9200

District of Columbia
1012 14th Street, N.W.
9th Floor
Washington, DC 20005-3410
(202) 393-8000

Florida
5830-142nd Avenue North
Suite B
P.O. Box 7950
Clearwater, FL 34620
(813) 842-5459 (Pasco City)
(813) 535-5522
(Pinellas County)
(813) 854-1154
(Hills, Tampa)
(813) 957-0093
(Sarasota, Manatee)
(800) 525-1447 (toll free
Hernando only) (all 24 hrs.)

2710 Swamp Cabbage Court
Fort Myers, FL 33901
(900) 225-5222 (24 hours,
$.95/minute)

7820 Arlington Expressway
Suite 147
Jacksonville, FL 32211
(904) 721-2288

16291 N.W. 57th Avenue
Miami, FL 33014-6709
(900) 225-5222 (24 hours,
$.95/minute)

P.O. Box 1511
Pensacola, FL 32503-2533
(904) 494-0222

1950 Port St. Lucie Boulevard
Suite 211
Port St. Lucie, FL
34954-5579
(407) 878-2010
(407) 337-2083

580 Village Blvd., Suite 340
West Palm Beach, FL 33409
(407) 686-2200
(407) 337-2083
(Martin County)

1011 North Wymore Road
Suite 204
Winter Park, FL 32789-1736
(Orlando)
(407) 621-3300 (24 hours)

Georgia
611 N. Jefferson Street
P.O. Box 808
Albany, GA 31701
(912) 883-0744

100 Edgewood Avenue
Suite 1012
Atlanta, GA 30303-3075
(404) 688-4910

310 7th Street
P.O. Box 2085
Augusta, GA 30901-1463
(706) 722-1574

208 13th Street
P.O. Box 2587
Columbus, GA 31901-2151
(706) 324-0712
(706) 324-0713

1765 Shurling Drive
Macon, GA 31211-2199
(912) 742-7999

6606 Abercorn Street,
Suite 108-C
P.O. Box 13956
Savannah, GA 31405
(912) 354-7521
(912) 354-7522

Hawaii
1600 Kapiolani Boulevard
Suite 201
Honolulu, HI 96814-3801
(808) 942-2355

Idaho
1333 West Jefferson
Boise, ID 83702-5320
(208) 342-4649

1575 South Boulevard
Idaho Falls, ID 83404-5926
(208) 523-9754

Illinois
211 West Wacker Drive
Chicago, IL 60606-1217
(900) 225-5222 ($.95/minute)

3024 West Lake
Peoria, IL 61615-3770
(309) 688-3741

810 East State Street, 3rd Floor
Rockford, IL 61104-1001
(900) 225-5222 ($.95/minute)

Indiana
722 West Bristol Street
Suite H-2
P.O. Box 405
Elkhart, IN 46514-2988
(219) 262-8996

4004 Morgan Avenue
Suite 201
Evansville, IN 47715-2265
(812) 473-0202
(812) 473-1425

1203 Webster Street
Fort Wayne, IN 46802-3493
(219) 423-4423
(800) 552-4631 (toll free in IN)

4189 Cleveland Street
Gary, IN 46408-2490
(219) 980-1511
(219) 769-8053
(800) 637-2118 (toll free in
northern IN)

Victoria Centre
22 E. Washington St., Suite 200
Indianapolis, IN 46204-3584
(317) 488-2222

207 Dixie Way North, Suite 130
South Bend, IN 46637-3360
(219) 277-9121
(800) 439-5313 (toll free in
northern Indiana)

Iowa
852 Middle Road, Suite 290
Bettendorf, IA 52722-4100
(319) 355-6344

505 5th Avenue, Suite 615
Des Moines, IA 50309-2375
(515) 243-8137

505 6th Street, Suite 417
Sioux City, IA 51101-1611
(712) 252-4501

Kansas
501 Southeast Jefferson
Suite 24
Topeka, KS 66607-1190
(913) 232-0454

328 Laura
Wichita, KS 67211
(316) 263-3146

Kentucky
410 West Vine Street
Suite 280
Lexington, KY 40507-1616
(606) 259-1008

844 South Fourth Street
Louisville, KY 40203-2186
(502) 583-6546 (24 hours)
(800) 388-2222 (toll free in
Kentucky and southern Indiana)

Louisiana
1605 Murray Street
Suite 117
Alexandria, LA 71301-6875
(318) 473-4494

2055 Wooddale Boulevard
Baton Rouge, LA 70806-1546
(504) 926-3010

1626 Barrow Street
Houma, LA 70360-6354
(504) 868-3456

100 Huggins Road
P.O. Box 30297
Lafayette, LA 70506
(318) 981-3497

3941-L Ryan Street
P.O. Box 7314
Lake Charles, LA 70605
(318) 478-6253

141 Desiard Street, Suite 808
Monroe, LA 71201-7380
(318) 387-4600

1539 Jackson Avenue
Suite 400
New Orleans, LA 70130-5843
(504) 581-6222 (24 hours)
(504) 528-9277

3612 Youree Drive
Shreveport, LA 71105-2112
(318) 861-6417

Maine
812 Stevens Avenue
Portland, ME 04103-2648
(207) 878-2715

Maryland
2100 Huntingdon Avenue
Baltimore, MD 21211-3215
(900) 225-5222 ($.95/minute)

Massachusetts
20 Park Plaza, Suite 820
Boston, MA 02116-4344
(617) 426-9000
(800) 4BBB-811 (toll free
802 area code)

293 Bridge Street, Suite 320
Springfield, MA 01103-1402
(413) 734 -3114

32 Franklin Street
P.O. Box 16555
Worcester, MA 01608-1900
(508) 755-2548

Michigan
40 Pearl, N.W., Suite 354
Grand Rapids, MI
46503-3001
(616) 774-8236
(800) 684-3222 (toll free
in western Michigan)

30555 Southfield Road
Suite 200
Southfield, MI 48076-7751
(Detroit)
(810) 644-9100 (24 hours)

Minnesota
2706 Gannon Road
St. Paul, MN 55116-2600
(612) 699-1111

Mississippi
4915 I-55 North
P.O. Box 12745
Jackson, MS 39206
(601) 987-8282

Missouri
306 E. 12th Street
Suite 1024
Kansas City, MO 64106-2418
(816) 421-7800

5100 Oakland, Suite 200
St. Louis, MO 63110-1400
(314) 531-3300 (24 hours)

205 Park Central East
Suite 509
Springfield, MO 65806-1326
(417) 862-4222
(800) 497-4222 (toll free in
southwestern Missouri)

Nebraska
3633 O Street, Suite 1
Lincoln, NE 68510-1670
(402) 476-8855

2237 North 91st Court
Omaha, NE 68134-6022
(402) 391-7612

Nevada
1022 East Sahara Avenue
Las Vegas, NV 89104-1515
(702) 735-6900

991 Bible Way
P.O. Box 21269
Reno, NV 89502
(702) 322-0657

New Hampshire
410 South Main Street
Suite 3
Concord, NH 03301-3459
(603) 224-1991
(603) 228-3789
(603) 228-3844

New Jersey
2 Sylvan Way, 3rd Floor
Parsippany, NJ 07054
(Newark)
(201) 539-8222

1721 Route 37 East
Toms River, NJ 08753-8239
(908) 270-5577

1700 Whitehorse-Hamilton
Square, #D-5
Trenton, NJ 08690-3596
(609) 588-0808

16 Maple Avenue
P.O. Box 303
Westmont, NJ 08108-0303
(609) 854-8467

New Mexico
2625 Pennsylvania, NE
Suite 2050
Albuquerque, NM
87110-3657
(505) 844-0500
(800) 873-2224 (toll free in New Mexico)

308 North Locke
Farmington, NM 87401-5855
(505) 326-6501

201 N. Church, Suite 330
Las Cruces, NM 88001-3548
(505) 524-3130

New York
346 Delaware Avenue
Buffalo, NY 14202-1899
(900) 225-5222 (24 hours, $.95/minute)

266 Main Street
Farmingdale, NY 11735
(900) 225-5222 (24 hours, $.95/minute)

257 Park Avenue, South
New York, NY 10010-7384
(900) 225-5222 (24 hours, $.95/minute)

847 James Street, Suite 200
Syracuse, NY 13202-2552
(900) 225-5222 (24 hours, $.95/minute)

30 Glenn Street
White Plains, NY 10603-3213
(900) 225-5222 (24 hours, $.95/minute)

North Carolina
1200 BB&T Building
Asheville, NC 28801-3418
(704) 253-2392

5200 Park Road, Suite 202
Charlotte, NC 28209-3650
(704) 527-0012 (24 hours)

3608 West Friendly Avenue
Greensboro, NC 27410-4895
(910) 852-4240 (24 hours)

3125 Poplarwood Court
Suite 308
Raleigh, NC 27604-1080
(919) 872-9240
(800) 222-0950 (toll free in eastern NC)

Eden Place
8366 Drena Drive
P.O. Box 69
Sherrils Ford, NC 28673
(704) 478-5622

500 West 5th Street
Suite 202
Winston-Salem, NC
27101-2728
(910) 725-8348

Ohio
222 W. Market Street
Akron, OH 44303-2111
(216) 253-4590

1434 Cleveland Avenue, N.W.
P.O. Box 8017
Canton, OH 44703-3135
(216) 454-9401
(800) 362-0494 (toll free in Ohio)

898 Walnut Street
Cincinnati, OH 45202-2097
(513) 421-3015

2217 East 9th Street
Suite 200
Cleveland, OH 44115-1299
(216) 241-7678

1335 Dublin Street, Suite 30A
Columbus, OH 43215-1000
(614) 486-6336

40 West Fourth Street, Suite 1250
Dayton, OH 45402-1828
(513) 222-5825

112 North West High Street
P.O. Box 269
Lima, OH 45802-0269
(419) 223-7010
(800) 462-0468 (toll free)

425 Jefferson Avenue, Suite 909
Toledo, OH 43604-1055
(419) 241-6276

600 Mahoning Bank Building
P.O. Box 1495
Youngstown, OH 44501-1495
(216) 744-3111
(216) 424-5522 (Lisbon)
(216) 394-0628 (Warren)

Oklahoma
17 South Dewey
Oklahoma City, OK
73102-2400
(405) 239-6081 (inquiries)

6711 South Yale, Suite 230
Tulsa, OK 74136-3327
(918) 492-1266

Oregon
610 S.W. Alder Street
Suite 615
Portland, OR 97205-3690
(503) 226-3981
(800) 488-4166 (toll free in Oregon and
southwest Washington)

Pennsylvania
528 North New Street
Bethlehem, PA 18018-5789
(215) 866-8780
(215) 372-2005 (Berks County)

29 E. King Street, Suite 322
Lancaster, PA 17602-2852
(900) 225-5222 (24 hours, $.95/minute)

1930 Chestnut Street
P.O. Box 2297
Philadelphia, PA 19103-0297
(900) 225-5222 (24 hours, $.95/minute)

300 6th Avenue
Suite 100-UL
Pittsburgh, PA 15222-2511
(412) 456-2700

129 N. Washington Avenue
P.O. Box 993
Scranton, PA 18501-0993
(717) 342-9129
(717) 655-0445

Puerto Rico
1608 Bori Street
P.O. Box 363488
San Juan, PR 00936-3488
(809) 756-5400

Rhode Island
Bureau Park
Box 1300
Warwick, RI 02887-1300
(Providence)
(401) 785-1212 (inquiries)
(401) 785-1213 (complaints)

South Carolina
2330 Devine Street
P.O. Box 8326
Columbia, SC 29202-8326
(803) 254-2525

113 Mills Avenue
Greenville, SC 29605-4077
(803) 242-5052

1601 North Oak Street
Suite 403
Myrtle Beach, SC
29577-1601
(803) 626-6881

Tennessee
P.O. Box 1178 TCA, #121
Blountville, TN 37617-1178
(615) 323-6311

1010 Market Street
Suite 200
Chattanooga, TN 37402-2614
(615) 266-6144

2633 Kingston Pike, Suite 2
P.O. Box 10327
Knoxville, TN 37919
(615) 522-2552

6525 Quall Hollow
Suite 410
P.O. Box 17036
Memphis, TN 38121
(901) 759-1300 (24 hours)

Nations Bank Plaza
414 Union Street
Suite 1830
Nashville, TN 37219-1778
(615) 242-4222 (24 hours)

Texas
3300 S. 14th Street, Suite 307
Abilene, TX 79605-5052
(915) 691-1533

1000 South Polk
P.O. Box 1905
Amarillo, TX 79101-3408
(806) 379-6222

2101 So. IH35
Suite 302
Austin, TX 78741-3854
(512) 445-2911 (24 hours)

476 Oakland Avenue
P.O. Box 2988
Beaumont, TX 77701-2011
(409) 835-5348

4346 Carter Creek Parkway
Bryan, TX 77802-4413
(409) 260-2222

216 Park Avenue
Corpus Christi, TX 78401
(512) 887-4949

2001 Bryan Street
Suite 850
Dallas, TX 75201-3093
(900) 225-5222 (24 hours, $.95/min.)

State National Plaza
Suite 1101
El Paso, TX 79901
(915) 577-0191

1612 Summit Avenue
Suite 260
Fort Worth, TX 76102-5978
(817) 332-7585 (24 hours)

2707 North Loop West
Suite 400
Houston, TX 77008-1085
(900) 225-5222 (24 hours, $.95/minute)

1206 14th Street
Suite 901
Lubbock, TX 79401-3922
(806) 763-0459 (24 hours)

10100 County Road
118 West, P.O. Box 60206
Midland, TX 79711-0206
(915) 563-1880
(800) 592-4433 (toll free in Texas)

3121 Executive Drive
P.O. Box 3366
San Angelo, TX 76904
(915) 949-2989

1800 Northeast Loop 410
Suite 400
San Antonio, TX 78217-5296
(210) 828-9441

3600 Old Bullard Road
Suite 103A
P.O. Box 6652
Tyler, TX 75701
(903) 581-5704

6801 Sanger Avenue
Suite 125
P.O. Box 7203
Waco, TX 76710
(817) 772-7530

609 International Boulevard
P.O. Box 69
Weslaco, TX 78599-0069
(210) 968-3678

4245 Kemp Boulevard
Suite 900
Wichita Falls, TX 76308-2830
(817) 691-1172

Utah
1588 South Main Street
Salt Lake City, UT
84115-5382
(801) 487-4656 (24 hours)
(800) 456-3907 (toll free in Utah)

Vermont
(Contact Boston Office)
20 Park Plaza
Suite 820
Boston, MA 02116-4344
(617) 426-9000
(800) 4BBB-811 (toll free in 802 area code)

Virginia
11903 Main Street
Fredericksburg, VA 22408
(703) 373-9872

3608 Tidewater Drive
Norfolk, VA 23509-1499
(804) 627-5651
(804) 722-9101 (Peninsula area)

701 East Franklin
Suite 712
Richmond, VA 23219-2332
(804) 648-0016 (24 hours)

31 West Campbell Avenue
Roanoke, VA 24011-1301
(703) 342-3455

Washington
1401 N. Union
Suite 105
Kennewick, WA 99336-3819
(509) 783-0892

4800 South 188 Street
Suite 222
P.O. Box 68926
Seatac, WA 98188
(206) 431-2222
(900) 225-4222 (24 hours, $4 flat fee)

East 123 Indiana
Suite 106
Spokane, WA 99207-2356
(509) 328-2100

222 Washington Mutual Building
P.O. Box 1584
Yakima, WA 98901
(509) 248-1326

Wisconsin
740 North Plankinton Avenue
Milwaukee, WI 53203-2478
(414) 273-1600 (inquiries)
(414) 273-0123 (complaints)

APPENDIX 6

List of Attorneys General for the United States and Jurisdictions

The following list of State Attorneys General is provided for your protection. If you have doubts about doing business with a company you should check their credibility. By contacting the Attorney General's office you can learn if complaints have been lodged against the company in question. Conducting research of this kind can reduce your odds of being victimized by an unscrupulous business.

This list, provided by the National Association of Attorneys General, is current as of October 1, 1997:

National Association of Attorneys General
750 First Street NE, Suite 1100
Washington, DC 20002
(202) 326-6000
Fax (202) 408-7014

Attorneys General by State:

Alabama
Honorable Bill Pryor
Attorney General of Alabama
Office of the Attorney General
State House
11 South Union Street
Montgomery, AL 36130
(334) 242-7300

Alaska
Honorable Bruce M. Botelho
Attorney General of Alaska
Office of the Attorney General
Post Office Box 110300
Diamond Courthouse
Juneau, AK 99811-0300
(907) 465-3600

American Samoa
Honorable Toetagata Albert Mailo
Attorney General of American Samoa
Office of the Attorney General
Post Office Box 7
Pago Pago, AS 96799
(684) 633-4163

Arizona
Honorable Grant Woods
Attorney General of Arizona
Office of the Attorney General
1275 West Washington Street
Phoenix, AZ 85007
(602) 542-4266

Arkansas
Honorable Winston Bryant
Attorney General of Arkansas
Office of the Attorney General
200 Tower Building
323 Center Street
Little Rock, AR 72201-2610
(501) 682-2007

California
Honorable Daniel E. Lungren
Attorney General of California
Office of the Attorney General
1300 I Street
Suite 1740
Sacramento, CA 95814
(916) 324-5437

Colorado
Honorable Gale A. Norton
Attorney General of Colorado
Office of the Attorney General
Department of Law
1525 Sherman Street
Denver, CO 80203
(303) 866-3052

Connecticut
Honorable Richard Blumenthal
Attorney General of Connecticut
Office of the Attorney General
55 Elm Street
Hartford, CT 06141-0120
(860) 566-2026

Delaware
Honorable M. Jane Brady
Attorney General of Delaware
Office of the Attorney General
Carvel State Office Building
820 North French Street
Wilmington, DE 19801
(302) 577-3838

District of Columbia
Honorable John M. Ferren
DC Corporation Counsel
Office of the Corporation Counsel
441 4th Street NW
Washington, DC 20001
(202) 727-6248

Florida
Honorable Robert A. Butterworth
Attorney General of Florida
Office of the Attorney General
The Capitol
PL 01
Tallahassee, FL 32399-1050
(904) 487-1963

Georgia
Honorable Thurbert E. Baker
Attorney General of Georgia
Office of the Attorney General
40 Capitol Square, S.W.
Atlanta, GA 30334-1300
(404) 656-4585

Guam
Honorable Charles H. Troutman
Acting Attorney General of Guam
Office of the Attorney General
Judicial Center Building
120 West O'Brien Drive
Agana, GU 96910
(671) 475-3324

Hawaii
Honorable Margery S. Bronster
Attorney General of Hawaii
Office of the Attorney General
425 Queen Street
Honolulu, HI 96813
(808) 586-1282

Idaho
Honorable Alan G. Lance
Attorney General of Idaho
Office of the Attorney General
Statehouse
Boise, ID 83720-1000
(208) 334-2400

Illinois
Honorable Jim Ryan
Attorney General of Illinois
Office of the Attorney General
James R. Thompson Center
100 West Randolph Street
Chicago, IL 60601
(312) 814-2503

Indiana
Honorable Jeffrey A. Modisett
Attorney General of Indiana
Office of the Attorney General
Indiana Government Center South
Fifth Floor
402 West Washington Street
Indianapolis, IN 46204
(317) 233-4386

Iowa
Honorable Tom Miller
Attorney General of Iowa
Office of the Attorney General
Hoover State Office Building
Des Moines, IA 50319
(515) 281-3053

Kansas
Honorable Carla J. Stovall
Attorney General of Kansas
Office of the Attorney General
Judicial Building
301 West Tenth Street
Topeka, KS 66612-1597
(913) 296-2215

Kentucky
Hon. Albert Benjamin "Ben" Chandler III
Attorney General of Kentucky
Office of the Attorney General
State Capitol
Room 116
Frankfort, KY 40601
(502) 564-7600

Louisiana
Honorable Richard P. Ieyoub
Attorney General of Louisiana
Office of the Attorney General
Department of Justice
Post Office Box 94095
Baton Rouge, LA 70804-4095
(504) 342-7013

Maine
Honorable Andrew Ketterer
Attorney General of Maine
Office of the Attorney General
State House Station Six
Augusta, ME 04333
(207) 626-8800

Maryland
Honorable J. Joseph Curran, Jr.
Attorney General of Maryland
Office of the Attorney General
200 Saint Paul Place
Baltimore, MD 21202-2202
(410) 576-6300

Massachusetts
Honorable Scott Harshbarger
Attorney General of Massachusetts
Office of the Attorney General
One Ashburton Place
Boston, MA 02108-1698
(617) 727-2200

Michigan
Honorable Frank J. Kelley
Attorney General of Michigan
Office of the Attorney General
Post Office Box 30212
525 West Ottawa Street
Lansing, MI 48909-0212
(517) 373-1110

Minnesota
Honorable Hubert H. Humphrey, III
Attorney General of Minnesota
Office of the Attorney General
State Capitol, Suite 102
St. Paul, MN 55155
(612) 296-6196

Mississippi
Honorable Mike Moore
Attorney General of Mississippi
Office of the Attorney General
Department of Justice
Post Office Box 220
Jackson, MS 39205-0220
(601) 359-3692

Missouri
Honorable Jeremiah W. (Jay) Nixon
Attorney General of Missouri
Office of the Attorney General
Supreme Court Building
207 West High Street
Jefferson City, MO 65101
(573) 751-3321

Montana
Honorable Joseph P. Mazurek
Attorney General of Montana
Office of the Attorney General
Justice Building
215 North Sanders
Helena, MT 59620-1401
(406) 444-2026

Nebraska
Honorable Don Stenberg
Attorney General of Nebraska
Office of the Attorney General
State Capitol
Post Office Box 98920
Lincoln, NE 68509-8920
(402) 471-2682

Nevada
Honorable Frankie Sue Del Papa
Attorney General of Nevada
Office of the Attorney General
Old Supreme Court Building
100 North Carson Street
Carson City, NV 89701
(702) 687-4170

New Hampshire
Honorable Philip McLaughlin
Attorney General of New Hampshire
Office of the Attorney General
State House Annex
25 Capitol Street
Concord, NH 03301-6397
(603) 271-3658

New Jersey
Honorable Peter Verniero
Attorney General of New Jersey
Office of the Attorney General
Richard J. Hughes Justice Complex
25 Market Street
CN 080
Trenton, NJ 08625
(609) 292-4925

New Mexico
Honorable Tom Udall
Attorney General of New Mexico
Office of the Attorney General
Post Office Drawer 1508
Santa Fe, NM 87504-1508
(505) 827-6000

New York
Honorable Dennis C. Vacco
Attorney General of New York
Office of the Attorney General
Department of Law—The Capitol
2nd Floor
Albany, NY 12224
(518) 474-7330

North Carolina
Honorable Michael F. Easley
Attorney General of North Carolina
Office of the Attorney General
Department of Justice
Post Office Box 629
Raleigh, NC 27602-0629
(919) 716-6400

North Dakota
Honorable Heidi Heitkamp
Attorney General of North Dakota
Office of the Attorney General
State Capitol
600 East Boulevard Avenue
Bismarck, ND 58505-0040
(701) 328-2210

N. Mariana Islands
Honorable Robert B. Dunlap II
Acting Attorney General of the Northern
Mariana Islands
Office of the Attorney General
Administration Building
Saipan, MP 96950
(670) 664-2341

Ohio
Honorable Betty D. Montgomery
Attorney General of Ohio
Office of the Attorney General
State Office Tower
30 East Broad Street
Columbus, OH 43266-0410
(614) 466-3376

Oklahoma
Honorable W. A. Drew Edmondson
Attorney General of Oklahoma
Office of the Attorney General
State Capitol
Room 112
2300 North Lincoln Boulevard
Oklahoma City, OK 73105
(405) 521-3921

Oregon
Honorable Hardy Myers
Attorney General of Oregon
Office of the Attorney General
Justice Building
1162 Court Street NE
Salem, OR 97310
(503) 378-6002

Pennsylvania
Honorable Mike Fisher
Attorney General of Pennsylvania
Office of the Attorney General
Strawberry Square
Harrisburg, PA 17120
(717) 787-3391

Puerto Rico
Honorable José Fuentes-Agostini
Attorney General of Puerto Rico
Office of the Attorney General
Post Office Box 192
San Juan, PR 00902-0192
(787) 721-7700

Rhode Island
Honorable Jeffrey B. Pine
Attorney General of Rhode Island
Office of the Attorney General
150 South Main Street
Providence, RI 02903
(401) 274-4400

South Carolina
Honorable Charles Molony Condon
Attorney General of South Carolina
Office of the Attorney General
Rembert C. Dennis Office Building
Post Office Box 11549
Columbia, SC 29211-1549
(803) 734-3970

South Dakota
Honorable Mark Barnett
Attorney General of South Dakota
Office of the Attorney General
500 East Capitol
Pierre, SD 57501-5070
(605) 773-3215

Tennessee
Honorable John Knox Walkup
Attorney General of Tennessee
Office of the Attorney General
500 Charlotte Avenue
Nashville, TN 37243
(615) 741-6474

Texas
Honorable Dan Morales
Attorney General of Texas
Office of the Attorney General
Capitol Station
Post Office Box 12548
Austin, TX 78711-2548
(512) 463-2191

Utah
Honorable Jan Graham
Attorney General of Utah
Office of the Attorney General
State Capitol
Room 236
Salt Lake City, UT 84114-0810
(801) 538-1326

Vermont
Honorable William H. Sorrell
Attorney General of Vermont
Office of the Attorney General
109 State Street
Montpelier, VT 05609-1001
(802) 828-3171

Virginia
Honorable Richard Cullen
Attorney General of Virginia
Office of the Attorney General
900 East Main Street
Richmond, VA 23219
(804) 786-2071

Virgin Islands
Honorable Julio A. Brady
Attorney General of the Virgin Islands
Office of the Attorney General
Department of Justice
G.E.R.S. Complex
48B-50C Kronprinsdens Gade
St. Thomas, VI 00802
(809) 774-5666

Washington
Honorable Christine O. Gregoire
Attorney General of Washington
Office of the Attorney General
P.O. Box 40100
1125 Washington Street, SE
Olympia, WA 98504-0100
(360) 753-6200

West Virginia
Honorable Darrell V. McGraw, Jr.
Attorney General of West Virginia
Office of the Attorney General
State Capitol
Charleston, WV 25305
(304) 558-2021

Wisconsin
Honorable James E. Doyle
Attorney General of Wisconsin
Office of the Attorney General
State Capitol
Post Office Box 7857
Suite 114 East
Madison, WI 53707-7857
(608) 266-1221

Wyoming
Honorable William U. Hill
Attorney General of Wyoming
Office of the Attorney General
State Capitol Building
Cheyenne, WY 82002
(307) 777-7841

APPENDIX 7
Federal Information Center

The Federal Information Center (FIC) is a resource available to everyone who is seeking information about the federal government's agencies, services and programs. When you don't know where to turn for help, the FIC will tell you which office to call. Calling hours are 9:00 A.M. to 5:00 P.M. local time.

The following list of toll-free numbers is for the specific metropolitan area listed. If you are calling from other areas, you must dial (301) 722-9000. The toll-free TDD/TTY number is (800) 326-2996 if you use a Telecommunications Device for the Deaf.

Alabama
Birmingham, Mobile
(800) 688-9889

Alaska
Anchorage (8 A.M.-4 P.M.)
(800) 688-9889

Arizona
Phoenix
(800) 688-9889

Arkansas
Little Rock
(800) 688-9889

California
Los Angeles, Sacramento, San Diego, San Francisco, Santa Ana
(800) 688-9889

Colorado
Colorado Springs, Denver, Pueblo
(800) 688-9889

Connecticut
Hartford, New Haven
(800) 688-9889

Delaware
Wilmington
(800) 688-9889

Florida
Ft. Lauderdale, Jacksonville, Miami, Orlando, St. Petersburg, Tampa, West Palm Beach
(800) 688-9889

Georgia
Atlanta
(800) 688-9889

Hawaii
Honolulu (7 A.M.-3 P.M.)
(800) 688-9889

Idaho
Boise
(800) 688-9889

Illinois
Chicago
(800) 688-9889

Indiana
Gary, Indianapolis
(800) 688-9889

Iowa
All locations
(800) 688-9889

Kansas
All locations
(800) 688-9889

Kentucky
Louisville
(800) 688-9889

Louisiana
New Orleans
(800) 688-9889

Maine
Portland
(800) 688-9889

Maryland
Baltimore
(800) 688-9889

Massachusetts
Boston
(800) 688-9889

Michigan
Detroit, Grand Rapids
(800) 688-9889

Minnesota
Minneapolis, St. Paul
(800) 688-9889

Mississippi
Jackson
(800) 688-9889

Missouri
All locations
(800) 688-9889

Montana
Billings
(800) 688-9889

Nebraska
All locations
(800) 688-9889

Nevada
Las Vegas
(800) 688-9889

New Hampshire
Portsmouth
(800) 688-9889

New Jersey
Newark, Trenton
(800) 688-9889

New Mexico
Albuquerque
(800) 688-9889

New York
Albany, Buffalo, New York
City, Rochester, Syracuse
(800) 688-9889

North Carolina
Charlotte
(800) 688-9889

North Dakota
Fargo
(800) 688-9889

Ohio
Akron, Cincinnati,
Cleveland, Columbus,
Dayton, Toledo
(800) 688-9889

Oklahoma
Oklahoma City, Tulsa
(800) 688-9889

Oregon
Portland
(800) 688-9889

Pennsylvania
Philadelphia, Pittsburgh
(800) 688-9889

Rhode Island
Providence
(800) 688-9889

South Carolina
Greenville
(800) 688-9889

South Dakota
Sioux Falls
(800) 688-9889

Tennessee
Chattanooga, Memphis,
Nashville
(800) 688-9889

Texas
Austin, Dallas, Forth
Worth, Houston, San
Antonio
(800) 688-9889

Utah
Salt Lake City
(800) 688-9889

Vermont
Burlington
(800) 688-9889

Virginia
Norfolk, Richmond,
Roanoke
(800) 688-9889

Washington
Seattle, Tacoma
(800) 688-9889

West Virginia
Huntington
(800) 688-9889

Wisconsin
Milwaukee
(800) 688-9889

Wyoming
Cheyenne
(800) 688-9889

APPENDIX 8

U.S. Government Bookstores

As an information resource, the U.S. government is unequaled. Countless federal employees labor to collect, research, analyze and publish information on an unbelievably wide range of topics. As an entrepreneurial inventor you can benefit from this vast repository of information. Of particular value are publications that explore topics such as patenting and intellectual property rights, business and marketing.

This collection of information is available for sale through each of the 24 *U.S. Government Bookstores*. A visit to one of their convenient locations will allow you to browse through many of the titles you are most likely to be looking for. Though each store cannot stock all 10,000-plus titles in their inventory, their helpful store personnel can fill your orders and send your purchase directly to your home or office.

The *U.S. Government Bookstores* accept major credit cards such as Visa, MasterCard, Discover/NOVUS as well as Superintendent of Documents deposit account orders. The stores are open for business Monday through Friday.

List of U.S. Government Bookstore Sites

U.S. Government Bookstore
First Union Plaza
999 Peachtree Street NE Suite 120
Atlanta, GA 30309-3964
(404) 347-1900
Fax (404) 347-1897

U.S. Government Bookstore
O'Neill Building
2021 3rd Avenue N
Birmingham, AL 35210-1159
(205) 731-1056
Fax (205) 731-3444

U.S. Government Bookstore
Thomas P. O'Neill Building
10 Causeway Street Room 169
Boston, MA 02222-1047
(617) 720-4180
Fax (617) 720-5753

U.S. Government Bookstore
One Congress Center
401 South State Street Suite 124
Chicago, IL 60605-1225
(312) 353-5133
Fax (312) 353-1590

U.S. Government Bookstore
Federal Building
1240 E 9th Street Room 1653
Cleveland, OH 44199-2001
(216) 522-4922
Fax (216) 522-4714

U.S. Government Bookstore
Federal Building
200 N High Street Room 207
Columbus, OH 43215-2408
(614) 469-6956
Fax (614) 469-5374

U.S. Government Bookstore
Federal Building
1100 Commerce Street Room IC50
Dallas, TX 75242-1027
(214) 767-0076
Fax (214) 767-3239

U.S. Government Bookstore
1660 Wynkoop Street Suite 130
Denver, CO 80202-1144
(303) 844-3964
Fax (303) 844-4000

U.S. Government Bookstore
Federal Building
477 Michigan Avenue Suite 160
Detroit, MI 48226-2500
(313) 226-7816
Fax (313) 226-4698

U.S. Government Bookstore
Texas Crude Building
801 Travis Street Suite 120
Houston, TX 77002-5727
(713) 228-1187
Fax (713) 228-1186

U.S. Government Bookstore
100 West Bay Street Suite 100
Jacksonville, FL 32202-3811
(904) 353-0569
Fax (904) 353-1280

U.S. Government Bookstore
120 Bannister Mall
5600 E Bannister Road
Kansas City, MO 64192-0001
(816) 765-2256
Fax (816) 767-8233

U.S. Government Printing Office
Retail Sales Outlet
8660 Cherry Lane
Laurel, MD 20707-4907
(301) 953-7974
(301) 792-0262
Fax (301) 498-8995

U.S. Government Bookstore
ARCO Plaza C-Level
505 S Flower Street
Los Angeles, CA 90071-2101
(213) 239-9844
Fax (213) 239-9848

U.S. Government Bookstore
Reuss Federal Plaza
310 W Wisconsin Avenue
Suite 150
Milwaukee, WI 53203-2200
(414) 297-1304
Fax (414) 297-1300

U.S. Government Bookstore
Federal Building
26 Federal Plaza Room 2-120
New York, NY 10278-0004
(212) 264-3825
Fax (212) 264-9318

U.S. Government Bookstore
Robert Morris Building
100 N 17th Street
Philadelphia, PA 19103-2736
(215) 636-1900
Fax (215) 636-1903

U.S. Government Bookstore
Federal Building
1000 Liberty Avenue Room 118
Pittsburgh, PA 15222-4003
(412) 644-2721
Fax (412) 644-4547

U.S. Government Bookstore
1305 SW 1st Avenue
Portland, OR 97201-5801
(503) 221-6217
Fax (503) 225-0563

U.S. Government Bookstore
Norwest Banks Building
201 W 8th Street
Pueblo, CO 81003-3038
(719) 544-3142
Fax (719) 544-6719

U.S. Government Bookstore
Marathon Plaza
303 2nd Street Room 141-S
San Francisco, CA 94107-1366
(415) 512-2770
Fax (415) 512-2276

U.S. Government Bookstore
Federal Building
915 2nd Avenue Room 194
Seattle, WA 98174-1001
(206) 553-4270
Fax (206) 553-6717

U.S. Government Bookstore
U.S. Government Printing Office
710 N Capitol Street NW
Washington, DC 20401
(202) 512-0132
Fax (202) 512-1355

U.S. Government Bookstore
1510 H Street NW
Washington, DC 20005-1008
(202) 653-5075
Fax (202) 376-5055

BIBLIOGRAPHY/
RECOMMENDED READING

We've sought to provide a compendium of information about inventing and the patent system which hasn't been well known nor widely available. Many other aspects of inventing, the patent system, business start-up and operation, marketing and sales and so forth need to be in your arsenal of knowledge if you plan to be successful. We highly recommend any of these books for further study by any inventor or creative person. The more knowledge you possess, the greater your chances for success. Good reading!

Patent and Invention Publications

American Intellectual Property Law Association, *How to Protect and Benefit From Your Ideas*
Price: $10. Includes a free 30-minute consultation with a patent attorney.
AIPLA, 2001 Jefferson Davis Highway, Suite 203, Arlington, VA 22202.

Boorstin, Daniel J., *The Discoverers*
New York: Random House, 1983.

Clark, R. W., *Edison, the Man Who Made the Future*
New York: Putnam, 1977.

Conot, Robert, *A Streak of Luck*
New York: Bantam Books, Inc., 1979.

DeCamp, L. Sprague, *The Heroic Age of American Invention*
Garden City, New York: Doubleday, 1961.

Drucker, Peter, *Innovation and Entrepreneurship*
New York: Harper & Row, 1985.

Elias, Stephen, *Patent, Copyright and Trademark: A Desk Reference to Intellectual Property Law*
Berkeley, CA.: Nolo Press, 1996, 1st edition.

Foltz, Ramon D. and Thomas A. Penn, *Protecting Engineering Ideas and Inventions*
Cleveland: Penn Institute, 1988.

Hanks, Kurt and Larry Belliston, *Getting Good Ideas*
Information Design, Inc., 1980.

Harman, W. and H. Rheingold, *Higher Creativity—Liberating the Unconscious for Breakthrough Insights*
J. P. Tarcher, 1984.

Heyn, Ernest V., *Fire of Genius*
Garden City, NY: Doubleday, 1976.

Jewkes, John, David Sawers and Richard Stillerman, *The Sources of Invention*
New York: Norton, 1969.

Johnson, Clifton, *The Rise of the American Inventor*
Garden City, NY: Doubleday, 1935.

Kivenson, Gilbert, *The Art and Science of Inventing*
New York: Van Nostrand Reinhold, 1982.

Knapp, Philip B., *Inventing: Creating and Selling Your Ideas*
Blue Ridge Summit, PA: Tab Books, Inc., 1989.

Lessing, *Man of High Fidelity: Edwin Howard Armstrong*
Philadelphia: Lippincott, 1956.

MacCracken, Calvin D., *A Handbook For Inventors: How to Protect, Patent, Finance, Develop, Manufacture, and Market Your Ideas*
New York: Charles Scribner's & Sons, 1983.

Moore, Arthur D., *Invention, Discovery And Creativity*
Garden City, NY: Doubleday, 1969.

Mosley, Thomas E. Jr., *Marketing Your Invention*
Dover, NH: Upstart Publishing Company, Inc., 1992.

National Inventors Hall of Fame, *Biographies of Inductees*
NIHF Foundation, Room 1D01, Crystal Plaza 3, 2001 Jefferson Davis Highway, Arlington, VA 22202. Free publication.

Paige, R. E., *Complete Guide to Making Money With Your Ideas and Inventions*
New York: Barnes & Noble, 1976.

Pressman, David, *Patent It Yourself*
Berkeley, CA.: Nolo Press, 1995, 4th edition.

Rabinow, Jacob, *Inventing for Fun and Profit*
San Francisco: San Francisco Press, 1990.

Rosenbaum, David G., *Patents, Trademarks and Copyrights*
Hawthorne, N.J.: Career Press, 1994, 2nd edition.

U.S. Department of Commerce, Patent and Trademark Office, *General Information Concerning Patents*
Washington: Government Printing Office, 1995.

Von Oech, Roger, *A Whack on the Side of the Head*
Atherton, CA: Creative Think, 1983.

Zadig, Ernest A., *Invent and Get Rich*
New Jersey: Prentice-Hall, 1985.

Inventing: How the Masters Did It
Durham, NC: Moore Publishing, 1974.

The Inventor's Desktop Companion
Detroit, MI: Visible Ink Press.

Smithsonian Book of Invention
Washington, DC: Smithsonian Books, 1978.

Business Publications

Bivins, Thomas, *Handbook for Public Relations Writing*
Lincolnwood, IL: NTC Publishing Group, 1991.

Bodian, Nat G., *Encyclopedia of Mailing List Terminology and Techniques*
Winchester, MA: Bret Scot Press, 1986.

Burton, Philip Ward and Scott C. Purvis, *Which Ad Pulled Best?*
Lincolnwood, IL: NTC Business Books, 1987.

Cohen, William A., *The Entrepreneur and Small Business Problem Solver*
New York: John Wiley & Sons, 1990.

Comiskey, James C., *How to Start, Expand and Sell a Business*
San Jose, CA.: Venture Perspectives Press, 1985.

Covey, Stephen R., *7 Habits of Highly Effective People*
New York: Simon & Schuster, 1989.

Dible, D. M., *Up Your Own Organization*
New York: Entrepreneur Press, Hawthorn Books.

Eichenbaum, Ken, *How to Create Small-space Newspaper Advertising That Works*
New York: Unicom Publishing Group, 1987.

Friedman, Scott E., *How to Profit by Forming Your Own Limited Liability Company*
Chicago: Upstart Publishing, 1996.

Gnam, Rene, *Creating Effective Response Ads in Publications*
Rene Gnam Consultation Company, 1984.

Greene, Gardiner G., *How to Start and Manage Your Own Business*
New York: New American Library, 1983.

Henderson, Carter F., *The Successful Strategies Entrepreneurs Use to Build New Businesses*
New York: Holt, Rinehart and Winston, 1985.

Hopkins, Tom, *How to Master The Art of Selling*
New York: Warner Books, Inc., 1982.

Hurley, Brian and Peter Birkwood, *A Small Business Guide to Doing Big Business on the Internet*
North Vancouver, British Columbia: International Self-Counsel Press Ltd., 1996.

Jessup, Claudia and Genie Chipps, *The Woman's Guide to Starting a Business*
New York: Holt, Rinehart and Winston, 1979.

Kishel, Gregory F. and Patricia G. Kishel, *How to Start, Run and Stay in Business*
New York: Wiley, 1981.

Kremer, John, *Mail Order Selling Made Easier*
Fairfield, IA: Ad-Lib Publications, 1990.

Lant, Dr. Jeffrey, *Money Making Marketing*
Cambridge, MA: JLA Publications, 1987.

Lesko, Matthew, *Government Giveaways for Entrepreneurs*
Information USA, 1992.

Levinson, Jay and Seth Godin, *The Guerrilla Marketing Handbook*
New York: Houghton Mifflin Company, 1994.

Mancuso, Joseph R., *How to Start, Finance, and Manage Your Own Small Business*
Englewood Cliffs, NJ: Prentice-Hall, 1984.

Mancuso, Joseph R., *The Small Business Survival Guide*
Englewood Cliffs, NJ: Prentice-Hall, 1980.

McKeever, M., *How to Write a Business Plan*
Berkeley, CA: Nolo Press, 1994, 4th edition.

Phillips, Michael and Salli Raspberry, *Marketing Without Advertising*
Berkeley, CA: Nolo Press, 1988, 1st edition.

Pride, William M., *Marketing: Basic Concepts and Decisions*
Boston: Houghton Mifflin, 1985, 4th edition.

Stevens, Mark, *Thirty-six Small Business Mistakes and How to Avoid Them*
Englewood Cliffs, NJ: Prentice-Hall, 1982.

Stone, Bob, *Successful Direct Marketing Methods*
Lincolnwood, IL: NTC Business Books, 1988.

Timmons, Jeffrey A., *New Venture Creation: Entrepreneurship for the 21st Century*
Boston: IRWIN, 1994, 4th edition.

Tom Bellavance   **Roger Bellavance**

ABOUT THE AUTHORS

Tom Bellavance co-owns and operates Quiet Corner Press, publishing and marketing *Inventing Made Easy: The Entrepreneur's Indispensable Guide To Creating, Patenting and Profiting From Inventions* and developing other products. With degrees in biology and electrical engineering, he has worked for 16 years in the medical field. He is a member of the Inventors Association of New England and the Small Publishers Association of North America. In his spare time he engages in his passion—writing feature length movie scripts. Look for him in the Martin Brest film *Meet Joe Black. Inventing Made Easy* is his first book. He resides in a bucolic corner of God's country—the quiet corner of northeastern Connecticut.

Roger Bellavance co-owns and operates Quiet Corner Press, contributing his extensive experience from over 20 years of inventing. He is the proud owner of several patents and copyrights, and a member of the Inventors Association of New England. A veteran, he graduated from the University of South Vietnam. His great adventure in southeast Asia included a tour of duty as a M48 tank crewman and human target for rocket shrapnel. Look for him in the Steven Spielberg film *Amistad.*

INDEX

Give the Gift of Profitability to Your Friends and Colleagues

CHECK YOUR LEADING BOOKSTORE OR ORDER HERE

❏ **YES**, I want_____ copies of *Inventing Made Easy* at $24.95 each, plus $3 shipping per book (Connecticut residents please add $1.68 sales tax per book). Canadian orders must be accompanied by a postal money order in U.S. funds. Allow 15 days for delivery.

My check or money order for $_____ is enclosed.
Charge my: ❏ MasterCard   ❏ VISA

Name _____

Organization _____

Address _____

City/State/Zip _____

Phone _____

Card Number _____

Exp. Date_____ Signature _____

Please make your check payable and return to:
Quiet Corner Press, L.L.C.
318 Sterling Hill Road
Moosup, CT 06354-2034

Or call your credit card order to 1-800-917-6689

275